The Christian and Judaic Invention of History

AR

American Academy of Religion
Studies in Religion

Editor
Lawrence S. Cunningham

Number 55
THE CHRISTIAN AND JUDAIC
INVENTION OF HISTORY

edited by
Jacob Neusner

THE CHRISTIAN AND JUDAIC
INVENTION OF HISTORY

edited by
Jacob Neusner

Scholars Press
Atlanta, Georgia

THE CHRISTIAN AND JUDAIC INVENTION OF HISTORY

edited by
Jacob Neusner

© 1990
The American Academy of Religion

Library of Congress Cataloging in Publication Data
The Christian and Judaic invention of history / [edited by] Jacob Neusner.
  p. cm. -- (Studies in religion / American Academy of Religion ; no. 55)
  Contents: The birth of history of Christianity and Judaism / Jacob Neusner -- A myth of innocence / Burton L. Mack -- The pagan background / Glenn F. Chesnut-- Christianity in the Roman forum / Mark S. Burrows -- Eusebius / Glenn F. Chesnut -- Pagan and Christian historiography in the fourth century A.D. / Arnoldo Momigliano -- The tannaism and history / Nahum N. Glatzer -- History fabricated / William Scott Green -- History transcended / Jacob Neusner -- History invented / Jacob Neusner The theory of history of Genesis Rabbah / Jacob Neusner -- The role of history in Judaism / Jacob Neusner.
  Includes index.
  ISBN 1-55540-320-4. -- ISBN 1-55540-321-2 (pbk.)
  1. Church history--Primitive and early church, ca. 30-600- -Historiography. 2. Rabbinical literature--History and criticism. 3. Judaism--History--Talmudic period, 10-425--Historiography. 4. Historiography--History. I. Neusner, Jacob, 1932-   .
II. Series: AAR studies in religion ; no. 55.
BR166.C52 1989
270'.01--dc19   89-6045
                                                              CIP

Printed in the United States of America
on acid-free paper

For

CHARLES WINQUIST

Executive Director of
The American Academy of Religion
during history-making times,
who laid the firm foundations for
the Academy's current eminence.

The editors salute a scholar, teacher, and friend,
and offer homage to
one of the courageous and honest leaders of
the Academy,
whose vision shapes the perspective of us all.

TABLE OF CONTENTS

PREFACE vii

INTRODUCTION

I. THE BIRTH OF HISTORY IN CHRISTIANITY AND JUDAISM 3
Jacob Neusner

PART ONE
THE CHRISTIAN INVENTION OF HISTORY

II. A MYTH OF INNOCENCE 19
Burton L. Mack

III. THE PAGAN BACKGROUND 29
Glenn F. Chesnut

IV. CHRISTIANITY IN THE ROMAN FORUM: TERTULLIAN AND THE APOLOGETIC USE OF HISTORY 51
Mark S. Burrows

V. EUSEBIUS: THE HISTORY OF SALVATION FROM THE GARDEN OF EDEN TO THE RISE OF THE ROMAN EMPIRE 77
Glenn F. Chesnut

VI. PAGAN AND CHRISTIAN HISTORIOGRAPHY IN THE FOURTH CENTURY A.D. 103
Arnaldo Momigliano

PART TWO
THE JUDAIC INVENTION OF HISTORY

VII. THE TANNAIM AND HISTORY 125
Nahum N. Glatzer. Translated by Brigette Kern-Ulmer.
Edited by Caroline McCracken-Flesher

VIII. HISTORY FABRICATED: THE SOCIAL USES OF NARRATIVE IN EARLY RABBINIC JUDAISM 143
William Scott Green

IX. HISTORY TRANSCENDED: THE MISHNAIC USES OF THE PAST 157
Jacob Neusner

X.	HISTORY INVENTED: THE CONCEPTION OF HISTORY IN THE TALMUD OF THE LAND OF ISRAEL	181
	Jacob Neusner	
XI.	THE THEORY OF HISTORY OF GENESIS RABBAH .	209
	Jacob Neusner	

PART THREE

CONCLUSION

XII.	THE ROLE OF HISTORY IN JUDAISM: THE INITIAL DEFINITION................................	233
	Jacob Neusner	
INDEX		249

PREFACE

Thoughtful people, wanting to make sense of things, have been writing history from the time of Herodotus. The Hebrew Scriptures (Old Testament) from Genesis through Kings appeal to history as the medium of religious discourse, as much as the Israelite prophets call upon the testimony of history in setting forth truth. But for Christianity and Judaism as we in the West have known them both, history was reinvented at a particular time, for a distinctive purpose, and in response to a singular event. Before that time and event, Christianity had come to intellectual expression in many kinds of writing, but not in historical narrative. And the Judaism that was taking shape in the first seven centuries A.D. produced its first historical reflections in writing only after Christianity did. That is what we mean when we speak of the Christian and Judaic invention of history. First came Christian, then came Judaic, history-writing. And both found the stimulus in an event of such consequence that only through rethinking in the forms of history the entire experience of humanity (on the Christian side) and of Israel, the holy people (on the Judaic side) was it possible to think intelligibly and constructively about that event. Then people sought the pattern of events—their meaning and end—and so wrote history. In the introduction the precise moment at which Christian and Judaic thought became historical in its form is identified and explained.

Precisely how do we represent the important developments in historical media for theological thought that we characterize as "the invention of history"? To place into context the appeal to history in Christian and Judaic writings, we turn to Burton Mack's opening lines of his now-classic *Myth of Innocence*. We see his remarks as paradigmatic for what is at stake in all historical thought within the two religious traditions of the West. For a picture of pagan historiography we rely on Glenn Chesnut's account, since that is framed in such a way as to underline the issues that would occupy Christian historians. Mark Burrows' paper on the apologetic use of history shows us how theologians appealed to historical considerations even without actually writing history. Then we turn to Eusebius, the first Christian historian (a designation refined by Momigliano at the end) and review Chesnut's picture of the basic traits of that initial piece of history-writing in

Christianity. To sum up what changes, and what remains the same, in Christian history in the setting of pagan historiography, we turn to the account of Arnaldo Momigliano. He tells us how the fourth century historians carried forward a tradition of thinking and how they also innovated and initiated a new tradition.

On the Judaic side we begin with Nahum N. Glatzer's picture of the sayings of a historical character attributed to authorities whose names appear in the Mishnah and related writings, authorities who bear the title Tanna, or repeater of traditions, and, for the plural, Tannaim. These sayings occur in diverse writings, some of them compiled and closed long after the period in which the named authorities flourished. Glatzer's account provides one approach to the problem before us, with results that continue to merit attention. The other approach to the use of the rabbinic evidence, applied by the Mishnah, Talmud of the Land of Israel, and Genesis Rabbah, describes a problem or theme, here, the uses of history, as a given document sets forth that matter. William Scott Green shows how the raw material of historiography is turned into not history but the statement, through hagiography, of social norms. That is part of the account of how the Judaic share of the invention of history describes the development of history and such history-writing as went on in the earlier rabbinic writings. The authorship of the Mishnah did not produce history, whether narrative or even hagiographical. Its approach to the past called for transcending events, concrete and specific, and uncovering the iron laws of society, which were general and universal. Then whence history in Judaism? The next two papers provide a picture of the same matter in the writings of the late fourth and early fifth centuries. Chapters Ten and Eleven, which speak of the fourth century writings in Judaism (some of them closed only in the fifth century) therefore form the counterpart to Chesnut's and Momigliano's picture of the fourth century historians and show us how, for Judaism, authorships reinvented history as a mode of thought and discourse.

The editors acknowledge with thanks permission to publish the following copyrighted materials:

Chapter

II. A MYTH OF INNOCENCE BY BURTON L. MACK. From Burton L. Mack, *A Myth of Innocence* (Philadelphia, 1987: Fortress Press), pp.xi-xiii, 3-9. © 1987 by Fortress Press. Reprinted by permission.

III. THE PAGAN BACKGROUND BY GLENN F. CHESNUT. From Glenn F. Chesnut, *The First Christian Histories* (Macon, 1986: Mercer University Press), pp.7-32. © 1986 by Mercer University Press. Reprinted by permission.

IV. CHRISTIANITY IN THE ROMAN FORUM: TERTULLIAN AND THE APOLOGETIC USE OF HISTORY BY MARK S. BURROWS. From *Vigiliae Christianae. A Review of Early Christian Life and Language* 1988, 42:209-235. © 1988 by E.J. Brill. Reprinted by permission.
V. EUSEBIUS: THE HISTORY OF SALVATION FROM THE GARDEN OF EDEN TO THE RISE OF THE ROMAN EMPIRE BY GLENN F. CHESNUT. From Glenn F. Chesnut, *The First Christian Histories* (Macon, 1986: Mercer University Press), pp.66-95. © 1986 by Mercer University Press. Reprinted by permission.
VI. PAGAN AND CHRISTIAN HISTORIOGRAPHY IN THE FOURTH CENTURY BY A.D. ARNALDO MOMIGLIANO. From Arnaldo Momigliano, ed., *The Conflict Between Paganism and Christianity in the Fourth Century* (Oxford, 1963: At the Clarendon Press), pp.79-99. © 1963 by Oxford University Press (Clarendon). Reprinted by permission.
VII. THE TANNAIM AND HISTORY BY NAHUM N. GLATZER. TRANSLATED BY BRIDGET KERN-ULMER. From Nahum Norbert Glatzer, *Untersuchungen zur Geschichtsleher der Tannaiten* (Berlin, 1933: Schocken Verlag), pp. 10-31. © 1933 by Schocken Verlag. Reprinted by permission of the author. Translation © 1989 by Brown University Program in Judaic Studies.

JACOB NEUSNER
*Graduate Research Professor of Religious Studies,
University of South Florida
St. Petersburg, Florida*

INTRODUCTION

CHAPTER ONE

THE BIRTH OF HISTORY IN CHRISTIANITY AND JUDAISM

Jacob Neusner

For Christianity and Judaism, history was born in the fourth century. History, meaning, the representation of intelligible sequences of purposeful events presented as narrative, was born, or reborn, because of a very particular and stunning event. It was the Emperor Constantine's favoring Christianity after three hundred years of barely licit, and often illicit, existence. Now, from the first third of the fourth century onward, great Christian theologians turned attention to politics, hence to public events involving this-worldly power and its disposition. They wanted to explain the supernatural and social experience of salvation, such as they identified with Constantine's realignment of the state with the Christian faith and Church, and that meant explaining the sequence of one-time events, the composition of a narrative of how the world had come to the state it now had reached. For Constantine's Christian politics marked a turning so utterly unanticipated and hitherto so unimaginable that new modes of thought had to help Christians to make sense of the world as they know perceived and experienced that world. It was to historical modes of thinking that they turned, explaining through an orderly account of related and sequential events how matters had come about. And, for Jews, the same event presented a crisis that none could have expected, and that prior reading of the course of events had scarcely led people to anticipate. The Christians asked of history one set of questions, the Judaic thinkers, the opposite ones. Accordingly, Christianity reinvented history, from Eusebius forward, and Judaism at the same time rediscovered the historical mode of religious-theological discourse as well.

Let us underline the novelty of history-writing: narratives with beginnings, middles, endings, and, in the context of ancient Israel's Scriptures, the narrative of humanity from creation to redemption (now or coming, as Christianity and Judaism respectively phrased matters). Before the fourth century, for Christianity, and writings closed in the fifth century, for Judaism, sustained historical narrative simply did not serve as a medium for Christian discourse. The study of history and telling of historical stories did not mark Judaic discourse. The New Testament for example contains no history-writing. The Judaism that was taking shape, beginning with the Mishnah, a late second century philosophical work in the form of a law code, did not encompass in its canonical writings a single historical work. The writings it did produce, moreover, rarely contained much narrative or even biography of a sustained order. It follows that from the initial writings of both Christianity and the Judaism of the dual Torah, exemplified for the later first century by the Gospels and Letters of Paul and related documents, on the one side, and, for the later second century, by the Mishnah and Tosefta, on the other, to the advent of Constantine in the fourth century, neither Christian nor Judaic writers wrote history.

That is not to say that prior to the age, and among Judaisms in the same period, people did not write history. The opposite is the fact. In the case of other, earlier Judaisms besides the Judaism represented by the Mishnah and its successor-compositions, to be sure, history-writing had gone forward, but the Judaism that appealed to the Mishnah as the writing down of the Oral Torah revealed by God to Moses at Sinai before the late fourth- and fifth-century documents yielded no history. No concern for history as a mode of religious thought and expression produced historical narratives. But, as a matter of fact, from Constantine onward, both the Judaism aborning in late antiquity and dominant thereafter, as well as the main stream of Christianity identified history as a fundamental mode of thought and discourse, each party in accord with the prevailing idiom of its community. In these papers we present an account of the advent of history as a mode of thought for both Christianity and Judaism, hence, the Christian and Judaic invention of history.

It would carry us far afield to speculate on why Constantine's favoring Christianity and the ultimate establishment of Christianity as the religion of the state made such a difference. It suffices to note from the change we can perceive that the difference was enormous. The age of Constantine, the fourth century (dates for convenience: from 312, when Constantine extended toleration to Christianity, to 429, when the Jewish government of the Land of Israel ceased to enjoy the recognition of the state) marks the century in which Christianity joined the political world of the Roman Empire. In that century Christianity gained power, briefly lost it, and, finally, regained the throne and assured its permanent domination of the state. Christians saw Israel as God's people, rejected by God for rejecting the Christ. Israel saw Christians, now embodied in Rome, as Ishmael, Esau, Edom: the brother and the enemy. The political revolution marked by Constantine's conversion not only forced the two parties to discuss a single agendum and defined the terms in which each would take up that agendum, as I have shown in my *Judaism and Christianity in the Age of Constantine* (Chicago, 1987: University of Chicago Press). It also made each party investigate the entire past in making sense of the unprecedented and uncertain present. When emperors convert and governments shift allegiance, the world shakes under peoples' feet.

Enormous shifts in the political facts of the world, represented by the growing control of Christianity over the institutions of state and government, raised for both Judaic sages and Christian theologians issues that, to begin with, the Scriptures of ancient Israel ("the Written Torah," "the Old Testament") had defined. These issues focused on the meaning of history, viewed by epoches, each with its message; the identity of the Messiah; and the definition of Israel, God's people, with special reference to the social metaphor and theological value imputed to that "Israel after the flesh" constituted by the Jews of the day. These three issues proved paramount specifically because the political revolution effected in the course of the fourth century by the Christianization of the Roman Empire made them urgent and transformed them into matters of public policy. Prior to that political change, Judaic and Christian thinkers had had no common argument.

All of these issues, by nature political, resolved themselves in part through the writing of history and the rethinking of the meaning of human destiny. Now matters of public policy, specifically, the ideology of state (empire, for the Christians; supernatural nation or, as we shall see, family, for the Jews) demanded a clear statement on the questions at hand. When the Roman empire and Israelite nation had to assess the meaning of epochal change, when each had to reconsider the teleology of society and system as the identity of the Messiah defined that teleology, when each had to reconsider the appropriate metaphor for the political unit, namely, people, nation, extended family, only then did chronic disagreement become acute difference. It was the progressive but remarkable change in the character of the Roman government, at the beginning of the century pagan and hostile to Christianity, at the end of the century Christian and hostile to paganism, that was decisive. In the age of Constantine the terms of the fifteen-hundred-year confrontation between Judaism and Christianity reached conclusive formulation. And it was through the invention of history that the issues would be formulated.

The character of the shift is clearly discerned when we compare the sort of religious writing prior to Constantine with the kind done afterward. Prior to the fourth century, Christian writiers referred to past events, but they did not produce linear, harmonious, pointed historical narrative, formed around the theological teleology that later historians would frame. The New Testament tells stories and provides biography, but it does not organize in a sustained historical narrative the history of its times or prior ages. A comparison of Genesis with Matthew tells the tale. This matter is expressed by Glenn W. Chesnut in the following way:

> Eusebius of Caesarea's *Church History* was the first full-length, continuous narrative history written from a Christian point of view . . . Eusebius's *Church History* . . . gave an account of the history of Christianity in its first three centuries of trial and persecution, from the coming of Jesus to the final triumph of Constantine. Several generations later, two lawyers in Constantinople, Socrates Scholasticus and Sozomen, and Theodoret the bishop of Cyrrhus in Euphratensis, each wrote a history continuing Eusebius's narrative from the time of Constantine down to the early fifth century . . . Nevertheless, the problem of working out a method for applying those ideas to the actual writing of an extended historical narrative was left for Eusebius himself to resolve. Moreover, the principal problems that he had to solve were primarily created by his predecessor historians, the great pagan authors like Herodotus, Thucydides, and Polybius, not the subsequent commentaries of theologians or philosophers. . . .[1]

The problems on which Eusebius centered his discussion were the motifs of fate and fortune, of critical interest to Graeco-Roman historians, and the issue of Rome and its emperor. He rejected the classical historians' understanding of fate and defended free will; these concerns, as Chesnut says, "shaped the narative style and explanatory methods of the first Christian historians." We see, therefore, how history-writing served as a medium for theological thought and discussion.

If Eusebius lived today in an American university, he would occupy professorships in departments of political science, sociology, history, religious and theological studies, and, of course, classics. But I think his particular department would be political science. For Eusebius, though the founder of Christian historiography, confronted an essentially political problem and organized his thought in response to it. The reason he turned to history is the same as the reason people today study history: to understand how things have come to their present pass. And, for Eusebius, that constituted a towering political fact. So Eusebius wrote history in order to develop a political theory, as Chesnut explains:

> The reformulation of Christian political theory necessitated by the legitimization of Christianity under Constantine was given official form in the writings of Eusebius . . . The Roman empire suddenly became a government within which Christians could take more active part, but for which they had to take more active responsibility. Some set of ideals for

---

[1] Glenn F. Chesnut, *The First Christian Histories* (Macon, 1986: Mercer University Press), second edition, p. 2.

The Birth of History

the Christian monarch had to be developed and given shape, by which men could live their lives in the new Christian world.[2]

Eusebius saw his work as fresh, a first of its kind. He says he has no antecedents, no models. That is so not only of his profession but also of his life. Eusebius saw himself as living in a new era, one without precedent.

Eusebius drew on history to derive proof for rules of theology. He organized facts in order to make points that transcended specific instances. Accordingly, he worked as a kind of social scientist, in that the concrete instance demonstrated a general rule. The rules, of course, derived from theology. But the historical method was rigorous and consistently applied. His account of Constantine, for example, proved the point that God honors pious princes but destroys tyrants (Life of Constantine 1:3). But his main interest was to demonstrate that from the creation of the world, all events formed a single pattern, leading up to the moment at which the Church would inherit the universal empire:

> It is my purpose to write an account of the successions of the holy apostles, as well as of the times which have elapsed from the days of our Savior to our own; and to relate the many important events which are said to have occurred in the history of the Church . . .[3]

To carry out his purpose, however, Eusebius starts with the time before the creation of the world, specifically, with the pre-existence and divinity of "our savior and Lord Jesus Christ." His name was known from the beginning and honored by the prophets. His religion was not new. In these arguments, Eusebius provides from the church a history from the very beginning of the world. The striking point is his stress that the Christians formed a new nation, more numerous (Church History 1:4):

> But although it is clear that we are new and that this new name of Christians has really but recently been known among all nations, nevertheless our life and our conduct, with our doctrines of religion, have not been lately invented by us, but from the first creation of man . . . have been established by the natural understanding of divinely favored men of old.

Eusebius therefore links the Christian nation to the ancients, some before the flood, others descendants of Noah, Abraham, and onward. Christian religion begins with Abraham:

---

[2] Chesnut, p. 34.
[3] *Church History* 1:1,1.

> But that very religion of Abraham has reappeared at the present time, practiced in deeds, more efficacious than words, by Christians alone throughout the world. What then should prevent the confession that we who are of Christ practice one and the same mode of life and have one and the same religion as those divinely favored men of old? Whence it is evident that the perfect religion committed to us by the teaching of Christ is not new and strange . . . but it is the first and the true religion.[4]

Abraham provides more than precedent. In the view of the historian, he proves social rules. He lived that life of virtue that produced in God the response of blessing. What is striking in Eusebius's picture is his powerful faith that Christianity began with the beginning of history and made its original statement through Abraham. No wonder then that sages too turned back to the same story and found in it the foundations for their faith too.

His principal stress was on the creation of a political philosophy based on the unity of the church and the empire under the providence of God. In the year of Constantine's conversion, Eusebius published his *Ecclesiastical History* (312), and his *Life of Constantine* after 337. Other lives of holy men followed in sequence. Pagan writing of history and hagiography came in sequence, so Momigliano: "The Christians attack. The pagans are on the defensive."[5] But with power and responsibility, Christian historians had to account for the past. So Momigliano characterizes matters:

> The new history could not suppress the old. Adam and Eve and what follows had in some way to be presented in a world populated by Deucalion, Cadmus, Romulus, and Alexander the Great. This created all sorts of new problems. First, the pagans had to be introduced to the Jewish version of history. Secondly, the Christian historians were expected to silence the objection that Christianity was new. . . . Thirdly, the pagan facts of life had to get into the Jewish-Christian scheme of redemption. . . . It soon became imperative for the Christians to produce a chronology which would satisfy both the needs of elementary teaching and the purposes of higher historical interpretation. . . . Christian chronology was also a philosophy of history. . . . Christian elementary teaching of history could not avoid touching upon the essentials of the destiny of man. . . .

Accordingly, as I have already stressed, no one can imagine that Christians began writing history only in the aftermath of the conversion of Constantine. A Christian scheme for describing the history of the world, beginning to end, did not await Eusebius. On the contrary, he reworked what he had in hand. But he laid stress on the pattern of

---

[4] Church History 1:4.
[5] Momigliano, given below.

history,[6] and that is why he is important. For it was in the discerning of patterns that history crossed the border into theology, and theology in the form of apocalypse at that.

Even though Jews wrote history, Josephus for example, and other Judaisms expressed their ideas through historical narrative and systematic allusion to the pattern of ancient and contemporary events, e.g., marrying Scripture to contemporay history as in the Essene Judaism attested by the Dead Sea Scrolls, the Judaic system first attested by the Mishnah and related writings did not. Scriptural history was treated as typology or simply amplified without yielding contemporary conclusions. No pattern of history emerged to impose articulated meaning on contemporary events. Rather than seeing historical events as patterned and therefore producing one-time and unique, yielding lessons on their own, the authorship of the Mishnah classified events in accord with the shared taxonomic traits among them. So history as a sequence of unique, linear events, coming from somewhere and going to some other goal, played no articulated role in the writing at all. And, accordingly, the authorship of the Mishnah did not make its points through telling historical stories. The authorship of the Mishnah identified regularities in discrete events, seeking the laws of the social order. They produced the opposite of history: not unique, linear happenings but patterns that applied in any age.

The framers of the Mishnah, for their part, explicitly refer to very few events, treating those they do mention with a focus quite separate from the unfolding events themselves. They rarely create narratives; historical events do not supply organizing categories or taxonomic classifications. We find no tractate devoted to the destruction of the Temple, no complete chapter detailing the events of Bar Kokhba nor even a sustained celebration of the events of the sages' own historical lives. When things that have happened are mentioned, it is neither to narrate nor to interpret and draw lessons from the events. It is either to illustrate a point of law or to pose a problem of the law—always *en passant*, never in a pointed way. Narrative, in the Mishnah's limited rhetorical repertoire, is reserved for the narrow framework of what priests and others do on recurrent occasions and around the Temple. In all, that staple of history, stories about dramatic events and important deeds, provides little nourishment in the minds of the Mishnah's jurisprudents. Events, if they appear at all, are treated as trivial. They may be well known, but are consequential in some way other than is revealed in the detailed account of what actually happened.

The Mishnah absorbs into its encompassing system all events, small and large. With them the sages accomplish what they accomplish in

---

[6] Momigliano, given below.

everything else: a vast labor of taxonomy, an immense construction of the order and rules governing the classification of everything on earth and in heaven. The disruptive character of history—one-time events of ineluctable signficance—scarcely impresses the philosophers represented by the Mishnah. They find no difficulty in showing that what appears unique and beyond classification has in fact happened before and so falls within the range of trustworthy rules and known procedures. Once history's components, one-time events, lose their distinctiveness, then history as a didactic intellectual construct, as a source of lessons and rules, also loses all pertinence. So working like social scientists, as much as did Eusebius, sages sorted out events and classified them. In that way they looked for points of regularity—lessons, laws, and rules—which would explain and made sense of new episodes. In discovering out of anecdotes a larger system of historical—we would say, theological—laws, sages treated history as the raw material for social science. The parallel to the mode of thought displayed by Eusebius is clear.

To this labor of taxonomy, the historian's way of selecting data and arranging them into patterns of meaning to teach lessons proves inconsequential. For history-writing, by contrast, what is important is to describe what is unique and individual, not what is ongoing and unremarkable. History is the story of change, development, movement, not of what does not change, develop, or move. For the thinkers of the Mishnah, on the other hand, historical patterning emerges through taxonomy, the classification of the unique and individual, the organization of change and movement within unchanging categories. In the Mishnah's system one-time events are not important. The world is composed of nature and supernature. The laws that count are those to be discovered in heaven and, in heaven's creation and counterpart, on earth. Keep those laws and things will work out. Break them, and the result is predictable: calamity of whatever sort will supervene in accordance with the rules. But just because it is predictable, a catastrophic happening testifies to what has always been and must always be, in accordance with reliable rules and within categories already discovered and well explained. That is why the lawyer-philosophers of the mid second century produced the Mishnah—to explain how things are.

The events of the fourth century directed attention to trends and patterns, just as the framers of the Mishnah would have wanted. But in search of those trends, the detailed record of history—so far as that record made trends visible and exposed the laws of social history—demanded close study. That is why sages' response to the historical crisis of the fourth century required them to reread the records of history, as much as Eusebius resifted the facts of the past. The sedulous indifference to concrete events, except for taxonomic purposes, characteristic of the Mishanaic authorship provided no useful model. Concrete, immediate, and singular events now made a difference.

Like Eusebius sages turned to the story of the beginning to find out the meaning of the present moment. In the pages of this book we shall consider Genesis Rabbah, a work that came to closure sometime after 400, for that book forms a striking counterpart to the writing of Eusebius for one important reason. Its authors not only lived through that same period of radical political change, but also reconsidered the historical question, and they did so in the same way, by reverting to the record of Creation, the beginnings of Israel in particular. Once more I enter the necessary warning: whether sages found themselves impelled to do so by the triumph of Christianity we cannot show. We only know what they did, and which turn out to be precisely the same thing that Eusebius did. I see no inherent difference between the inquiry of Genesis Rabbah and the question of Eusebius: what patterns do we discern, now that (from Eusebius's perspective) we know where, all the time, things where heading? Since the method of the two parties proved identical, and the sources on which they drew were the same, we may proceed to examine the arguments adduced by parties who, we realize, shared one and the same issue and also concurred upon the premises and the proofs for the propositions that, in the mind of each, would settle the issue. Here therefore, we see how a genuine and authentic arguemnt could have been caried on by two parties to a single dispute.

In Genesis Rabbah, a commentary to the book of Genesis made up of episodic comments on verses and their themes, the Judaic sages who framed the document thus presented a profound and cogent theory of the history of Israel, the Jewish people. Let me briefly characterize their mode of thought in doing the work. In contrast to the approach of Eusebius, the framers of Genesis Rabbah interpreted contemporary history in the light of the past, which Eusebius read the past in light of the present. So the Israelite sages invoked the recurring and therefore cyclical patterns of time, finding in their own day meaning imparted by patterns revealed long ago. Eusebius, for his part, stood squarely in the tradition that saw events not as cyclical but as one-time and remarkable, each on its own. So the one side looked for rules, somewhat like the social scientist-philosopher, asking how events form patterns and yield theories of a deeper social reality. The other side looked not for rules but for the meaningful exceptions: what does this event, unique and lacking all precedent, tell us about all that has happened in the past.[7] But the two sides met with a single concern: what do the

---

[7] I think we should go too far were we to impute to Eusebius the notion that, just as the

events of the day mean for tomorrow.

Accordingly the framers of Genesis Rabbah intended to find those principles of society and of history that would permit them to make sense of the on-going history of Israel. They took for granted that Scripture speaks to the life and condition of Israel, the Jewish people. God repeatedly says exactly that to Abraham and to Jacob. The entire narrative of Genesis is so formed as to point toward the sacred history of Israel, the Jewish people: its slavery and redemption; its coming Temple in Jerusalem; its exile and salvation at the end of time. In the reading of the authors at hand, therefore, the powerful message of Genesis proclaims that the world's creation commenced a single, straight line of events, leading in the end to the salvation of Israel and through Israel all humanity. That message—that history heads toward Israel's salvation—sages derived from the book of Genesis and contributed to their own day. Therefore in their reading of Scripture a given story will bear a deeper truth about what it means to be Israel, on the one side, and what in the end of days will happen to Israel, on the other. True, their reading makes no explicit reference to what, if anything, had changed in the age of Constantine. But we do find repeated references to the four kingdoms, Babylonia, Media, Greece, Rome—and beyond the fourth will come Israel, fifth and last. So sages' message, in their theology of history, was that the present anguish prefigured the coming vindication of God's people.

It follows that sages read Genesis as the history of the world with emphasis on Israel. So the lives portrayed, the domestic quarrels and petty conflicts with the neighbors, all serve to yield insight into what was to be. Why so? Because the deeds of the patriarchs taught lessons on how the children were to act, and, it further followed, the lives of the patriarchs signaled the history of Israel. Israel constituted one extended family, and the metaphor of the family, serving the nation as it did, imparted to the stories of Genesis the character of a family record. History become genealogy conveyed the message of salvation. These propositions really laid down the same judgment, one for the individual and the family, the other for the community and the nation, since there was no differentiating. Every detail of the narrative therefore served to prefigure what was to be, and Israel found itself, time and again, in the revealed facts of the history of the creation of the world, the decline of humanity down to the time of Noah, and, finally, its ascent to Abraham, Isaac, and Israel.

So sages read Genesis as history. It was literally and in every detail

---

resurrection put all of history into a new light, so the advent of the Christian emperor likewise required the rereading of the entire past. But the point of contact in the otherwise extravagant comparison is simple. Both events were one-time, unique, and, for that reason, enormously important.

a book of facts. Genesis constituted an accurate and complete testimony to things that really happened just as the story is narrated. While, therefore, sages found in Genesis deeper levels of meaning, uncovering the figurative and typological sense underlying a literal statement, they always recognized the literal facticity of the statements of the document. In the fourth century the two heirs of ancient Israel's Scriptures, Judaism and Christianity, laid claim to the Land of Israel/the Holy Land. Constantine and his mother dotted the country with shrines and churches, so imparting to the geography of the land a Christian character. Israel, for its part, was losing its hold on the Land of Israel, as the country gained a Christian majority. Here, in Genesis, sages found evidence for Israel's right to hold the land. So the biography of Abraham, Isaac, and Jacob also constitutes a protracted account of the history of Israel later on. If the sages of Judaism could announce a single syllogism and argue it systematically, that is the proposition upon which they would insist.

This brings us to this anthology. As we shall see in the papers collected in Part One, for Christianity, and in Part Two, for Judaism, in the fourth century, for Christianity, and in writings generally assigned to the fifth century, for Judaism, with Eusebius, Socrates, Sozomen, Theodoret, and Evagrius, on the one side, and the Talmud of the Land of Israel and Genesis Rabbah, on the other, we have history: narrative formed to order and explain events and so to make sense of things. That is the point that the papers we have selected are meant to make.

Why do we think this anthology is important? It is because the simple proposition that we mean to set forth through the articles we have collected on Christian and Judaic history runs contrary to what people infer from the prevailing and correct view that history-writing had long been carried on in ancient Israel, to which both Christianity and Judaism traced their antecedents. Since, as we know, the Hebrew Scriptures ("Old Testament," "written Torah") conveys its messages through sustained narrative of past events, that is, through appeal to history as precedent for theology, in such books as Genesis and part of Exodus, Deuteronomy, Joshua, Judges, Samuel, and Kings, and since, moreover, much of prophecy concerns itself with events and their interpretation, doing history, thinking historically, are perfectly routine.

So ancient Israel thought about its life in historical ways and also put down the results of its thought in historical form, and if, in Christian terms, the Old Testament was deeply historical in its mode of thought, then why should the advent of Christian theology of history strike us as noteworthy? And why should we regard it as consequential and interesting that at a given time a Eusebius or an authorship such as that connected with Genesis Rabbah or important compositions in the Talmud of the Land of Israel should narrate events and draw conclusions from them? People ordinarily infer that both Christianity and Judaism (meaning, the Judaism of the dual Torah, deemed normative or classical) were as a matter of fact historical religions, in that they produced history and argued on the basis of events in behalf of their views of God and the social order alike. And so they became. But, in the case of both religious formations, in their initial writings they were not at all historical.

The reason is simple. In the case of each, the entire corpus of writings—the Gospels and indeed the New Testament as it had reached canonical status by the time of Constantine, on the Christian side, the Mishnah and Tosefta, and, if these be assigned to the third or fourth centuries as seems likely, Sifra, Sifré to Numbers and Sifré to Deuteronomy—simply bypassed historical narrative—whether long stories or strings of stories made into a complete tractate—as a medium of sustained theological discourse. But at a given point Christianity, then the Judaism attested by the writings of the age, invented history, each for its own important purposes. Take Judaism, for example. Sifra forms a sustained reflection and counterpoint to the book of Leviticus. In Chapter Twenty Six, the priestly authorship of Leviticus presents a historical-apocalyptic vision of Israel's history and destiny, making fundamental theological judgments through its account of what would happen. Here then is an opportunity for Sifra's authorship to think historically about historical events. But that is not what they did. Rather, they commented in a routine and *ad hoc* way, not in a systematic and urgent manner, upon the apocalyptic writings, even while those writings afforded the occasion to address urgent events of the time, e.g., the destruction of the Temple, the closure of Jerusalem to Judaic worship. Sifra's treatment of Leviticus Chapter Twenty-Six, not less than the Gospels' treatment of the destruction of the Temple, shows how important events were absorbed within a quite ahistorical framework of thought and exposition.

For three centuries, the first through the third, in the case of Christianity, the second through the fourth, in the case of Judaism, we find no important and sustained historical writings. That does not mean authorships did not take events seriously and adduce lessons from them, e.g., proof for propositions of a theological character. People could make points from events without turning events into history, and the authorships of Christianity and Judaism in the second, third, and fourth centuries (for Judaism) and in the first, second, and third centuries (for Christianity) did just that. Apocalypse, as in Revelation, found its counterpart in law, as in the Mishnah. In the latter, events were systematized and organized into laws, shown to exhibit common indicative traits and so to form a class of events subject to the same rule, for instance. The upshot is that we look in vain for history in the form of narrative of events, sustained exposition of sequences of events, story-telling of a teleological order, in the writings of Christianity and Judaism before the advent of Constantine. But, as we shall show in this book, from the advent of the Christian empire onward, first Christians, then Jews, did do history.

Nor do we mean to suggest that prior to that time people were indifferent to what happened in the "out-there" of world-historical happenings. That is not the case. As Burton Mack shows in the prologue, taken from his *Myth of Innocence*, the Gospels themselves appeal to a linear and one-time account of the beginnings of things. And that appeal—for apologetic purposes, as Mack shows—is one fundamental characteristic of historical thinking. Along these same lines Mark S. Burrows demonstrates in the case of Tertullian, who lived in 160/170-215/220, that appeal to precedent, to origins and the beginnings of things, characterized the great apologist. Anyone familiar with the importance of ancient Israelite saints to Christian writers, for example, Abraham to Paul and the author of the Letter to the Hebrews, David to Matthew, will find no difficulty in conceding that appeal to precedent, hence to the past, was commonplace. Nor can we open the pages of the Mishnah without on nearly every line asking about the relationship between Scripture and what the authorship of the Mishnah proposes to allege. But there is no counterpart to Samuel and Kings in the New Testament, and there is no parallel to be located between a single sentence of Isaiah or Jeremiah and the entire composition of the Mishnah and the Tosefta. But after 300, for Christianity, and after 400, for Judaism, there were ample counterparts and parallels, in conception and structure, among Christian and Judaic writers of the age and the historical thinkers of the olden times. Living in a new age of history-writing in the world of religious thought, we turn back to the beginnings of the conception that history forms a medium for God's address to humanity.

PART ONE

THE CHRISTIAN INVENTION OF HISTORY

CHAPTER TWO

A Myth of Innocence

Burton L. Mack

Since Foucault published his *Archaeology of Knowledge*, New Testament scholars have thought of their work as digging. I have therefore tried to imagine my task as sifting through the layers of accumulated constructions upon a certain site. The image is attractive in some respects and disconcerting in others. An aura of archeology is gratifying mainly because it seems to bless the labor as worthwhile. But textual sites differ somewhat from tells, cemeteries, and village dumps. And in the case of the mass of traditions, texts, and commentaries that make up the mound for doing biblical archeology, the site is still inhabited. That complicates the digging. Worse still, the site has already been dug up so many times no stone has been left unturned. Diggers keep looking for the foundations even while the builders keep busy at the surface of the heap as if the foundations were there, solid, and known. Thus the layers of accretion are constantly being disturbed and rearranged, and hardly an artifact is found embedded in its proper stratum. Given this living tell of textual tradition, it is to our credit, I suppose, that we New Testament scholars have managed to reconstruct any outline at all of the earliest layers of the edifice called Christianity.

It is disconcerting nonetheless to see what happens when the metaphor is pressed too far. One catches sight of a very messy dig and of diggers in disagreement about what they are looking for. Not only is there confusion about what counts as an artifact, there is no clarity about what a firm foundation might be were one ever to be found. This, at any rate, has been my own uneasiness with the jumble of mystifying conclusions regularly drawn at the end of scholarly books and articles in quest of Christian origins. I fear, frankly, that we have been picking away at the wrong layer looking for stones that were never there.

It has usually been thought that the laying of the foundations, stone of stumbling and all, happened with the historical Jesus. That is how the gospels paint the picture and that is what scholars have somehow been content to imagine, though in other terms. Something unique and powerful, it is assumed, must have taken place then in order to account for the novelty of Christianity. Even if that dramatic moment cannot be located, described, or comprehended, so the logic seems to run, it must be posited in order to make sense of all the stories that came to be told about divine events at the beginning.

I found that odd, for the notion of an incomprehensible origin is clearly mystifying and mythological, and all critical scholars say that they know the gospels to be mythic. When the gap between what we know about myth-making, symbols, and social formation on the one hand, and the tedious rehearsal of apologies for not adequately grasping the mysterious originary moment on the other became unbearable, I decided to switch sites.

What if one acknowledged that the gospel story was Christianity's charter document and regarded its formation as an essential moment in the "laying of the foundations"? Then the focus would not fall solely on the life of Jesus as the stratum within which all of the crucial, originary events are to be found. Instead it would be the later occasions for imagining Jesus that way which one should want to understand. Complex social histories of many diverse groups and movements would have intervened as all scholars know. Complicated textual histories would have to be traced and situated within these social histories in order to locate points of contact, conflict, and accommodation that may have determined the way in which a group construed its world. The gospels were put together two and three generations later than the time of Jesus out of very diverse traditions, lore, and even full-blown myths. If the social circumstances of that later time were regarded as the "foundational" stratum, and the composition of the gospel taken as the "originary" moment of significance for Christian origins, the fantastic events depicted in the gospel might actually begin to make sense. They would not make the kind of sense New Testament scholars have hoped to find at the beginnings of Christianity. But they might make very good sense of the kind myths make in general. Supposing that the gospels were myths of origin for social formations in need of a charter, the scholar's quest would have to be to understand the moment when the gospel was designed. Foucault's archeology refers, after all, not to a quest for extraordinary events of generation prior to social formation, but to critical moments of social interest within a given discourse. . . .

. . . .The goal of New Testament scholarship has been to give an account of the origins of Christianity. For more than two hundred years an amazingly rigorous and critical discourse has pursued this goal, probing the texts produced by early Christians in order to get behind them. Some event, it is thought, or moment, or impulse, needs to be discovered as the source for the novelty Christianity introduced into the world. In spite of this concentrated effort, however, there is no agreement about what that mysterious moment was or had to have been. One might think that the failure to reach an agreement on such a fundamental objective would eventually call attention to itself and force a reconceptualization of the discipline. That has never happened and the quest continues unabated.

To the historian who has no theological proclivity, such persistence in the quest for a singular genesis of Christianity is curious. The very notion of an origin within history is strange if taken to the extreme as is the case in New Testament studies. It is doubly strange because, though the notion of a radically new beginning is pervasive throughout this scholarly discourse, it has never been taken up for examination by those who posit it as the goal of their intellectual pursuits. Silence on this subject is odd, especially so because the discipline of biblical studies is known for its care about methods and the precision with which it seeks to define them and their objectives. If one asks further how it could be that such a careful discipline could sustain a problematic assumption as its stated objective, the peculiar nature of this scholarship is compounded once again. That is because everyone seems to know that the objective is ultimately beyond reach. The origins of Christianity are known to lie on the other side of limits set by the nature of the texts at the scholar's disposal and the nature of the history that can be reconstructed from them. Thus the methods of historical literary criticism, the hallmark of this discipline, are tacitly acknowledged to be inadequate from the start. It is as if the scholar's texts and tools are known only to scratch the surface of the social histories stemming from Jesus; they cannot account for their generation. To do that, it is assumed, one must introduce yet another kind of reflection, either about the texts in hand, in which case the reflection will be called hermeneutics, or about the history learned, in which case the reflection will be called theology. That which counts does not lie on the surface of things, but beneath it, or beyond it, or prior to it.

The reason for this unusual situation—a scholarship in quest of an objective known to be unreachable by scholarly tools and methods—is not difficult to understand. It stems from basic assumptions about Christianity that underlie the discipline, motivate its energies, and influence the way in which texts are taken up for investigation. The fundamental persuasion is that Christianity appeared unexpectedly in human history, that it was (is) at core a brand new vision of human existence, and that, since this is so, only a startling moment could account for its emergence. The code word serving as sign for the novelty that appeared is the term unique (meaning singular, incomparable, without analogue). For the originary event the word is transformation (rupture, breakthrough, inversion, reversal, eschatological). For the cognitive effect of this moment the language of paradox is preferred (irony, parable, enigma, the irrational). It is this startling moment that seems to have mesmerized the discipline and determined the applications of its critical methods. All of the enormous labor devoted to the preparation of texts, the honing of linguistic instruments, and the devisement of methods has been organized just in order to approach as closely as possible that moment of mystery even if, in the last analysis, some leap of the imagination will be required to posit its presence.

Where to locate the mystery has been the unacknowledged question guiding the twists and turns of the scholarship. There has been a general agreement that it was the appearance of Jesus that made all the difference, but efforts to be more definite have invariably run into horrendous complications. That is because the image of Jesus presented by early Christian texts is so complex that decisions cannot be made as to the exact reason for his influence without distorting other features of the picture. The options run from superior personhood (whether because of character or charisma), through startling activity (whether as a manifestation of uncommon compassion or a display of miraculous power), and the marvelous words (whether as announcement, pronouncement, or invitation to enlightenment), to his remarkable death, unexpected resurrection, and overpowering appearances to his followers as the new society was formed. At one time or another each of these manifestations of the unusual has been championed as the moment that made the critical difference. None has held the field for long, though, without revision. Shifts in perspective and changes in method mark the junctures of a very restless search for some way to determine which factors were the more or most significant. At each juncture something more was learned about the early histories, of course, but new knowledge about the histories has not settled the question of origination.[1]

The hardest lesson has always been that the texts in hand are "late," the product of many moments of memory and imagination that occurred between the time of Jesus and the time of their writing. This fact, underscored in any first lecture on the critical study of the New Testament, has frequently been stated as the problem and challenge of

---

[1] *History of scholarship.* The standard handbook on the history of New Testament scholarship is Werner G. Kümmel, *The New Testament.* Kümmel charts the shifts in critical approaches to a fairly small set of issues that have guided scholarly interests from the beginning. The book follows the German tradition primarily and breaks off about the time of the Second World War, but it can be used nevertheless to make observations about the discipline wherever pursued and the nature of the questions it has entertained. To cover the period since the war, Scholars Press has promised a series of volumes on The Bible and Its Modern Interpreters.

the discipline. Jesus was active in the late twenties of the first century C.E. The earliest evidence of his influence comes from the fifties, the Pauline correspondence with communities of believers in Asia Minor, Greece and Rome. Even then, however, there are no reminiscences of Jesus' activity, but only fragments from a Christ cult that had formed around myths and rites in memory of his death and resurrection. The first surviving document to contain reminiscences of Jesus and his activity in Galilee comes from the early seventies, the Gospel of Mark, a full forty years removed from Jesus' time. The document known as the Source (Q) for Jesus' sayings, though thought to contain some authentic words of Jesus, presents a problem of even greater magnitude. It must first be reconstructed by comparing the ways in which Matthew and Luke employed it in the writing of their gospels during the last decades of the century. Because the data available to historians for reconstructing the life of Jesus come from documents removed in time by one, two, or even three generations of social history, New Testament scholarship can be described as an archeology of early traditions about Jesus and the Christ: the attempt to work back from later texts to earlier memories closer to the source. Early traditions and events have always been associated with the originary, late compositions always regarded as developments of earlier traditions.

The archeological efforts of two hundred years of scholarship can be thematized by tracing two main tracks along which the quest for Christian origins has traveled. The one has been the quest for the historical Jesus, working back through the gospel accounts to retrieve some picture of the man as he appeared in Galilee. The other has been the quest for the earliest christology, working back through layers of mythic interpretations to determine the first identification made. Each of these quests has been pursued somewhat in isolation from the other, not only because the literary corpora seem to divide that way, with the gospels providing the Jesus materials and the letters the earliest christological formulations, but also for strategic reasons. Those who have concentrated upon the figure of the historical Jesus have always hoped to discover something about him that could account for his crucifixion and the beliefs of early Christians in his continuing influence among them. Those who have worked back toward the first visions, experiences, or interpretations of his death and/or resurrection have always hoped to find some connection between those startling claims and the kind of person Jesus may have been. The strategy has been to close the gap, if possible, on those events that must have taken place between the appearance of the man Jesus and the first formation of the Christian community after his death. Most of the methods designed for reading New Testament texts, therefore, have aimed explicitly at sorting out the earliest traditions in order to gain some access to those crucial events suspicioned to have inaugurated the Christian time.[2]

The quests have produced a huge amount of learning, but they have not pinned down the inaugural event. Undaunted, New Testament scholars have pressed ahead, taking sides on this or that preference and working out ever more sophisticated ways of imagining how it all must have begun. Currently, those who emphasize the effectiveness of Jesus' way with words on the imagination are using the languages of presence, immediacy, "nakedness," and even silence in order to name the critical moment of transformation. Others, also concerned to pinpoint the significant moment in the life of the historical Jesus, rather than in the events of his death and resurrection, have begun to confess openly that the miracle stories told about him have to be given their due. The term most often used in this regard to indicate that about Jesus which instigated change is charismatic power. Those who think that Jesus' death made the difference, the way he died and how it affected his followers, are not talking openly at the moment. Not too long ago, however, scholars commonly used the term Christ event. Preference for a theology of the cross is still strong enough among New Testament scholars in the German Lutheran tradition to influence the way in which both texts and history continue to be read.

---

[2] *Quest for the historical Jesus.* The classical study of the lives of Jesus that were written during the nineteenth century is Albert Schweitzer's *The Quest of the Historical Jesus.* Underlying the quest were assumptions about myth and history that were severely criticized in the first two decades of the twentieth century. James M. Robinson, in *A New Quest of the Historical Jesus,* discusses the reasons for this critique, especially from the point of view of Rudolf Bultmann and his students, a proposal for a renewed attempt along existentialist lines. Anglo-American scholars did not react dramatically to the trauma in Germany created by the end of the nineteenth-century quest, nor did they swing easily to existentialist methods to interpret the mythic language found embedded in New Testament texts. For a recent statement that reflects more the Anglo-American tradition, though sobered somewhat by the continental discussion, see Howard C. Kee, *Jesus in History.* The difficulty scholars have had in agreeing upon a reconstruction of the historical Jesus has given rise to a burgeoning literature on the fringes of the discipline. Novelistic works have taken advantage of scholarly uncertainties to romanticize the history; others have begun to appear that express extreme skepticism about the possibility of knowing anything at all about the historical Jesus. An example of the later genre is the book by G. A. Wells, *The Historical Evidence for Jesus.* Scholars with theological interests have scarcely taken note of this literature.

Quest for the earliest christology. Summarizing half a century of scholarship, major studies appeared in the sixties: Reginald H. Fuller, *The Foundations of New Testament Christology;* Werner Kramer, *Christ, Lord, Son of God;* Ferdinand Hahn, *The Titles of Jesus in Christology.* Many scholars have thought to find the bridge between the two quests in the description of the Son of Man attributed to Jesus in the synoptic tradition of the gospels. One of the more sophisticated attempts of this type is that of Willi Marxsen, *The Beginnings of Christology.*

All scholars seem to agree, however, on the importance of the resurrection. Three terms are frequently used, each encoded by custom within the discourse of the discipline, to refer euphemistically to the resurrection of Jesus from the dead: Easter, appearance, and spirit. The casual reader may not notice how often recourse is made to these terms in the language of New Testament scholarship, thinking perhaps that their occurrence is to be attributed to the idiosyncrasy of an occasional confessional writer. After reading seriously into the field and at length, however, the repetition of these terms creates a crescendo that becomes quite shrill. These coded signs, usually capitalized, do not enlighten because they mark the point beyond which the scholar chooses not to proceed with investigation, indeed, the point beyond which reasoned argument must cease. They serve as ciphers to hold the space for the unimaginable miracle that must have happened prior to any and all interpretation. They have become an all too convenient rhetorical device for evoking the myth of Christian origins without having to explain it.[3]

The reader who dares to enter this discourse from the humanities,

---

[3] *The resurrection.* Appeal to "the resurrection" is the most mystifying of all the ciphers used to protect the myth of Christian origins from critical investigation. The notion is used regularly to distinguish "pre-Easter" from "post-Easter" performances of Jesus' sayings, for instance, as if the resurrection were a datable piece of evidence. By allowing the mystery of Easter and the appearances to mark the point from which the Spirit effected the new age of Christian experience and mission, everything else can be examined rigorously without threatening the notion of originary uniqueness. A statement recently made by Helmut Koester, a New Testament scholar highly regarded for his critical acumen, can serve as an example of this strange compartmentalization: "The content and effect of the appearances were decisive.... It is presupposed, of course, that the Jesus of Nazareth who died on the cross is now alive. But this is not a fact of any significance for Jesus and his fate. Nor is the statement that he now lives identical with a clear and unanimous explanation of the significance of Jesus' mission.... The resurrection and the appearances of Jesus are best explained as a catalyst which prompted reactions that resulted in the missionary activity and founding of the churches, but also in the crystallization of the tradition about Jesus and his ministry. But most of all, the resurrection changed sorrow and grief, or even hate and rejection, into joy, creativity, and faith. Though the resurrection revealed nothing new, it nonetheless made everything new for the first Christian believers.... They were radically different ... from other Jews in Jerusalem because of their enthusiastic consciousness of the possession of the spirit; this was the spirit of God which was to be poured out at the end of times, which brought the gift of tongues and of prophecy, worked miracles, and granted assurance to the members of the community that they belonged to God's elect people" (*Introduction to the New Testament* 2:84-87). If the historian hardly knows what to make of such a statement, its purpose, apparently, has been achieved. A point of origin has been established that is fundamentally inaccessible to further probing or clarification. It guarantees the uniqueness of early Christianity by locating its novelty beyond data and debate. Koester's scenario simply reproduces the Lukan myth of Christian origins written around the turn of the first century or later. Koester agrees to the later dating of Luke-Acts, *Introduction to the New Testament* 1:310.

or from the social sciences, cannot avoid coming to a certain conclusion. The events that center the massive amounts of scholarly learning are exactly those that haunt the average Christian imagination as well. They are exactly those suggested by the Christian gospel, the gospel that sets them forth as inaugural and foundational for Christian history and faith. The Christian gospel, it is well known, claims that the same events serve, at one and the same time, to grant the church its charter and to offer to the individual Christian transformation or renewal. They are those events at the beginning where, according to Christian teaching, God entered into human history. The private contemplation of these events draws the imagination of the believer, not only to the symbols of personal salvation, but to the originary chapter of the history of the church. Social and personal interests intersect there, as well as mythic schemes for joining history and heaven. Insofar as Christianity actually is peculiar as a religion, and thus the scholarly hunch on target, it is certainly due to just this notion of an event within history that interrupted the normal course of human social activity and created a new kind of time and society. For the church, it should be noted, the events all go together—Jesus, his teachings and activities, the supper, cross, and resurrection. These, it should then be emphasized, are just those moments thought by scholars to be candidates for the point of Christian origins. They are taken from the gospel, actually, the gospel that Mark wrote, others enlarged, and the church eventually claimed for its charter. So the suspicion cannot be avoided that the scholarly quest for the origins of Christianity has, in effect, been driven by the Christian imagination. Though the gospel story has been critically analyzed at the level of its textual history, at another level, the level of the scholarly imagination of Christian origins, the claims of the gospel have been accepted as self-evident.

What if the notion of a single, miraculaous point of origin was acknowledged for what it was, not a category of critical scholarship at all, but an article of faith derived from Christian mythology? Then the quest would have to be turned around. Not the mythic events at the beginning, but the social and intellectual occasions of their being imagined would be the thing to understand. To ask when, where, and why early followers of Jesus dared to think such audacious thoughts, that would be to learn something. The task would be to account for the formation of the gospel itself in the context of a later social history, not to use it as a guide to conjure up chimeras at the beginning. Instead of assuming eruptions of inexplicable energy penetrating the human scene from without, giving shape to certain vehicles of influence ("traditions," "trajectories," "messages," "syntagmatic structures") that could bear the aura of mystique and spiritual empowerment, then stream out in all directions from a common source, commissioning, transforming, spreading, and pressing to fill the whole world with a novel presence, one would look for historical circumstances, intellectual resources, and social motivations for early Christians to have imagined such a cosmic drama. What if the historical origins of the Jesus movements were not all that dramatic? What if the formation of the gospel were regarded as the origin of the Christian notion of dramatic origins? Then the "later" texts would be just as interesting as the earlier ones, perhaps even more interesting because of their greater degree of fantasy. To understand the original purpose of the belated gospel would be to understand the social function of the Christian claim to pure origination, unique vision, and novel social order. The fantasy of an order of things without precursor might actually be capable of explanation. If so, Christian and scholarly obsession with the notion, whether in full or partial mythic dress, might be explained as well. It might even be possible to say something about the persistence of such a fantasy in modern times, a fantasy that, apparently, modernity has not been able to challenge.

CHAPTER THREE

THE PAGAN BACKGROUND

Glenn F. Chesnut

It is impossible to comprehend the full set of problems confronting the first Christian historians without understanding the background that lay behind them. History writing in the early Christian period was dominated by the pagan Graeco-Roman historiographical tradition that went back to Herodotus. Within that tradition various historians held that the historical process was controlled by acts of Fortune, that human free will was under the rule of Fate, and that the gods intervened in history with omens, retribution, and vindictive acts of jealousy. In order to work out a coherent Christian understanding of history and the forces that shaped it, Eusebius and his successors first of all had to deal with those overwhelming issues. Fortune, Fate, omens, retribution, and the envy of the gods were discussed so often and played such a major role in Greek and Roman historiography that a Christian historian was almost forced to make some explicit statement about these issues and either attack them as pagan or adapt them to Christian purposes. Because of the importance of these ideas, it will be useful to begin with a brief survey of their varied roles in Greek and Roman history writing through the centuries.

The concept of Fortune (Τύχη) in particular lay at the very center of traditional pagan thought about history. It could be regarded in either supernatural or natural terms. Herodotus believed that the gods intervened in history to control the course of the fortunes of human beings.[1] Even though his successor Thucydides completely rejected any notion of divine intervention in history, he also used the

---

[1] Her. 1.124, 1.32; see also 1.126, 3.139. J.L. Myres (*Herodotus: Father of History* [Oxford: Clarendon Press, 1953] 48-49, 55) discusses the degree to which Herodotus personified Fate and Fortune. He feels this to have been slight. For an even more impersonal interpretation, see R.G. Collingwood, *The Idea of History* (Oxford: Clarendon Press, 1946) 22-23. Nevertheless, Fortune and Fate were for Herodotus clearly manifestations of the *divine*. For discussions of this, see Harry Elmer Barnes, *A History of Historical Writing* (New York: Dover, 1962) 29; Joseph Wells, *Studies in Herodotus* (Oxford: Basil Blackwell, 1923) 194; R.W. Macan, "Herodotus and Thucydides," in *Cambridge Ancient*

word τύχη—twenty-eight times in his speeches, and eleven times in his narrative sections.² In contrast to Herodotus, clearly, he did not imply anything supernatural by his use of the word, rather, he simply identified unforeseen chance occurrences that disrupted human plans. Later on, in the Hellenistic period, Polybius's use of the concept of Fortune was particularly notorious, and a vast modern scholarly literature discusses the question of what this historian in fact meant by the term, and whether he thought of Fortune in different ways at different stages in his own intellectual development.³ Polybius proclaimed that Fortune had directed the overall historical process whereby Rome had gradually conquered the entire Mediterranean world.

> I therefore thought it quite necessary not to leave unnoticed or allow to pass into oblivion this the finest and most beneficent of the performances of Fortune. For though she is ever producing something new and ever playing a part in the lives of men, she has not in a single instance ever accomplished such a work, ever achieved such a triumph, as in our own times.⁴

In at least some passages he seems to have spoken of Fortune as itself a personified divine power deliberately guiding the course of world events. This development is not strange, since in the Hellenistic period Tyche was widely worshiped as a goddess, sometimes as a sort of tutelary genius of a particular city, and her statues are found in great number.

When the Romans began to write history, they took over the concept of Fortune as an intrinsic part of the Greek models they were following. As Sallust put it, "Fortune" (*fortuna*) is she "whose irrational whim [*lubido*] controls the nations."⁵ Fortune's personification grew as one passed further into the Roman imperial period. In Dio

---

History (1927) 5:407; W.C. Greene, *Moira: Fate, Good, and Evil in Greek Thought* (New York: Harper and Row, 1963) 270.

² Plus one use in a treaty (4:118:11). See M.H.N. von Essen, *Index Thucydideus* (Berlin: Weidmannos, 1887).

³ See for example, Rudolf von Scala, *Die Studien des Polybios* (Stuttgart: Kohlhammer, 1890) 1:159ff., 167-68, 174-81; Otto Cuntz, *Polybius und sein Werk* (Leipzig: Teubner, 1902) 43-45; J.B. Bury, *The Ancient Greek Historians* (London: Macmillan, 1909) 200-203; Richard Laqueur, *Polybius* (Leipzig: Teubner, 1913) 250-60; Walter Siegfried, *Studien zur geschichtlichen Anschauung des Polybios* (Leipzig: Teubner, 1928) 1-7, 37-39, and 47-67; F.W. Walbank, *Historical Commentary on Polybius* (Oxford: Clarendon, 1957) 1:23-26; Paul Pédech, *La méthode historique de Polybe* (Paris: Les Belles lettres, 1964) 331-38. Unfortunately, this work has not usually been done with sufficient sensitivity to the textual problems in some of the crucial passages most often cited. For a modern survey of the state of the text of Polybius's history, see John M. Moore, *The Manuscript Tradition of Polybius* (Cambridge: Cambridge University Press, 1965).

⁴ Polyb 1.4.3-5.

⁵ Sall. *Cat.* 51.25. Compare *Jug.* 102.9, *Cat.* 8.1, and so forth.

Cassius (late second and early third century C.E.) Fortune had become personified so completely that an individual worshiper could now devote his life to this goddess and receive special revelations from her. In his dreams, Dio tells us, the goddess Fortune commanded him to write his history, and he wrote of her with admiration in that work: "This goddess gives me strength to continue my history when I become timid and disposed to shrink from it; when I grow weary and would resign the task, she wins me back by sending dreams.... I have dedicated myself to her."[6]

In short, hardly any pagan historian in the Graeco-Roman world could have conceived of writing a history in which the concept of Fortune did not play some role. It intruded into every sort of historical circumstance. It could be interpreted as a personal deity, or as a mechanical combination of natural circumstances, or anything in between, depending on the degree of piety in the historian.

But even if we find differing opinions on the question of whether or not acts of Fortune were ultimately controlled by some supernatural power, on a more phenomenological level it is possible to describe clearly the sorts of historical events that were apt to be called "acts of Fortune" by ancient historians, and explain why these particular events were so regarded. Basically, Fortune to them meant the way in which history was dominated by combinations of forces outside any single human being's prediction or control. On the one hand it meant the *conjuncture* of two or more independent chains of historical events—independent in that no one single human being was in control of all the important factors involved, nor were all the events part of some single, simple natural process. On the other hand there was usually some element of the *unexpected* involved, so that the final turn of events came as a surprise and a shock to the human actors involved.

Herodotus tells us that at the very point when Croesus had temporarily disbanded most of his army, Cyrus decided to make a sudden attack on Sardis. This conjuncture of events was an act of Fortune, and it proved disastrous for Croesus, whose kingdom was consequently destroyed.[7] Polybius tells us that Hannibal's one attempt to make a surprise attack on Rome itself happened to come on the very day when Gnaeus Fulvius and Publius Sulpicius had ordered the recruits for two newly formed legions to assemble there in the city. One chain of events began when Hannibal secretly began moving towards Rome; the other, originally unconnected, chain of events began when the two Roman officials published that particular date as the time for the new recruits to report for enrollment and active duty. They had no idea

[6] Dio Cass. 73(72).23.2-4.
[7] Her. 1.77, 79.

that Hannibal was planning an attack. The conjuncture of these two chains of events was entirely an act of Fortune, but Rome, which otherwise would have been undefended, was saved by it.[8] The concept of Fortune, as can be seen, in no sense implied the inability to give a complete causal explanation of the events involved; in this sense it was quite different from what a modern person often means by "chance." An act of Fortune was not "inexplicable" or "uncaused"; it was uncontrollable, which is a quite different kind of statement.

An act of Fortune was also usually unpredictable. It was the element of the unexpected in history. However carefully human plans for the future were laid, unforeseen factors continually cropped up to produce results different from those that were planned or expected. As we find the idea expressed in Thucydides' history, "We commonly lay upon fortune (τὴν τύχην) the blame for whatever turns out contrary to our calculations (παρὰ λόγον)."[9] Polybius regarded this as the principal fascination of the topic he had chosen for his great historical work: "the very element of unexpectedness (τὸ παράδοξον) in the events I have chosen as my theme will be sufficient to challenge and incite everyone, young and old alike, to peruse my systematic history."[10] Even with the greatest wisdom and preparation, a finite human mind could never calculate all the possible avenues for catastrophe. By repeated bitter experience, history taught "a lesson to humankind never to discuss the future as if it were the present, or to

---

[8] Polyb. 9.6.5-7. Compare the passage in J.B. Bury's historiographical essay, "Cleopatra's Nose" (in *Selected Essays* [Cambridge: Cambridge University Press, 1930] 60-69): "I visit Paris. I meet an American friend, whom I had not seen for years, in the Rue de la Paix. We were mutually ignorant of each other's presence in Paris, and we describe our meeting as a happy chance. My visit to Paris and my walking in the Rue de la Paix at a particular hour were the result of a sequence of causes and effects. His visit to Paris and his presence in the same street at the same hour followed upon another sequence of causes and effects. The collision, as we may say, of these two independent chains made what we call the chance of our meeting."

[9] Thuc. 1.140.1. Compare 6.23.3 and 7.67.4, where Fortune is contrasted with those factors that the human actors have knowingly prepared for in advance. F.M. Cornford (*Thucydides Mythistoricus* [London: Routledge and Kegan Paul, 1965] 167-68, 222) emphasized this aspect of Fortune: "The future is dark and uncertain, and although rational foresight (γνώμη) can see a little way into the gloom, Fortune, or Fate, or Providence, is an incalculable factor which at any moment may reverse the purposes and defeat the designs of man." "Not only in the great catastrophes, in flood and avalanche and earthquake, but again and again in the turns of daily experience, man finds himself the sport of an unseen demon. Now, by some unforeseen stroke, his long-cherished design is foiled; now, with equally unintelligible caprice, goods are heaped on him which he never expected."

[10] Polyb. 1.1.4. In his history, words meaning "unexpected," like παράδοξος and παράλογος, occur with almost wearisome repetition, for example 1.6.8, 24.1, 44.5, 54.8, 58.1-2, 58.3, 61.7, 82.3-8, 87.1 (connected with περιπέτεια); 2.17.3, 18.6, 37.6, 70.2-3; 9.6.5-7, 16.2-4; 15.15.5; 30.10.1-2.

have any confident hope about things that may still turn out quite otherwise. We are but human beings, and should in every matter assign its share to the unexpected (τῷ παραδόξῳ)."[11]

One of the most useful and sensitive analyses of Fortune in ancient Greek thought was drawn up by Aristotle in one section of the *Physics*.[12] A man went to the market, he said, on an unusual errand (he did not usually go to that part of the market) and unexpectedly met a man from whom he wanted to collect some money. The successful collection of the money was not due to some intentional choice of a particular course of action (προαίρεσις) based upon intelligent planning (διάνοια) and directed to the end of collecting the money. The man did not go to the market with any idea or expectation of finding the one from whom he wanted money, but, while there on some other purpose, just happened to run into him. In normal Greek usage, one would say that it was simply a matter of fortune (τύχη), Aristotle said. "Clearly, therefore, fortune is an accidental cause affecting those happenings which are for the sake of some purpose or end, and which also involve free choice."[13] Only human beings could experience fortune, Aristotle said, and indeed only human beings out of infancy and old enough to form purposeful plans and to decide on courses of action by rational choice. Fortune was a much more highly specialized concept than the sort of crude mechanical principle of chance that governed whether a tossed coin, for example, came down heads or tails. Inanimate objects could not suffer Fortune, only human beings. Fortune, Aristotle said—using one of his most important philosophical terms— was "the accidental," τὸ κατὰ συμβεβηκός, which made human purposeful action produce results different from those that were planned and expected. This exact technical phrase[14] was to be used more than six centuries later by Eusebius, the first Christian historian, in his own

---

[11] Polyb. 2.4.3-5. Compare 2.7.1-2, "For we are but human beings, and to meet with some unexpected (παραλόγως) blow is not the sufferer's fault, but that of Fortune (τῆς τύχης) and those who inflict it on him."

[12] 2.4.195b-6.198a. Compare the discussion in John Herman Randall, *Aristotle*, 182-84.

[13] *Physics* 2.5.197a: δῆλον ἄρα ὅτι ἡ τύχη αἰτία κατὰ συμβεβηκὸς ἐν τοῖς κατὰ προαίρεσιν τῶν ἕνεκά του.

[14] Mediated perhaps through Middle Platonic sources. One sees Tyche referred to as τὸ κατὰ συμβεβηκός for example, in works like the essay "On Fate" in Plutarch's *Moralia*, 571e-572c. See vol. 7 of the LCL edition of the *Moralia* (where Plutarch's authorship of the piece is, however, questioned, 303), trans. P.H. DeLacy and B. Einarson (London: Heinemann, 1959) 303-59. We also find here succinct descriptions of both aspects of Fortune. For Fortune as the unexpected we get the classic Stoic definition of it as "a cause unforeseen and not evident to human calculation" (572a). For Fortune as historical conjuncture we have a Platonic example in which we are told that "the outcome resulted from a concourse of causes (ἐκ συνδρομῆς τινος αἰτίων), each of them having a different end" (572c).

analysis of the fortuitous, so Aristotle's discussion of this issue must be carefully noted.

One finds a similar definition from Eusebius's own century in Nemesius of Emesa. One should note the way both sides of the idea are brought out, Fortune as conjuncture of two or more independent chains of historical events, and Fortune as the unexpected in history.

> For fortune is defined as the coincidence and concurrence (σύμπτωσιν καὶ (συνδρομὴν) of two actions each of which arises from some particular purpose, to produce something quite different from what was intended by either, as when a man digs a ditch and finds a buried treasure. For one man buried the treasure, but not that the other man might find it. Nor did the other man dig for the purpose of finding treasure. The first intended, in his own time, to dig the treasure up again, while the second intended to dig a ditch. What fell out was something different from what either had intended.[15]

The Stoics also had a famous definition of Fortune. "Chance is a cause obscure to the human mind," they said, "and thus the same event appears to one as chance and to another not, depending on whether one knows the cause or does not know it."[16] But this definition did not give a true picture of all that Greek historians had meant by the term. It was distorted by Stoic metaphysics, which insisted that the universe was completely deterministic. Unlike Aristotelians or Platonists, Stoics had no room for genuine chance or accident in their philosophy, and so they had to "explain away" part of what a Greek historian would usually have meant by the word Fortune. Aristotle, and the Middle Platonist Nemesius, are therefore better guides to usual Graeco-Roman historical practice.

But it is important to remember that "Fortune" was not just an abstract concept to be discussed and defined at the academic, philosophical level. Within Greek culture especially, this motif was an expression of a basic, fundamental attitude toward life.[17] It dominated

---

[15] Nemesius of Emesa, *De natura hominis* 39 (Migne *PG* 40, cols. 761b-764a) trans. by W. Telfer in the Library of Christian Classics.

[16] Alexander Aphrodisiensis, *De anima* 179.6, quoted in S. Sambursky, *Physics of the Stoics* (London, 1959) 76, 135.

[17] As Collingwood said (*The Idea of History*, 22), the Greek historical consciousness was one "of violent περιπέτειαι, catastrophic changes from one state of things to its opposite, from smallness to greatness, from pride to abasement, from happiness to misery. This was how they interpreted the general character of human life in their dramas, and this was how they narrated the particular parts of it in their history. The only thing that a shrewd and critical Greek like Herodotus would say about the divine power that ordains the course of history is that it is φανερὸν καὶ ταραχῶδες: it rejoices in upsetting and disturbing things. He was only repeating (i. 32) what every Greek knew: that the power of Zeus is manifested in the thunderbolt, that of Poseidon in the earthquake, that of

Greek drama as much as Greek history. Human beings were never in complete control of their lives or their futures. Powerful forces were at work in history that could destroy the strongest king as quickly as the poorest member of his kingdom. No person ever enjoyed a life of good unmixed with evil. The wise person accepted every good event with a certain tincture of sadness and pessimism; in some way, unforeseeable at the present, what he enjoyed would eventually be taken away, or counterbalanced with some terrible misfortune, unless death first brought him an escape of sorts. "Count no man blessed until he is dead" was one of the most famous summaries of classical Greek pessimism about the world.[18] A wise person set his plans for the future with a mixture of pragmatic precaution and humility. The use of reason and caution would sometimes lead to ruin, but the failure to do so would nearly always bring destruction. A refusal to acknowledge in his heart the inescapability of uncertainty and death was what was truly at the core of the tragic hero's self-willed drive towards his own tragic downfall. These widespread assumptions about the nature of life were so much a part of Greek culture that the first Christian historians were practically driven by necessity to thinking about these issues.

But we must not minimize the role of human decisions. History to the Greeks was a complicated interplay between the power of Fortune and the willful actions of hundreds of individual human beings. If the classical Greek history was an account of the disrupting power of the fortuitous, it was equally a history of decisions. The ancient historians analyzed these decisions in terms of motives and purposes; they illustrated the consequences of each decision; they discussed the alternative possibilities open to the decision makers. One need only think of the marvelous speeches in Thucydides here. This emphasis upon human decisions as the basic stuff of history is one of the features that give ancient Greek histories their characteristic flavor. It is the thing that makes them look so different from those histories of our own period that put such a stress on impersonal social and economic forces. Even those caught in a situation like the Spartans at Thermopylae could still make certain basic choices, and Herodotus in typical Greek fashion focused carefully on these men caught in the ultimate hour of decision and recorded how they chose between death and dishonor.[19]

Although the power of Fortune held sway over most of history, it was nevertheless true that Fortune herself could create a certain exceptional situation—the καιρός or "critical moment"—in which a sin-

---

Apollo in the pestilence, and that of Aphrodite in the passion that destroyed at once the pride of Phaedra and the chastity of Hippolytus."
[18] Her. 1.32; Aeschylus, *Agamemnon* 928-929; Aristotle, *Nicomachean Ethics* 1.10 (1100a-1101a).
[19] Her. 7.201-233.

gle decision by a single human being affected the whole subsequent course of history. Graeco-Roman historians lovingly analyzed such crucial events.[20] Herodotus wrote that the decision of a single man, Callimachus, made the Greeks stay and fight at Marathon.[21] On five different occasions, he tells us, Themistocles took actions that determined the whole subsequent course of the Persian war.[22] Thucydides ascribed an even greater importance to Pericles—had he lived, the Peloponnesian war would not have caused the Athenian spirit to fall apart.[23] Polybius prefaced his account of the great battle between Hannibal and Scipio at Zama with the statement that "Fortune" had never "offered to contending armies a more splendid prize of victory," since the victor in this single battle in Africa would win as a reward the entire world.[24] Sallust turned this idea of the key man who knew how to seize the opportune moment into a generalized theory of the great man in history. At times he almost approached the hero worship of a Thomas Carlyle. Sallust used his "great man" theory to explain, for example, why the early Romans had been able to carry out their magnificent deeds.

> After long reflection I became convinced that it had all been accomplished by the eminent merit of a few citizens; that it was due to them that poverty had triumphed over riches, and a few over a multitude. But after the state had become demoralized by extravagance and sloth ... for a long time, as when mothers are exhausted by child-bearing, no one at all was produced at Rome who was great in merit. But within my own memory there have appeared two men of towering merit, though of diverse character, Marcus Cato and Gaius Caesar.[25]

But it was rare to displace this theory of the great man, as Sallust did,

---

[20] See again Bury's amusing historiographical essay, "Cleopatra's Nose," for a series of examples of such key figures and key events drawn from history at large: Antony and Cleopatra, the invasion of the Huns, George III and the American Revolution, Napoleon's military genius, and Constantine's decision to support Christianity.
[21] Her. 6.109-110.
[22] Whether there would be any Greek resistance to the Persians depended on whether the Athenians decided to fight or to give in (Her. 7.139), and Themistocles also played a key role in the development of the Athenian decision to fight at sea (7.140-144). Three times, Themistocles alone got the Greeks to stand and fight instead of fleeing (8.4-5, 56-64, 74-76).
[23] Thuc. 2.65. Note especially 65.9: Pericles kept the spirits of the Athenian people at all times in line with reason and the καιρός of the moment.
[24] Polyb. 15.9.2-5. Compare 9.22.1, "of all that befell both nations, Romans and Carthaginians, the cause was one man and one mind—Hannibal."
[25] Sall. *Cat.* 53.2-6. Thomas Carlyle's work *On Heroes, Hero-Worship, and the Heroic in History* (1841) was very influential on the more popular nineteenth-century English historical literature, and had a profound indirect effect on the writing of standard textbooks for schools.

so completely from its roots. The great man existed, in usual Graeco-Roman historiographical practice, only because a καιρός had occurred—an "opportune moment" or "critical moment"—in which one human decision had a shaping effect on all subsequent history. This basic concept of the καιρός was everywhere present in Graeco-Roman histories. In Polybius one finds it in passage after passage;[26] Thucydides[27] and Sallust[28] both invoked it. But even though it raised human decision making to ultimate historical significance, the important point was that the καιρός was simply another face of Fortune.[29]

As I shall later demonstrate, the second major Christian historian, Socrates Scholasticus, used this word καιρός as a way to talk about the fortuitous in history without bringing in all of the pagan associations that the word τύχη raised. Well before Socrates' century, Tyche had become a widely known goddess whom many pagans worshiped; but Kairos (in spite of one altar to him at Olympia) never developed a widespread cult. The word καιρός could be used by a Christian in a way that the word τύχη could not.

On a simple phenomenological level, an act of Fortune did not involve miracles. A straightforward account of historical events would not show any laws of nature being broken. But in other situations (where the word Fortune significantly was *not* used) some Graeco-Roman historians would tell miracle tales. An ancient historian would call such an event an act that went "against nature." The ancient world did not think in terms of a highly articulated set of "laws of nature" such as we assume in our own scientific age. The scale of our knowledge today is so much greater that it is different in kind. But the Graeco-Roman period did have a clear concept, in its own way, of φύσις or "nature." At roughly the same time Herodotus was producing the first piece of Greek history writing, the medical scholars of the Hippocratic school at Cos were trying to give more precise theoretical form to the concept of φύσις.[30] The island of Cos was situated within eyesight of Herodotus's birthplace, Halicarnassus, and the possible connections have been noted by modern scholars.[31] At any rate, Herodotus's own writing gives ample evidence as to what he understood

---

[26] For example, Polyb. 3.109.12; 5.101.5-10, 104.2-4, and 104.7-8; 7.12; 9.2.5, 12.3-5, 13.7, 15.1; 10.5.8; 15.14.7, 16.1; 18.22.8, 24.7, 26.2 (three critical moments in the course of the same battle), 36.8; 27.20.1-2; 29.27.8; 32.13.4.
[27] See Thuc. 2.42.4, where it is connected with τύχη.
[28] See Sall. *Jug.* 6.3 (*opportunitas*), 56.4 (*fortunam, casum*).
[29] In Polybius for example, see 2.49.7-8 (τύχη); 5.26.12-13 (sudden reversals of fortune, that is, περιπέτειαι); 34.2-3 (τύχη); 9.6.5-7 (παράδοξος, τυχικός, αὐτομάτως); 11.24a.3 (τύχη); 15.29.5 (synergesis of ταὐτόματον at the proper καιρός).
[30] W.H.S. Jones, introduction to the LCL edition of Hippocrates, 1:xvi.
[31] Joseph Wells, *Studies in Herodotus*, 188-89. See also Myres, *Herodotus*, 2-3, T.R. Glover, *Herodotus* (Berkeley: University of California Press, 1924) 14.

by the term "nature." When he said, for example, that he ws going to tell the reader about the φύσις of the crocodile, he talked about its body, scales, and jaws; the way it lived its life along the riverbanks; its reproductive cycle; and the way it related to other animals and birds of its region.[32] The word φύσις, in other words, implied normal process, growth, functioning, and behavioral patterns.[33] One would say that a crocodile acted "against nature" if it had two heads, flew through the air, lived in the middle of a desert, or spoke with a human voice. In that sense, one finds a number of "miracle stories" in Herodotus and some of the other Graeco-Roman historians. We are told that the dust and chanting of thousands marching in an Eleusinian procession was seen and heard after Attica had been completely evacuated of its people and lay vacant before the Persians; that when Darius conquered Babylon, a mule gave birth to a foal; that whenever disaster threatened the people of Pedasa, the priestess of Athene grew a long beard.[34]

But there was also a good deal of skepticism within the Graeco-Roman historiographical tradition. Even Herodotus showed this more than is frequently acknowledged. When he reported the story that the deep-sea diver Scyllias deserted the Persians and got safely over to the Greek side by swimming underwater from Aphetae to Artemisium without coming up for air, he immediately went on to poke fun at the tale: "It is my opinion, which I hereby declare, that he came to Artemisium in a boat!"[35] Herodotus gave ample warning to his readers in 7.152: "For myself, though it be my business to set down that which is told me, to believe it is none at all of my business; let that saying hold good for the whole of my history." Thucydides rejected the whole notion of miracle completely, and refused even to include such stories in his history at all. His skepticism is famous. In the introduction to his history he acknowledged that "it may well be that the absence of the fabulous from my narrative will seem less pleasing to the ear."[36] Polybius also said, in some very sharp and critical passages, that superstitious nonsense about miracles and the intervention of gods and demigods in human history had no place in an intellectually respectable historical work.[37] A crafty politician or general could use the credulity of the uneducated masses to manipulate them to his own

---

[32] Her. 2.68.
[33] John L. Myers, *Herodotus*, 47-48. It was this commonplace Greek idea that lay behind Aristotle's more technical definition, later on, of φύσις as something that grew, moved, or changed, and had within itself its own source of movement; see *Physics* Beta 1.192b and *Metaphysics* Delta 4.1014b-1015a.
[34] Her. 8.65; 3.151-153; 1.175.
[35] Her. 8.8.
[36] Thuc. 1.22.4.
[37] Polyb. 3.47.7-9 and 48.7-10; 10.5.8; 12.24.5; 16.12.

advantage,[38] but woe to the statesman or military commander who, like Nicias, let superstition affect his own mind.[39] It was common in later historians for a few miracle stories to be included in the narrative, but it was also quite customary for the miracle story to be prefixed with a phrase like "some people say" or concluded with a phrase like "let the reader judge for himself."[40]

The first Christian historians therefore found that the existing pagan historiographical tradition did give some room for miracles, but that this was mixed with a good deal of scepticism. In particular, even pagan historians who told large numbers of miracle stories would not usually claim that a miracle had itself altered the basic course of history at any point in their narratives. Consequently, the first Christian histories could defend the possibility of miracles on the grounds of Christian piety, but it did not help them any in solving the basic problem, that of giving God real, omnicompetent control over the fundamental course of human history. Appeal to the miraculous has never been a good theological device for introducing any continuous divine presence into human history. God is absent more often than he is present in that way. Furthermore the concept of miracles in the simple sense (men walking on water, and so forth) does not get a church historian very far in an analysis, say, of the course of the fourth-century Arian controversy. So even though the first Christian historians did believe in miracles, this was a surprisingly peripheral question in terms of the development from pagan to Christian historiography. They found the debate over Fortune and Fate moved one much closer to the central problem of God and history.

The matter of miracles was of great importance in pagan historiography in one regard, however. If one surveys a list of all the miracle tales that a pagan historian like Herodotus recorded in his history, one notes that the majority of them were either stories of omens and portents, or stories about acts of retribution against human beings who committed sacrilege against the gods who gave these omens and portents.[41] And in addition to miraculous signs such as water boiling without fire, horses eating snakes, and mules giving birth to foals, there were also other ways of predicting the future. The proclamations of the Delphic oracle and other such oracular predictions played a promi-

---

[38] Polyb. 10.2.8-12; 10.4-5; 10.11.7-8; 10.14.
[39] Polyb. 9.19.1-3.
[40] See the comments, for example, on Dionysius of Halicarnassus, Josephus, and Lucian's *Quomodo hist. sit conscribenda* in H. St. John Thackeray, *Josephus: The Man and the Historian* (New York: Jewish Institute of Religion Press, 1929) 57-58.
[41] Omens and portents: Her. 1.59, 78, 175; 3.151-153; 8.65; 9.120. Other miracle tales: 1.19 and 22, 23-24, 86-87; 8.35-39; 9.65.

nent role in Herodotus's history.⁴² The Athenians were told that their city would be saved by the Athenian fleet, the "wooden wall"; poor Croesus was told that if he attacked the Persians "he would destroy a mighty empire," and then forgot to ask whether it would be his or theirs.⁴³ Dreams were another important way of predicting the future. Croesus dreamed at one point that his son Atys would be killed by an iron spear, and in spite of all his precautions the terrible prophecy came true.⁴⁴ One important variety were "kingship dreams"— what Bischoff called *Dynastienträume*⁴⁵—that foretold either the accession of a new king to the throne or the downfall of a king, or both.⁴⁶

Portents, oracles, and dreams were dismissed as a matter of course by the most skeptical among the Graeco-Roman historians. Thucydides declared contemptuously that the only Greek oracle that ever came true in the whole Peloponnesian war was the one that predicted the number of years it would last!⁴⁷ But Xenophon, his successor, took a position closer to that of the average person of that time. The ancient Greeks as a whole were a superstitious people in certain matters. An army, one remembers, did not go out of its home country or enter into battle or start any other major project without sacrificing animals and having a professional fortune-teller (μάντις) inspect the livers to see whether the future looked favorable.⁴⁸ Xenophon himself was a pious man,⁴⁹ and seems to have believed that this really worked.⁵⁰ It was the gods who revealed the future to human beings, through the signs, the omens, the pronouncements of oracular shrines, and the inspection of the livers of sacrificial victims. For everything was known to the gods, "who see all things both now and forever."⁵¹ In Polybius one found a more Thucydidean mood, so that classical Greek historiography ended on a skeptical note at the Roman conquest. But in the subsequent centuries of Roman historiography, the signs and portents and oracles and prophecies came back in again. Sallust, for example, made the accurate prediction of Marius's future by the haruspex play a key role in the development of the plot in the *Jugurthine War*.⁵² Roman historiography was further affected by the new religious mood

---

⁴² Her. 1.13, 53-56, 62-63, 66, 91; 2.152; 3.57-58; 7.140-144, 220; 8.77, 96; 9.43.
⁴³ Her. 7.141; 1.53.
⁴⁴ Her. 1.34.
⁴⁵ Heinrich Bischoff, *Der Warner bei Herodot* (Borna-Leipzig: R. Noske, 1932) 41.
⁴⁶ Her. 1.107 and 108, 209; 3.30, 124; 7.19.
⁴⁷ Thuc. 5.26.3-4. Compare 2.21.3, 47.4; 5.103; 8.1.1.
⁴⁸ Among the many examples in Xenophon, see *Hell.* 3.1.17 and 19, 4.15; 4.1.22, 2.18, 4.5, 7.2 (at the frontier of one's home country), 7.7 (setting up a fortified post).
⁴⁹ See, for example, *Hell.* 3.4.18, and Xenophon's praise of Agesilaus in *Hell.* 4.3.20.
⁵⁰ *Anabasis* 7.8.8-10 and 21-22. *Hell.* 4.8.36-37, 7.2.20-23.
⁵¹ *Hell.* 6.5.41.
⁵² *Jug.* 63.1. See also 64.1; 90.1; 92.1-2, 6; 93.1; 94.6.

that began to take over the empire in the late second century C.E. The historian Dio Cassius actually produced as his first literary work a small book of dreams and signs predicting the rise to power of the then reigning emperor, Septimius Severus.[53]

In the fourth century C.E. Ammianus Marcellinus, the last great Latin historian, gave his readers a careful catalogue of the many different ways he approved for predicting the future. In Ammianus's work one had reached the twilight of paganism, and there one moved through a particularly dim and gloomy world, dark with foreboding, as signs and portents appeared to the horrified eyes of men abandoned by the guardian daemons to their Fate. By secret theurgic rituals, these last pagans tried to probe the future behind locked doors. "The elemental powers, when propitiated by divers rites, supply mortals with words of prophecy, as if from the veins of inexhaustible founts." Augury and auspice could also be used. "A god so directs the flight of birds that the sound of their bills or the passing flight of their wings in disturbed or in gentle passage foretells future events." The livers of sacrificial animals could also be inspected with the same intent. By this century, the rationale had begun to assume the forms of a Neoplatonized sun worship of the sort that one also sees in the writings of Ammianus's hero, the emperor Julian. "The Sun, the soul of the universe, sending out our minds from himself after the manner of sparks," is able to make the human mind "blaze up" in ecstatic prophecy like that of the Sibyls. Other techniques of predicting the future involved observing thunder, or lightning, or the stars. "And dreams, as Aristotle declares, are certain and trustworthy, when the person is in a deep sleep and the pupil of the eye is inclined to neither side but looks directly forward."[54] Here in Ammianus one is in contact with an immediate contemporary, a pagan whose lifespan overlapped with those of most of the first Christian historians. This was the sort of paganism they had to argue against.

Implicit in the belief in omens, dreams, and portents was the doctrine of Fate. What the gods revealed of the future had necessarily to come true. "None may escape his destined lot, not even a god."[55] Sometimes an oracle was conditional, and provided an avenue of escape if certain actions were avoided. But often there was only inevitable doom, and as the Greeks knew, "it is the hatefulest of all human sorrows to have much knowledge and no power."[56] The oracle or

---

[53] Dio Cassius 73(72).23.1-2, 75(74).3. Dio was significant because he was a rather proto-Byzantine figure, pointing towards the ideas and attitudes of the future in many ways—see Fergus Millar, *A Study of Cassius Dio* (Oxford, 1964) vii.
[54] Ammianus Marcellinus 21.1.8-12.
[55] Her. 1.91.
[56] Her. 9.16.

omen was itself sent by the divine, but from that point on no miracle occurred. In some mysterious fashion the person's fate would be worked out in the natural course of events. The person went to his foreordained doom by a series of acts of his own free will. But his choices always seemed to conspire against him. Much as in acts of Fortune, the catastrophe normally broke upon the person in some unexpected conjuncture of events.

There was another current of thought also present in the classical concept of Fate. This was a particular kind of psychological theory used to explain certain types of self-destructive action. In the mechanism involved, the person's own free decisions produced consequences whose possibility he *ought* to have foreseen. He did not anticipate what he ought to have foreseen because he had fallen into a certain kind of dangerous state of mind, which made him act unreasonably in certain crucial situations. One could be suddenly overcome by a powerful emotional state. Blind rage, insane jealousy, or uncontrollable lust could make a person act in the heat of a sudden moment in foolish and tragic ways. Or a person could fall into a frame of mind that caused him consistently to make unwise decisions in certain kinds of situations, until he slowly but inexorably led himself to his own doom. But there was no infringement of free will in the normal Greek understanding of the term. The unhappy consequences came as a result of the tragic victim's own decisions. It was not his will but his understanding that was the cause of his misfortune.[57] On the other hand, these dangerous states of mind tended to have a self-perpetuating component, in that a person caught up in such a frame of mind tended systematically to overlook or discount precisely that sort of information that could break him out of it. Only the experience of the traumatic act of self-destruction itself could clear the mind to reawakened self-knowledge. This was the standard *pattern of tragic downfall.* It was the basis, of course, of the Greek tragic drama, but it had an influence on Greek history writing as well.

One could have either or both aspects of Fate present in the story. Fate could mean the mysterious oracular prediction of some event long in advance, or it could mean only a kind of semideterministic psychological theory, but quite often it meant a combination of the two: the oracle spoke, but then the tragic flaw in the principal character actually produced the fated outcome. The story of King Croesus in Herodotus was an excellent example of the combination. The Delphic

---

[57] As Collingwood says (*The Idea of History*, 23-24), "This conception of history was the very opposite of deterministic, because the Greeks regarded the course of history as flexible and open to salutary modification by the well-instructed human will. Nothing that happens is inevitable. The person who is about to be involved in a tragedy is actually overwhelmed by it only because he is too blind to see his danger."

oracle foretold his end, but then his own character led him into the fatal decisions that destroyed his kingdom.[58] John L. Myres has argued that not only Croesus, but also Cyrus, Cambyses, Polycrates, Darius, Cleomenes, and Mardonius were all portrayed in Herodotus's history as tragic figures in the style of the Attic drama.[59]

Thucydides' sceptical method naturally excluded all notions of oracular fatalism or supernatural guiding forces. But F. M. Cornford argued that the purely *psychological* theory of tragic downfall influenced the basic plot of his history. The power and might of Athens led it into a fatal hybris that got the Athenian army destroyed on the foolish Sicilian expedition.[60] Later, in Polybius, the pattern of tragic downfall showed up in its simplest form in the story of Marcus Atilius Regulus and also in the story of Queen Teuta:[61] good Fortune caused a person to start acting cruelly and arrogantly and unmercifully, and then a sudden reversal of Fortune in the other direction sent the person to his or her destruction. When the Romans began to write history, Sallust for example took over this basic theme from the Greek world, particularly the idea that extremes of prosperity or of poverty were a temptation of Fortune that could lead men into the grips of overriding passions that could destroy them. When Rome became prosperous and powerful, he argued, the internal corruption began that would lead to her decline and fall.[62] On the other side, the revolutionary Catiline had found his most willing helpers among men rendered desperate by poverty, the other dangerous extreme.[63] In one form or another, therefore, the idea of Fate and psychological patterns of tragic self-destruction influenced Greek and Roman history writing

---

[58] Croesus's tragic character flaw was ἐλπίζειν, the pathological Hope of the compulsive gambler who squanders everything he or she has (and more) on foolish bets—Her. 1.54, 55-56, 75, 77, 80; also in Her. 1.30, where Bischoff, *Der Warner bei Herodot*, 32, speaks of "die Spannung, die zwischen der ἐλπίς des Fragers und den Antworten des Gefragten besteht." As Cornford points out (*Thucydides Mythistoricus*, 167-68), "Elpis had not to the Greeks the associations which Christianity has given to 'Hope'; she is not a virtue, but a dangerous passion.... Elpis is the passion which deludes man to count on the future as if he could perfectly control it."

[59] Myres, *Herodotus*, 77-78. "It is probably to Athenian influence that Herodotus owes his debt to the literary technique of tragedy. His residence at Athens comes midway in his career and affected him profoundly in other ways." See also 92, 137, 151, 169, and 218.

[60] Cornford, *Thucydides Mythistoricus*.

[61] Polyb. 1.31-35; 2.4.6-12.6.

[62] Sall. *Cat.* 10.1-3; 11; 12.2; 13.2-5; *Jug.* 41.1 and 3, 9 (vice leading to tragic downfall). Changes occurred in the new Roman context. Sallust offered a rationale for this that had a Latin flavor quite different from the Greek psychological theory of tragic downfall. To him, it was the vices of the flesh that led from prosperity to corruption and downfall. *Cat.* 13.2-5; 14.1-3; *Jug.* 1.1-4; 2.3-4.

[63] Sall. *Cat.* 14.1-3; 16.4; 18.4; 21.1-2; 37.

deeply. Even if it were only the trite statement that prosperity bred arrogance, it was a regular, frequent constituent of historical narratives in the pagan world.

In addition to this classical idea of Fate, with its Delphic oracles, and tragic heroes storming with majestic violence and passion against the onward sweep of destiny, there were other currents of fatalism present in the Roman world of the early Christian era. The practice of astrology began to invade the Roman empire from the East in the first century B.C.E. Astrologers taught that the position of the seven planets in the twelve signs of the zodiac and the twelve houses, together with the positive and negative aspects of the planets to one another, gave each person, at birth, a characteristic emotional signature. One could predict how that person would be angry, they said, and in what spheres of life; how the person would sense opportunity, and in what areas; the kinds of inner emotional turmoil the person would experience in certain situations; the person's ability to pursue long-term goals, and the style in which the person would pursue them (confrontationally, circuitously, analytically, intuitively, or whatever). In addition, the astrologers claimed that the planets in their circling set up cycles, spreading out over months and years of a person's life, in which the influence of Mars on anger, or Mercury on intellectual discrimination, or Saturn on defensiveness, would wax and wane in positive and negative fashion, and sometimes overlap disastrously, emotionally propelling the person uncontrollably into predictable actions in predictable directions. The ancient Graeco-Roman world was uncomfortable about the realm of the human emotions to begin with, and found the claims of astrology quite frightening. Astrology also exacerbated an already profound discomfort over the role of Fate in human life.

The first major discussion of astrology in a Graeco-Roman history was not until Tacitus, in the second century C.E., and the Christian historians later on rarely mention it explicitly. When Eusebius speaks of Fate, he usually chooses the oracles in Herodotus as his explicit target. But then one suddenly notes Eusebius claiming, in a quick aside, that the daemons who dwelt in the pagan oracular shrines, as at Delphi, actually gained their ability to predict the future from their knowledge of astrology, and one realizes that even when he seems to be using purely classical language about the role of Fate, he is doing this from the viewpoint of a postclassical world.[64] And even if the or-

---

[64] Tacitus, *Annals* 6.20-22; Eus. *PE* 6 pref. 1-3(236bc) and 6.1.6-7(237d-238a). Ancient horoscopes could be amusing. One was told that Sagittarians had square foreheads and profuse eyebrows, and that they were companionable people who were "jovial when they were drunk." Those born under Aries, on the other hand, were said to have contracted eyebrows and drawn cheeks, and had to be treated with caution since they were "quarrellers in a brawl" (Hippolytus, *Refutation of All Heresies* 4.23 and 4.15. A Gemini

thodox Christian theologians of the first several centuries did not obtain a fear of the possible influence of the stars directly from the astrologers themselves, they had always to deal with astrological beliefs at least secondhand, through the many heretical Christian gnostic systems that taught that the human ψυχή, the seat of the emotions, was enchained by the seven planetary archons and their rule of εἱμαρμένη. Astrology was an important and prevalent form of fatalistic belief that was often buried underground and not raised to the level of explicit discussion in orthodox Christian authors, but with which a Christian historian had to contend, at some level, in formulating his own understanding of history.

Another important form of fatalistic belief was the Stoic philosophical system, which had set up its own highly developed metaphysical view of the universe, in which Fate or εἱμαρμένη ultimately ruled the world. The Stoic Fate was equated with Zeus, and also with what we today would call the laws of nature. It was not quite what Herodotus or the Greek tragic dramatists had meant by Fate, but the Stoics did defend popular faith in oracles and the validity of oracular predictions of the future, partly as an attempted proof of their own philosophical theory of determinism. Stoicism was important from the Hellenistic period down to the second century of the early Roman empire. Even though it had no important supporters by the time of the first Christian histories, nevertheless Stoic ideas and terminology had entered the philosophical tradition of Middle Platonism, and in this indirect form, Stoicism still had to be confronted intellectually by Eusebius in the fourth century. Originally Stoic terms, like the distinction between τὸ ἐφ' ἡμῖν and τὸ οὐκ ἐφ' ἡμῖν ("what is in our power" and "what is not in our power," that is, what is fated), were used by Euse-

---

was promised (if other configurations did not interfere) "a life of ease and unfading youth spent in the arms of love" (Manilius, *Astronomica* 4.157). It must be remembered that astrology in the full sense, with mathematically calculated horoscopes, was a relatively new idea in the ancient world. The earliest known calculation of a horoscope based on all the planetary positions dates back only to 410 B.C.E., found on a cuneiform tablet referring to the positions of the stars on 29 April of that year (Cramer, *Astrology in Roman Law and Politics* 3-5). As can be seen from the systematic collection made by O. Neugebauer and H.B. Van Hoesen (*Greek Horoscopes* [Philadelphia: American Philosophical Society, 1959]vii) the earliest full horoscopes did not begin to appear in Greek texts until the first century B.C.E. Christian gnosticism quickly began to pick up astrological ideas in the next two centuries. On Jewish astrology and its connection with later Jewish angelology—another area in which Christians came into contact with astrological beliefs—see E.A. Wallis Budge, *Amulets and Superstitions* (New York: Dover, 1978) 386-89, 393-94. See also Pierre Boyancé, "La religion astrale de Platon à Cicéron," *Revues des Etudes Grecques* 65 (1952): 312-50; Leroy A. Campbell, *Mithraic Iconography and Ideology* (Leiden: Brill, 1968) 49, 54-55, 66-67, 261-63, 392; and Franz Cumont, *Les mystères de Mithra* (Brussels: Lamertin, 1913) 145.

bius to set out his own quite different philosophy of free will.[65]

In the fourth centruy C.E., the oracular shrines experienced a resurgence as part of the new anti-Christian pagan revivals. It was the oracle of Apollo at Didyma near Miletus—in Classical times one of the most widely recognized oracular sanctuaries after Delphi itself—that commanded the Great Persecution under Diocletian and Galerius in 303.[66] Later in the century, the emperor Julian's attempt to revive paganism and push back Christianity involved massive support of the oracular shrines, such as that of Apollo at Daphne outside Antioch.[67] In the long battle in that century between Christianity and the new paganism (with its basically Late Neoplatonic inspiration), both sides regarded the use of oracles and other such fortune-telling techniques as a fundamental line of division between the two religions. What we could now call magical methods of predicting the future were an intrinsic and important part of the new paganism, but feared and rejected by orthodox and theologically sophisticated Christians. The dividing line was not necessarily so clear, of course, to many ordinary, uneducated Christians, which made the issue even more important to bishops and theologians who wanted to deliver their flocks from that evil.

When Eusebius therefore began writing the first Christian history, "Fate" meant a variety of things. The classical histories, with their oracles, dreams, and portents, were still read as masterpieces of literature, as were also the classical tragedies. The oracles pronounced at Delphi and preserved in Herodotus were especially well known. The concept of the tragic hero struggling against destiny was an intrinsic part of Greek culture. Astrology and gnosticism were also deeply fatalistic, though in a way different from the classical understanding of Fate. Stoic ideas still had to be fought intellectually because of their role in the Middle Platonic philosophical tradition, and the Stoics had supported oracular prediction of the future. Last of all, the resurgent neo-paganism of the fourth century revived the old oracular shrines and eagerly supported various other methods of divination. It was the combination of all these things that had to be combated in order to develop a Christian view of history, but in particular it was the central role of the concept of Fate in Greek and Roman historiography—a role

---

[65] For example, Eus. *PE* 6.6.22(245c). There were also linkages between astrology and Late Stoicism, as one sees in more specialized works like Manilius's *Astronomica*, but also in widely read Late Stoic authors like Seneca, *Quaestiones Naturales* 3.29.1, 27.1, and 30.8.

[66] Eusebius *VC* 2.50-51; Lactantius, *On the Deaths of the Persecutors* 11. See Henry Chadwick, *The Early Church* (Harmondsworth, England: Penguin, 1967) 121; W.H.C. Frend, *Martyrdom and Persecution in the Early Church* (Oxford: Blackwell, 1965) 129.

[67] Socrates *HE* 3.18-19; Sozomen *HE* 5.19-20; Theodoret *HE* 3.10-11; Ammianus Marcellinus 22.12.6-13.3; 25.4.17.

it had played from the very beginning—that made the issue almost unavoidable for Eusebius.

A notion of retribution was sometimes involved in the classical doctrine of Fate. Herodotus recounted many stories in which a human being was punished for having committed some enormous moral outrage. "The gods do greatly punish great wrongdoing."[68] But even though Herodotus said in one place that "no man on earth doth wrong but at last shall suffer requital,"[69] it was not petty offenses that were at stake for him but only great atrocities and infamous deeds of wanton cruelty and violence. A second variety of retribution stories concerned cases in which human beings committed an act of sacrilege against something that had been dedicated to the gods.[70] As Rudolf Otto pointed out, the "idea of the holy" in its primitive original form conveyed the idea of mysterious power and danger completely divorced from any moral component, so this second variety of retribution story was very important, but more primitive than the more moralistically conceived type.

A third type of retribution story involved the widespread Ancient Near Eastern notion of the jealousy ($\phi\theta\delta\nu o\varsigma$) of the gods. As Solon said to Croesus by way of warning, "Well I know how jealous is Heaven and how it loves to trouble us."[71] Any kind of human greatness or excellence or beauty was apt to arouse the irritation of some god. As Euripides pointed out in his *Hippolytus*, even piety towards the gods was dangerous if it caused one to stand out of the ordinary. An extreme, but widespread piece of advice throughout the general Ancient Near Eastern world was that the best way to get along with the gods was to avoid doing anything that would attract their attention. As Herodotus put it, in Greek fashion,

> You see how God strikes with his lightning those living beings who stand out above the rest, and does not permit them to make an ostentatious show, while the smaller ones do not irritate him at all. You see how it is always the biggest houses and the tallest trees at which he hurls his thunderbolts. For God loves to cut short everything that stands out above the rest. In the same way a large army is completely destroyed by a small one whenever God is jealous and sends them fear or thunder, by which they perish in a manner unworthy of themselves. For God does not permit anyone besides himself to have high and mighty ideas.[72]

---

[68] Her. 2.120. For examples see 1.13, 86, 118-119 and 130, 166-167, 212-214; 4.202 and 205; 6.72, 75 and 84; 7.133-137; 8.105-106.
[69] Her. 5.56.
[70] Her. 1.105; 3.29-30, 33, 64; 6.75 and 84; 8.129.
[71] Her. 1.32.
[72] Her. 7.10. For examples, see 1.8-12, 34; 8.13, 109.

This notion of the jealousy of the gods was a basic and characteristic mode of ancient thought.

Thucydides naturally rejected all ideas of divine retribution. He did not regard the fundamental structures of the universe as being either personal or moral. The plague at Athens showed, he believed, that moral constraints existed only on a surface layer even of the human psyche.[73] His successor Xenophon spoke more piously. "The gods do not overlook either those who act impiously or those who do wicked, unholy things."[74] Polybius had two retribution stories, but in general did not think in those terms,[75] while Sallust went so far as to say that Fortune acted only *ex lubidine*, on the basis of arbitrary, irrational whim.[76] So as these examples illustrate, in the pre-Christian period historians were more apt to view the basic structures of history in fairly amoral terms, but the pious ones could and did introduce into their histories notions of moral judgment, or "jealous" retribution against human pride and presumption.

Ideas of divine moral retribution in history caused early Christians no trouble at all, of course—it fitted in smoothly with their own view of the divine justice. The concept of the jealousy of the gods raised more problems. This was a deeply felt expression of the general Greek pessimism towards existence. Joy over any kind of success or prosperity became tinged with apprehension that Fortune, or a jealous god, or some dark force intrinsic in the nature of things would strike in retribution. Over in the eastern, Greek-speaking half of the Roman empire, not even Christians could remove that dark fear completely from their minds. It was too fundamental a part of the Greek attitude towards life. Yet the Christian God could hardly be said to be an enemy of the good, the excellent, and the truly beautiful. So an interesting compromise was worked out, which the first Christian historians then used in their histories, as shall be seen in subsequent chapters. The idea of jealous supernatural powers was retained, but this function was assigned to daemons, who became totally evil beings in Christian teaching. The "jealousy" of "the daemons who hate the good" was then blamed in early Christian histories for certain kinds of events in a way closely analogous to earlier pagan teaching about the jealous and envious acts of the Olympian gods. The idea of the jealousy of the gods did not disappear, it was merely reinterpreted.

Ancient Graeco-Roman historiography therefore raised a series of serious problems for the first Christian historians. It was the intellectual tradition in which they had been cast. Yet it regarded the histori-

---

[73] Thuc. 2.52-53.
[74] Xen. *Hell*. 5.4.1. See also 2.4.14-15; 6.4.30-31.
[75] Polyb. 1.84.9-10; 15.20.5-8.
[76] Sall. *Cat.* 8.1; 51.25.

cal human being as one whose life was continuously at the mercy of the fortuitous. Oracles, dreams, and omens—as well as the stars—cast a web of fate upon the human future. The gods beheld the works of men and women through eyes of jealousy. This dark vision of reality was obviously alien to the Judaeo-Christian understanding of God and history, so that some sort of response was demanded, but various ancient Jewish and Christian historical thinkers developed quite different answers to this problem.

CHAPTER FOUR

Christianity in the Roman Forum: Tertullian and the Apologetic Use of History

Mark S. Burrows

Tertullian's *Apology* entered no empty world. The arena of late antiquity bristled with debates regarding the nature of religion, society, and the gods. As the empire expanded, those discussions inevitably came to question the status of "new" or "foreign" religions, such as Christianity. If we can rely on Dio Cassius' report of Maecenas' speech to the emperor Augustus, we have an early record of the Roman distrust of such aberrations: "Those who attempt to distort our religion you should abhor and punish, not merely for the sake of the gods, but because the emergence of new divinities in place of the old persuades many to adopt foreign practices, from which spring up conspiracies, factions, and political clubs which are far from profitable to a monarchy."[1] Within this world which was skeptical of intrusions on the hallowed ground of "tradition," Tertullian's treatise was by no means the first attempt at a Christian apology. Such responses could already by this time look to the precedent of a developing genre. Before this apologist's contribution had appeared, Christian apologetics already claimed a mature literary tradition in the Greek realm,[2] and the internal evidence of this first Latin apology suggests that Tertullian was not unaware of these arguments. Of course, it must also be said that Christianity was not the only religion which fell under severe criticism, nor were Christians the only ones who raised a critical voice regarding the "pagan" religious traditions. The Romans themselves had spoken criti-

---

[1] Dio Cassius, cited in Robert L. Wilken, *The Christians as the Romans Saw Them* (New Haven: Yale Univerity Press, 1984), pp. 62-3.

[2] The task of unravelling the possible connections between Tertullian's *Apology* and the earlier writings of Justin Martyr, Athenagoras, Theophilus, et al., lies beyond the scope of this study. Here we must be content to observe the strong parallels which exist between these sources; we can only suggest that the internal evidence, which we will refer to sparingly at various points in our study, supports the hypothesis that some direct link must be made between the Greek and subsequent Latin contributions to this genre.

cally of their myths and religious practices, subjecting them to scrutiny, revision, and even mockery by rhetors and playwrights, philosophers and emperors. Thus, in the broader sphere of Latin letters, a Christian writer such as Tertullian was by no means a pioneer in criticizing the Roman worship of the gods. He could depend, for example, upon the philosophical precedent of Cicero;[3] his own use of irony as a weapon against Roman traditions reflected a measure of the biting satire of Lucian.[4] Indeed, this was a world in which rhetoric spoils all sincerity.

Christian apologists were by no means unaware of the arguments levelled against them. In the case of Tertullian as among the earlier Greeks, the defense of Christianity became essentially a redefinition of "antiquity" and "novelty," of *vetera et nova*. Apologetics could not afford to avoid the question of history. The apologists in general did not see themselves as defenders of any "new" phenomena upon the landscape of religious cults or philosophical schools in the Roman world. Rather, they cast their defense upon the ancient foundations of the Jewish heritage, one which they held to be far superior to the novelty of Roman institutions and practices. Thus, the dialogue provided by such an apology became a complex web of arguments—with the defenders of Roman institutions, with indigenous critics of Roman traditions and practices, and with Jewish historians. The margins of Tertullian's text spill over with voices of a long, ongoing debate, belying his suggestion at the outset of his treatise that truth should be allowed to advance "by the hidden path of silent literature."[5] This world is no empty place, nor should we miss the irony of Tertullian's contention that literature was in any way "silent."

Tertullian's *Apology* is on the surface a forensic defense of the legitimacy of Christianity, a legal argument regarding the status of Christians within the Roman Empire. On a more profound level, however, it must be understood as a treatise on origins—the origin of Christianity, of course, but also origins having a more immediate bearing upon "pagan" society. Thus, the forensic "defense" of the Christian truth is interspersed with explanations regarding the origins of Roman worship and law, the origin and function of the demons, the cause of contemporary Roman "superstitions" and of the "irreligiosity" which

---

[3] We shall subsequently refer in greater detail to Tertullian's dependence on Cicero's *de natura deorum*; cf. for example, p. 221.

[4] Cf. below, pp. 221-2.

[5] Tertullian, *Apologeticus*, i. 1. All references are cited according to the text and translation of the Loeb edition; *Tertullian and Minucius Felix*, trans. by T. R. Glover, W. C. A. Kerr and G. H. Rendall (Cambridge, Massachusetts: Harvard University Press, 1931), i. 1. References to this treatise will be cited parenthetically within the corpus of the paper, noting chapter and verse only.

stood to condemn not Christian but Roman traditions. In this sense, Tertullian here articulates a complex historical argument which, breaking beyond the limits of strictly "intramural" categories, presses the criticism to the very heart of Roman religious sensibilities. Not only does this Latin apologist defend Christians from the legal charges set against them, as had his Greek predecessors, but he also forwards a positive argument, a startling "retorsion" of the Roman indictment which underscored the constructive role of Christianity in and for Roman society. With this "apology" we hear much more than a defensive reaction to an unjust persecution, even though this theme forms the outer structure of his argument; rather, Tertullian advances a full-fledged philosophy of history, one which exposes what he calls "the darkness of antiquity" (iv. 7) by accounting for the rise (and demise) of Roman morality, law, and religion.

The constructive edge of his argument is thus not merely meant as a plea for the survival of Christianity. Beneath the surface of this theme, it stands as an argument which projects Christianity as the ultimate hope of the survival of society itself. Tertullian's *Apology*, therefore, borrows the accepted form of forensic "retorsion" in order to ridicule the superficiality of the Roman condemnation of Christianity, arguing not merely for the legal status of Christianity but for the very survival of Rome itself. And, as we shall subsequently point out in greater detail, Tertullian develops this argument with specific and prominent attention given to the realm of history. This rhetor identifies the apologist's task in conjunction with the writing of history. His apology thus serves his case by interpreting the annals not only of Jerusalem and the emergence of the Christian community, but of Rome itself.

The thrust of this study will presume familiarity with recent scholarship regarding Tertullian's reliance on rhetoric.[6] Our focus shall be upon the historical method this apologist applies in his rhetorical argument, not upon the shape of the rhetoric itself. Yet our analysis of the historical arguments he advances depends to a large extent upon this work, primarily because the contribution of this work on Roman rheto-

---

[6] The bibliography on this question alone is immense. A representative survey of the salient contributions must include the following, listed here in order of appearance. Richard Heinze, *Tertullian's Apologeticum*, Vol. LXII: *Berichte über die Verhandlungen der königlich sächsischen Gesellschaft der Wissenschaften zu Leipzig, Philologische-historiche Klasse* (Leipzig: B. G. Teubner, 1910). Joseph Lortz, *Tertullian als Apologet*, Bds. 1 und 2 (Muenster: Aschendorffsche Verlagsbuchhandlung, 1927/8). Carl Becker, *Tertullians Apologeticum. Werden und Leistung* (Muenchen: Koesel Verlag, 1954). Timothy D. Barnes, *Tertullian. A Historical and Literary Study* (Oxford: Clarendon Press, 1971). Robert D. Sider, *Ancient Rhetoric and the Art of Tertullian* (Oxford: University Press, 1971). Sider provides a useful survey regarding the state of scholarship on this matter in his opening chapter, "The Problem," pp. 1-10.

ric locates Tertullian's writings squarely within the sphere of existing literary models. And, as we shall suggest, several of his key arguments are not inventions of his own design, but are derived from this rhetorical tradition. Consequently, we must acknowledge at least in a brief manner the contribution of earlier scholarship on this decisive matter.

Beginning early in this century, the *Apology* in particular has received three consecutive generations of careful scrutiny as a product of classical forms of rhetoric, a massive undertaking which we can only hope to summarize in its crudest outline here. In 1910, Richard Heinze published his ground-breaking piece entitled simply *Tertullians 'Apologeticum,'*[7] in which he argued that Tertullian's knowledge of Roman forensic practice enabled him to refashion the traditional apologetic material following legal precedent. In his detailed analysis of the text, Heinze argued that Tertullian was merely adopting well-established rhetorical divisions of argumentation: namely, an *exordium* (chs. i-iii), *partitio* and *propositio* (iv. 1-2), a *refutatio* (iv-xlv), and a final *peroratio* (xlvi-l).[8] Joseph Lortz, building upon the foundation of Heinze's work, argued that this strictly established external structure was the major feature elevating this apologist's argument above the "diffused," "largely polemic", and "crudely fashioned" material arguments of the Greek apologists. That is, the unique contribution of Tertullian lay not so much in the content as in the form of his argument. Describing the treatise as "a truly artistic inspiration" which stands as "the mature fruit of a long, interior development,"[9] Lortz faults Heinze only in failing to acknowledge the personal genius by which Tertullian enlivened the classical form of forensic rhetoric in arguing his case. Finally, and most recently, Robert Sider has devoted a major monograph to the consideration of the rhetorical background of Tertullian's writing.[10] In this thorough consideration of the rhetorical influences upon the broader spectrum of Tertullian's oeuvre, Sider refines Heinze's earlier thesis by arguing that Cicero and Quintilian stand as the primary sources upon which Tertullian drew, both for form and for the fundamental "patterns of argument" which were available from "the rhetoric of law courts."[11] His work defies a generalized analysis, proceeding as it does with meticulous attention to detail and nuance. In a word, the fruit of his study is the conclusion that Tertullian was "deeply concerned to integrate Christianity and classical culture," a commitment which Sider traces in this apologist's "deep absorption in the rhetorical habit of thought" and even in the "pro-

---

[7] Heinze, *op. cit.*
[8] *Ibid.*, pp. 13, 21ff.
[9] Lortz, Vol. II, pp. 152ff.; 169.
[10] Sider, *op. cit.*
[11] *Ibid.*, pp. 4, 38.

gramme of topics" which he inherited from the classical tradition.[12] The combined force of these studies confirms Jean-Claude Fredouille's recent claim that Tertullian represents "la première rhétorique chrétienne";[13] the intention of our study will be to explore his rhetoric in a different direction, directing primary attention to the arguments regarding history with which Tertullian filled those classical forms of rhetoric.

Form was not the only legacy which Tertullian inherited from his cultural surroundings. With regard to the style of his argument, these studies have also pointed to the manner in which this Latin apologist stands squarely in the mainstream of the Second Sophistic,[14] a "movement" which added virtuosity in argument to Quintilian's classic definition of the orator's task as that of instructing, moving, and pleasing.[15] As Barnes concludes on this subject, Tertullian is a fitting exemplar of this tradition because of "the lavish display of erudition and the prominence of philosophical themes" in his rhetoric. "The massive erudition [of his writing]," he contends, "was not designed as mere ostentation. Those who were familiar with the Sophistic Movement of the second century would not have expected less of an expert orator. Tertullian had shown himself at least the equal of an Apuleius."[16] Although Sider warns us against overemphasizing what he calls "the mere sophistical techniques of his argumentation,"[17] it is clear that the Second Sophistic not only provided this apologist with a "manual of style" for persuasive declamation.[18] but also equipped him with a reliable guide on how

---

[12] *Ibid.*, esp. pp. 128ff.

[13] Jean-Claude Fredouille, *Tertullien et la conversion de la culture antique* (Paris: Études Augustiniennes, 1972), p. 29. For a more detailed bibliography concerning this thesis, cf. *ibid.*, p. 29, n. 2.

[14] Cf. Barnes, p. 211; also, E. L. Bowie, "Greeks and Their Past in the Second Sophistic," *Studies in Ancient Society. Past and Present Series* (London: Routledge and Kegan Paul, 1974), pp. 166-209. Note here Bowie's insistence that "the archaism of language and style [which is present in the Latin as well as Greek world] is only part of a wider tendency, a tendency that prevails in literature not only in style but also *in choice of theme and treatment,*" p. 167 (my emphasis). He goes on to point out that "certainly by the second half of the first century A.D. declamation [in its role as public entertainment] seems to have moved into the first rank of cultural activities and acquired an unprecedented and almost unintelligible popularity." At the same time, he is intent on establishing that such rhetoric was anything but "purely artificial"; the late antique world did not distinguish "entertainment" from the category of the "inartificial" as modern sensibilities might be prone to do. Cf. pp. 168-9.

[15] Quintilian, *Inst. Orat.* III.5.2; also, cf. Barnes, p. 211.

[16] *Ibid.*, p. 109.

[17] Sider, p. 5.

[18] The distinction between "style" and "form" is not always made clear in discussions of Latin rhetoric and the Second Sophistic. Sider is nost helpful in defining "form" in terms of the argument's internal argument, whereas "style" has to do with the flourish with which such an argument is expounded by the rhetor.

to employ the *exempla* which occur with such frequency in his works. Barnes argues in this regard that "Quintilian defined an *exemplum* as the recalling of some action (historical or imaginary) which was useful for driving home the orator's point."[19] The lists and references—historical, philosophical, literary—abound at virtually every stage of Tertullian's argumentation, leading Barnes and Sider to conclude that he may have borrowed from standard florilegia to defend his argument as did other rhetors of the day.[20]

For the purposes of this paper, we will here accept the results of these studies of Tertullian's reliance on classical rhetoric; aside from an occasional reference to this work when germane to our subject matter, we will not indulge in a tedious rehearsal of the details produced by this prodigious scholarly gathering. The basis upon which our study proceeds, therefore, accepts Sider's claim that this apologist adopted "the age-old rhetorical techniques of sophistical argumentation" while borrowing the specific forms of his arguments from the well-spring of classical rhetoric, particularly as he drew from the elegant treatises of Cicero and Quintilian.[21] Indeed, we shall here accept Sider's carefully defended contention—which is a broader elaboration of the earlier arguments of both Heinze and Lortz on the same point—that this formal dependence establishes the superiority of Tertullian's treatise over his Greek predecessors. A mere repetition of this work would not substantially advance our appreciation of Tertullian's *Apology*. Rather, while we shall have recourse to speak of "form" at several points, the focus of this study will be upon the historical detail of Tertullian's apologetic argument, the elaborate fabric of themes by which he draws upon the varied threads of diverse historians' work to weave his own case for the legitimacy of Christianity. In this regard, we will first consider Tertullian's admonition to "consult [Roman] histories," considering in particular the emphasis he gives to earlier historical and philosophical arguments by which Romans and Greeks had understood—sometimes critically, at other times with conflicting evidence—their own religious traditions. That is, we will see that Tertullian's critique of Roman religion is often fashioned in the borrowed categories of earlier (classical) rhetorical arguments. We shall also consider Tertullian's use of Judaism as the historical foundation upon which he

---

[19] Barnes, pp. 217-8.

[20] *Ibid.* Barnes also adds a note of caution with regard to the apologist's use of Greek philosophy, however, pointing out that Tertullian's "dependence on excerpts alone could not account for [his] long quotations or for his knowledge of [the variety of] Platonic dialogues" which he introduces into his writings. Without commenting here upon the apologist's broader oeuvre, we would agree with this qualification as a fair conclusion to draw from the *Apology*.

[21] Sider, p. 5.

places the Christian claim for antiquity. From the vantage point of this historiographical perspective, he could articulate a strong argument for an "antiquity" which shamed the Romans in their false pride. His argument on the matter of the Judaeo-Christian historical tradition, which posits a theme of the "transfer" from things old to new, thus portrays Christianity as the rightful heir to Judaism's historical claims. Here we see the sharp polemic edge of his historical argument against Judaism, one which presumably spoke to the antipathies already held by earlier Roman historians of the empire.[22] Finally, we shall suggest that the broader framework in which Tertullian sets his forensic argument translates the immediate quest of his rhetoric into a broader eschatological framework. At stake is a judgment and a "case" of sorts, though here the "charge" levelled has nothing to do with the Christians and everything to do with the Romans—namely, in terms of their neglect not of "the gods," but of "the true religion of the true God." Eschatology defines "tradition" on an entirely new basis. On this point, we see the emerging outlines of a peculiarly Christian interpretation of history, a model which sets the entire forensic arena in the higher "court" of divine judgment at the final "day of judgment" (e.g., xxiii. 14-5).

Drawing upon an established form of forensic rhetoric in the *Apology*,[23] Tertullian acts as an advocate, bringing a carefully crafted and stylistically polished case for Christianity not simply before "the Roman magistrates" (i. 1), but before the literate Roman audience of his day. Indeed, it is entirely reasonable to assume—with Lortz, Barnes, Sider, et al.—that the genre of Christian apologetics developed in order to articulate the message of Christianity in a sophisticated form— and for a sophisticated audience—which Christian scriptures alone were unable to accomplish. Christianity here enters the Roman forum in a deliberate and forceful manner, thereby opposing Celsus' roughly contemporaneous portrait of Christianity as "an obscure and secret association"[24] or Lucian's caricature of this "new" religion as a flight

---

[22] Cf. Wilken, *Judaism and the Early Christian Mind. A Study of Cyril of Alexandria's Exegesis and Theology* (New Haven: Yale University Press, 1971), p. 43. Here Wilken argues that "the bond between Judaism and the Graeco-Roman culture was torn asunder by the Roman-Jewish wars. The epoch of Philo was the last in which the ideals of a brotherhood between Greeks and Jews could still be seriously envisaged." We shall subsequently see the subtle manner in which Tertullian made use of this estrangement to speak of the positive relationship of "Jewish antiquity" to Rome via the "new" legal consciousness of Christianity.

[23] Sider's thesis, shared by most commentators on Tertullian's rhetoric cited above, n. 7.

[24] Cited in Wilken, *Christians as the Romans Saw Them*, pp. 44-7. Nock also refers to Celsus' critique of Christianity as a "mass movement of falling away from 'tradition.'" *Conversion: The Old and New in Religion from Alexander the Great to Augustine of Hippo* (London, 1933), p. 207. Note that Tertullian's *Apology* is filled with references to

from rationality.²⁵ It now remains for us to consider the more specific manner in which Tertullian fashions his apologetic argument.

I. THE ROMANS AS WITNESSES AGAINST THEIR OWN CASE: "Consult your own histories . . ."

Tertullian prefaces his discussion of the origin of Roman laws against Christians by instructing his readers to "consult your histories"! (v. 3). Indeed, this early argument justifies our thesis that Tertullian's apology rests upon the foundation of historical evidence, borrowed from either earlier rhetors or Roman historians. On this point, he applies Quintilian's advice on the art of rhetoric concerning

> the advantage derived from the knowledge of historical facts and precedents, with which it is most desirable that our orator should be acquainted; for such knowledge will save him from having to acquire all his evidence from his client and will enable him to draw much that is germane to his case from the careful study of antiquity. And such arguments will be all the more effective, since they alone will be above suspicion of prejudice or partiality.²⁶

"The careful study of antiquity": on this basis Tertullian advances his case against the Roman persecution of Christians, here echoing a historiographical perspective already established in the argument of Melito of Sardis.²⁷ According to this "historical" argument,²⁸ Roman

---

the "openness" of both Judaism and Christianity—in terms of worship, the accessibility of their scriptures, etc. This becomes an integral part of the apologist's insistence that the "special revelation" of God to the Jews and Christians was mediated in written texts which could be scrutinized by all with equal measure.

²⁵ Lucian, cf. "Lover of Lies." Also, note Galen's notion of Christianity as a matter of the "uneducated"; Cicero, *De natura deorum*, I.117, II.72; Tacitus, *Annals*, xv. 4. A discussion of the Roman understanding of "superstition" would be helpful at this juncture. Note that Suetonius spoke of Christianity as "a new and mischievous superstition"; cited in Wilken, *Christians*, p. 50, and *ibid.*, pp. 49, 79ff. Stephen Benko, "Pagan Criticism of Christianity During the First Two Centuries," *Aufstieg und Niedergang der römischen Welt*. II/23.2.

²⁶ Quintilian, *Inst. Orat.*, x.1.34.

²⁷ Barnes, "Legislation against the Christians," *Journal of Religious Studies* 58 (1968): 34-5.

²⁸ Of course, we are using "historical" in a late antique sense, without commenting upon the reliability of such conclusions. An interesting note on the sincerity with which rhetors used "historical" arguments can be gleaned from Cicero's *Paradoxa Stoicorum*, in which he warns his reader against an indiscriminate use of rhetoric as mere "entertainment"; in a tone similar to later disclaimers of both Tertullian and Minucius Felix—who are not engaged in "mere dialectic," but in the pursuit of "truth"—Cicero had there argued that "our verdict must be the result of scrupulous balancing not of inflated eloquence but of hard facts." *Ibid.*, xv.

authorities accepted Christianity until the *institutum Neronianum*,[29] a piece of legislation which, attributed by Melito and subsequently by Tertullian to Nero, was held to be inadequate because of the widely accepted scorn cast upon this emperor's reputation. This argument was by no means one found only among Christian apologists. Tertullian is apparently also aware of the earlier precedent contributed to the literary record by Tacitus, presumably the Roman historian to whom the apologist's veiled challenge refers (i.e., *commentarios vestros*). In Tacitus' *Annals*, we find an explicit reference to Nero as the emperor who first persecuted Christians: ". . . it seemed that [the Christians] were destroyed not for the common good, but because of the cruelty of one man."[30] Yet Roman and Christian historiography agreed on one point of interpretation: namely, the general disdain cast upon this debauched emperor's reputation. In contrast to the Christian apologists, however, Roman historians were not as quick to attack legislation attributed to bad emperors, confining criticism to their person. Thus, a theme which for Tacitus had been an acknowledgement of an historical occurrence becomes an apologetic disclaimer for Melito and, following him, for Tertullian:

> But we glory—nothing less than glory—to have had such a man [as Nero] to inaugurate our condemnation. One who knows Nero can understand that, unless a thing were good—and very good—it was not condemned by Nero . . . . Such are ever our persecutors—men unjust, impious, foul—men whom you yourselves are accustomed to condemn; and those whom they condemn you have become accustomed to restore. (v. 3-5)

On the basis of this historical analysis, Tertullian does not miss the chance to extend his argument by indicting current legal practice: "What sort of laws, then, are those which are only used against us by the impious, the unjust, the foul, the fierce, the vain, the demented?" (v. 7). And, finally, in the same argument we hear Tertullian call upon Marcus Aurelius, whom he styles with an eccentric flair as the "protector" of Christians, to balance positively the argument from history regarding emperors. If Nero had condemned those whom Marcus Aurelius "protected," what attitude could the Romans possibly have toward Christians but one of toleration—if not of outright embrace? The historical argument thus focuses not upon the existence of laws which "raised the imperial sword against this [Christian] school" (v. 3), but upon the character of those emperors who created or enforced as contrasted with those who overlooked such legislation. History be-

---

[29] This is a phrase occurring not explicitly in the *Apology*, but in the earlier *Ad nationes*; see Barnes, "Legislation," p. 34.
[30] *Annals*, xv. 44.

comes an apologetic tool in Tertullian's hands, but only by moving within the orbit of established precedents of earlier Roman historians.

On the matter of the history of Roman law, Tertullian had also earlier commented on the apparently capricious process of selection by which some laws were maintained, others forgotten: "How many of your laws lie forgotten, still to be reformed? What recommends a law is not the number of its years nor the dignity of its makers, but its equity and nothing else" (iv. 10). Antiquity cannot be a viable defense of *any* law; in an insistent argument regarding the origins of Roman legislation, Tertullian directly opposes the notion that extant laws had fallen from the heavens (iv. 5). As creations of the human will, they are subject to error, and, if so proven, stand in need of reform. Again here the apologist forwards an argument from Roman history, citing a series of *exempla* which defend his claim that Roman law is currently reformable because already reformed by Romans *in the past* (cf. iv. 6-9). Tertullian extends his examination of "origins" to consider the manner in which laws, once created, were subsequently maintained. The reverence for antiquity is only credible, we hear him saying, if the traditions are also faithfully conserved. The argument is a compelling one, since Tertullian uses Roman *history*—rather than the "justice" involved in his specific case—to argue against the notion that Roman law was permanently binding, or irreformable. The history of Roman society had established the precedent that all law, including Roman law, is anything but inviolable, subject rather to the judgments of the present—i.e., to the dictates of the "magistrates," the influential senatorial class whom Tertullian addresses with the full force of his characteristic irony as "the most religious protectors and maintainers of laws" (vi. 1), those who are not invested with authority in order to enforce the laws but so that they might "do justice" (i. 1). Tertullian has focused the subject of that "justice" beyond the immediate concerns of his defense of Christianity, however; his deeper concern is that the Romans treat their own legal heritage with justice *and* consistency. Our apologist, a relentless historian as we have seen, hereby reveals his preference for "case law"!

As he unfolds his apology, it becomes increasingly clear that it is only in a superficial sense that the Christians are facing indictment; on a more profound level, Tertullian's argument has placed the law itself on trial, and the "stewards" of the Roman legal tradition are called upon to defend—or reform—the laws which "the mob"[31] enforces ac-

---

[31] We can only suggest at this point that Tertullian's opposition to "the mob" was one which struck at the heart of Roman fear of anarchy, of any disintegration of the *stabilitas* which the law was meant to maintain. Cf. here Tacitus' displeasure with the manner in which "the crowd" controlled public affairs; *Annals*, xv. 44, and the discussion in Benko, "Pagan Criticism," pp. 1062ff.

cording to its own anarchical devices. Sider reminds us that such an argument, with its insistent appeal to the responsibility of the judge (cf. iv. 10-13), was a commonplace for Roman forensic practice.[32] Thus, Tertullian subtly inverts the argument against Christians by defining "justice" rather than blind obedience as the basis of Roman law. Unlike Justin's argument, which contented itself with challenging the specific accusations against Christians (and the *nomen Christianorum*; see *First Apology*, 3-4), Tertullian answers the *nominis odium* (iii. 5) by launching his attack upon the very fiber of Roman legal practice insofar as it came to exert "an unjust tyranny from the citadel" (iv. 4). As he reminds his reader through his recitation of the history of the Roman legal tradition, law was not irreformable; it was the primary responsibility of the judge—in this case, the readers of the *Apology*—not merely to honor the legacy of the past, but to define justice in the present.

The remark of a recent scholar in defense of the historian's guild provides an apt summary of Tertullian's tactic here, when he pointed out that "unexamined history operates as fate."[33] This apologist's primary aim may well confront the problems facing Christians, but he pleads his case by turning his reader's attention to the past, insisting that Romans must understand the function of their own traditions if they are to act with justice and integrity in the present. Thus, Tertullian places the specific focus upon the anti-Christian legislation into the broader framework of a history of law, an arena in which Tertullian calls to his defense the redoubtable witness of the Romans themselves.

Tertullian presses this historical argument even further by challenging the integrity of the Roman veneration of "tradition." Addressing himself with an ironic intent only slightly veiled by flattery, Tertullian calls upon the "most religious protectors and maintainers of law and ancestral usages" to argue that Romans, and not Christians, were despisers of "ancestral tradition":

> Where is the religious awe, where is the veneration owed by you to your ancestors? In dress, habit of life, furniture, feeling, yes! and speech, you have renounced your ancestors. *You are forever praising antiquity, and every day you improvise some new way of life.* All of which goes to prove that, while you abandon the good usages of your ancestors, you keep and maintain the practices you should not have, and what you should have kept you have not maintained. (vi. 9-10 my emphasis)

Again here the thrust of Tertullian's defense arises from a "case law"

---

[32] Sider, pp. 75-6.
[33] David Steinmetz, "The Necessity of the Past," *Theology Today* 33 (1976): 173.

approach to the apologist's task, placing his specific argument within a broader philosophy of law. He is bent on proving that the Roman persecution of Christians is a relative novelty, one which reflects a broader contempt for the more ancient traditions which the decadence of Nero's reign and the wave of more recent persecutions under Domitian (cf. v. 4) had blurred. Here he echoes a well-established rhetorical theme: namely, historical memory unveils the steady sense of decline in Roman institutional, social, and moral life.[34] Indeed, Tertullian seems to be taking Tacitus here at his word when the earlier historian had left his readers with the challenge that the decadence of the present must always be measured in terms of past glories: "may the honorable competition of our present with our past long remain!" (*Annals* III. iv.). Tertullian stands with Tacitus in criticizing the decadence of the present, but he invokes this historical argument for his peculiar apologetic purpose to argue for Roman toleration of Christians.

In a later discussion, Tertullian addresses his apology to another argument which Roman historiography had advanced. Mentioning the condemnation of Christians as "the enemies of the human race" (cf. *Apol.* xxxvii. 8), the apologist may here have Tacitus' indictment in mind. In his *Annals*, this Roman historian had condemned Christians on the basis of their "hatred of the human race" (xv. 44), the same argument he elsewhere levelled against the Jews (cf. *Histories* v. 5.1.).[35] Tertullian's subsequent characterization of the Christian community must be interpreted in the shadow of this criticism; thus, it is no accident that we find him arguing in good Stoic fashion that Christians are "citizens . . . of the universe" (xxxviii. 3) and thereby respect public order by avoiding factiousness (xxxviii. 2), and that the Christian community is known by its commitment to the emperor (xxxix. 2; here we come upon the apologist's premise that the *pax romana* represents a universal peace) and by its "work of love" (xxxix. 7). In conjunction with this argument, Tertullian explicitly draws upon Christian scripture—the single direct biblical reference in the treatise!—as a defense against the Roman accusation that Christians were guilty of treason

---

[34] Cf. Michael Grant, *The Ancient Historians* (London: Weidenfeld and Nicolson, 1970), pp. 295-9. Grant here provides a succinct and penetrating discussion of Tacitus on this point of historiography.

[35] Also, note that Josephus had responded to the thrust of this accusation, arguing in the *Jewish Antiquities* that his purpose in writing was "to reconcile other people to us and to remove any reasons for that hatred which unreasonable people bear toward us. As for our customs, no nation observes the same practice as another; in nearly every city we encounter different ones. But justice is a universally admired practice and advantageous to all equally, whether Greek or barbarian. And for justice our laws have the greatest regard. These laws, therefore, if we observe them rightly, make us charitable and friendly toward all people. For this reason we have a right to expect similar treatment from others" (xvi. 7).

against the state (cf. xxxi. 2-3; here citing 1 Tim. 2.2). Indeed, the apologist goes to considerable length to counter Tacitus' argument, describing the character of the Christian "faction"[36] in its activities in and for the (Roman) world (cf. xxxix. 1ff.) and concluding that this community "should not be called a faction; it is a senate" (xxxix. 21; *non est factio dicenda, sed curia*). With this extended argument, Tertullian seeks to amend Roman historiography by revising this facet of one of the "commentaries" which otherwise provides evidence for his own case. That is, although he elsewhere draws freely upon Tacitus, this historical "source" is not beyond criticism. On this point of interpretation, Tertullian does not hesitate to correct the existing Roman authorities, identifying his role as an apologist and at the same time and as an historical "revisionist."

When we come to the question of religion, we find Tertullian returning to the fertile fields of historiography, here advancing an attack upon Roman myths which sought to move beyond the sensitive issues of piety in order to expose the "objective" history of their origin. Again we see that the apologetic argument becomes a direct application of Roman history. Tertullian looks to an earlier Greek authority, identifying the origins of myths on the basis of the well known arguments of Euhemerus. This tactic, as R. P. C. Hanson has pointed out,[37] opposes the veracity of Roman religious mythology on the basis of what Hanson calls "a historicizing theory." Standing in a long and ongoing apologetic tradition which includes Clement of Alexandria, Minucius Felix, Cyprian, Lactantius, and Eusebius,[38] Tertullian's reliance upon Euhemerus' theory attacks contemporary religious practice through the indirect route of an historical deconstruction of the mundane origin of the gods. Pagan religion, according to this theory, is nothing but "ancient history touched up by the poets."[39] Euhemerus' attack upon these myths, which had been translated into Latin by the poet Ennius and had reached a wide circulation in the "western" sector of the Empire by this time,[40] held that

> all gods whose cults can be identified were originally human beings who so impressed themselves on the memory of their contemporaries that on their death they were deified. They made this impression by their bene-

---

[36] Tertullian usually speaks of the Christian community as a "sect," or as the "divine sect," a term which Cicero and Quintilian had used to describe philosophical schools (cf. *Apology*, xxxvii. 3, 4; xxxviii. 1). He also subsequently refutes any suspicion that Christianity was a "faction"; cf. *Apology* xxxix. 11.

[37] R. P. C. Hanson, "The Christian Attitude to Pagan Religions up to the Time of Constantine the Great," ANRW, II/23.2, pp. 934-5.

[38] *Ibid.*

[39] *Ibid.*, p. 937.

[40] *Ibid.*, p. 934.

factions and achievements during their lives and in some instances by instituting cults of themselves during their lifetime. Some examples of this historicizing theory given by Euhemerus can be recovered, and indeed they must have been sufficiently shocking to pious ears when he produced them.[41]

In the hands of Tertullian, this "historicizing theory" received a measured treatment in his *Apology*. Beginning with Saturn, whom the apologist identified as "the original of all your pantheon" (x. 6; cf. also Minucius Felix, *Octavius*, xxi. 4ff.), Tertullian rehearses what earlier *auctores* had held regarding his origin: "As to Saturn, then, so far as books inform us, neither Diodorus the Greek nor Thallus, neither Cassius Severus nor Cornelius Nepos, nor any other author dealing with antiquities of that kind, has alleged that Saturn was anything but a man" (x. 7). The reference to "books [which] inform us" is not insignificant: Tertullian wishes to advance his argument on the basis of the ancient authorities which literate Romans—and, presumably, those in positions of power, whether in the Senate or in provincial administration—would have known and respected. But he does not stop with the legacy of literature. He also cites the "proof" displayed for all eyes on monuments, geographical references, and even coins, an accumulation of evidence which pointed to the diffused route by which these myths spread among the populace. As a rhetor adept at his task, the apologist relies on evidence which would not have been contested by his audience, again heeding Quintilian's advice to rely upon historical arguments which "alone will be above suspicion of prejudice or partiality."[42] History has become the apologist's primary tool. "So, as to your gods," concludes Tertullian, "I see merely the names of certain dead men of the past. I hear their stories; from their stories I understand their rituals. As to their actual images, I find nothing beyond material akin to what is in ordinary pots and tools. . . ." (xii. 1-2).

Tertullian does not evade the philosophical defense of this historical argument which Cicero had earlier offered. In *de natura deorum*, the rhetor had conceded that "the outpourings of the poets" had offered absurd notions of the gods which were "little less absurd" than those of the Stoic school, being "more like the dreams of madmen than the considered opinions of philosophers" (I. xvi [42]). Such misguided impressions of "the gods" Cicero had classed along with "the monstrous doctrines of the magi and the insane mythology of Egypt," relegating both to "a mere mass of inconsistencies sprung from ignorance" (I. xvi [42]). In *de natura deorum*, this rhetor sought to interpret the underlying truth of such myths, transcending such stories in order to

[41] *Ibid.*, p. 935.
[42] *Inst. Orat.*, x. 1.34.

discover a deity "above" the gods. On this point, Tertullian finds himself in essential agreement with Cicero. He also argues that there must be a supreme god who is "more sublime [*aliquem sublimiorem deum*], true owner in his own right of deity [*mancipem quendam divinitatis*], who made the gods out of men [*qui ex hominibus deos fecerit*]" (xi. 2). Yet this nobler conception of divinity abolishes the need for "the gods," according to Tertullian's logic. This "more sublime" deity, the "god beyond the gods," is the one whom the Christians worship—and, following Cicero's defense, the one to whom philosophers and Roman rhetors had also pointed. With this cautious agreement, however, Tertullian has not yet rested his case. He presses this argument further, reasoning that even if the populace accepted the veracity of the many gods, "on the basis of common consent" (*de aestimatione communi*) they nonetheless conceded that "there is a god, more sublime and more potent, Emperor as it were of the universe, of absolute power and majesty" (xxiv. 3). In other words, the apologist perceives the faith of the "crowd" more astutely than Cicero! As he goes on to argue, "most apportion divinity" by contending that "the control, the supreme sway, rests with one, the various functions of divinity among many." Here he calls upon Plato (*Phaedrus*, 246e) to secure his case, concluding that even the respected sources of the goldern era of Greek philosophy sought a higher deity *above* the pantheon of gods. Why, then, did the Romans seek to maintain such myths and neglect the true source of divinity? Could any philosophical argument dispel the disturbing evidence of history, the crude stories regarding the genesis of such myths?

In a similar vein, we hear Tertullian ridiculing the commercialism of the Roman religious practices, imitating the tradition of satire which Lucian had popularized. Thus, he mocks a religion which "knocks down deity to the highest bidder, and leases [it] out" (xiii. 6), one which "goes around the cookshops begging" (xiii. 6), concluding that among the Romans "one may not know the gods for nothing: *they are for sale*" (*non licit deos gratis nosse; venales sunt*; xiii. 6). The echo to the satire of Lucian's biting criticism in "Philosophies for Sale" would not have gone unnoticed by a sophisticated audience, though they would undoubtedly have been surprised to hear such an attack coming from the mouth of a Christian apologist. "When [the apologists] attacked the old myths," concludes Hanson, "they were following a much-worked vein" among Romans.[43] Blending satire with historical "evidence," Tertullian recounts the haunting memory of Socrates' execution because of his mockery of the gods (xiv. 7). Recalling as well the Athenians' subsequent "cancelling . . . of his condemnation," the apol-

---

[43] Hanson, pp. 920-1.

ogist again turns the burden of defense upon the authorities, whose hasty judgment of the philosopher who "destroyed the gods" was itself condemned in regret (xiv. 8). With these familiar witnesses from the history and literature of his audience, therefore, Tertullian's argument is no creation of his own design, nor does he suggest that the Christians stood alone against the "superstition" of the Roman religion. Rather, he located his argument within the established discourse of Roman historians, rhetors, and *literati*,[44] thereby echoing witnesses who, as *auctoritates*, needed no further defense. Tertullian's rhetorical method is thus a compelling instance of the kind of self-assured argument which Cicero had called "credible," one which the audience would accept without any further evidence.[45]

Several decades before Tertullian had composed his *Apology*, a Roman proconsul in North Africa had rebuked the Christians who stood trial before him, concluding with the abrupt threat that "if you ridicule things we hold sacred I will not allow you to speak."[46] It is not insignificant, therefore, that Tertullian's arguments relied upon accepted *Roman* sources, voices which even a proconsul could not silence. The apologist continued this line of attack by contrasting the chronology of Roman history with the chronology of the Roman gods, and by ridiculing the view of history which identified "piety" as the immediate cause of success. Cicero's earlier claim regarding the superiority of Roman religion furnished a ready-made argument against the Christians, particularly because he had linked Roman religiosity with military success:

> The fate of these men [i.e., the defeat of Gaius Flaminius who "ignored the claims of religion," and of Claudius and Junius whose demise had everything to do with their mockery of the gods] may serve to indicate that our empire was won by those commanders who obeyed the dictates of religion. Moreover, if we care to compare our national characteristics with those of foreign peoples, we shall find that, while in all other respects we are only equals or even the inferiors of others, yet in the sense of religion, that is, in reverence for the gods, we are far superior.[47]

Yet Tertullian challenges this contention directly and without any hesitation, arguing against Cicero and others who assumed that "it is a reward for their eminently religious attitude that the Romans have reached so high a point of grandeur as to hold the whole world, and that the gods are so conspicuously gods that those flourish beyond all others who beyond all others renders them obedience" (xxv. 2). Note

---

[44] *Ibid.*, p. 921.
[45] Sider, p. 15.
[46] Cited by Wilkens, *Christians* . . ., p. 63; Barnes, "Legislation," p. 50.
[47] *De natura deorum*, II.iii [8].

well: the apologist states his case not on the basis of any metaphysical argument, but by calling upon the testimony of *Roman history* to aid him in his defense. First, he points out the ridiculousness of even attempting to untangle the vicissitudes of political history, Roman or Greek. That is, history simply did not bear the claim that "the gods" always favored the Romans "on the score of gratitude" for their religious zeal (xxv. 3). "Whose side," he says in so many words, "were the gods on?"

> But how absurd it is to set down the glory of the Roman name as the reward of religious feeling, when it is only since the empire (or perhaps it was still kingdom) was achieved, that the religion made its forward strides! ... So the Romans were not 'religious' before they were great; and, it follows, they are not great because they were religious. How could they be great because of their religion, when *their greatness came from their irreligion?* Unless I am mistaken, all kingship or empire is sought in war and extended by victory. War and victory depend on the capture and generally the overthrow of cities. That business is not put through, without injury to the gods. Walls and temples have one destruction; citizens and priests alike are slain; the plunder of wealth is the same whether it is sacred property or that of laymen. Then the sacrileges of the Romans are exactly as many as their trophies; their triumphs over gods as many as over races; their spoils in war as many as the statues still left of captured gods. ... Certainly it cannot square with belief that they should be supposed to have grown great as a reward of religion, who, as we have shown, did religion wrong and so grew strong, or growing strong did it wrong. (xxv. 12-17)

The direct, historical argument by which Tertullian attacks the legitimacy of the *religio romana* as the source of Roman military success concerns the ignorance of history which was necessary to sustain such an hypothesis. The shadow of Cicero's argument pales in the light of the apologist's historical review.

Furthermore, he attacks the relative "novelty" of the Roman gods, thereby eroding the foundation of an argument that would identify worship of the gods as the source of imperial success. As he argues in an allusion to Roman letters, "Rome in the forest [cf. Virgil's *Aeneid*, viii. 347] is older than some of her gods; she reigned before she built that great circuit of the Capitol" (xxvi. 2). He concludes his argument by attacking as naive the notion that Roman gods—and Roman political history—stood in any position of historical preeminence. "Babylonians reigned before there were Roman pontiffs," he argues, "Medes before there were Quindecimviri, Egyptians before there were Salii, Assyrians before there were Luperci, Amazons before there were Vestal Virgins" (xxvi. 2). Tertullian applies himself vigorously to refute any suspicion that history might justify the equation of imperial success and Roman *pietas*, the reverence for the gods or ancestral traditions. History stands at the very heart of this apologist's argument. In measured steps, Tertullian calls the Romans to witness against their own case by "consulting [their] histories." But these arguments have by no means exhausted his case.

II. A JEWISH WITNESS ENTERS THE FORUM: On Jewish Antiquity and Roman Novelty

"In the Greek world, everything will be found to be modern and dating, so to speak, from yesterday or the day before."—Josephus[48]

At this juncture of our study we must turn our attention to the historical texture of Tertullian's apologetic argument from—and against—Judaism. Yet as our opening citation indicates, it is not sufficient for us to examine only the Christian historiography regarding Judaism; rather, we must also account for the Jewish apologetic, if only in a cursory manner, which had already been directed against the "novelty" of the Greek (to say nothing of Roman) history. Thus, we hear Tertullian repeating the argument which the Greek apologists had forwarded regarding the antiquity of Moses (cf. *First Apology*, 44, 54, 59; also, Theophilus, *To Autolycus* III. 20-29; Tatian, *Oration to the Greeks*, 36-41), though we must recall that Tertullian explicitly lines his argument behind the authority not of the earlier Christian witnesses but of Josephus, the towering historian whom he refers to as "the native champion of Jewish Antiquities" (xix. 6). The apologist's contention that Moses was older than Roman religion may well be culled from Josephus' claim that "he [i.e., Moses] was born two thousand years ago, to which ancient date the poets never ventured to refer even the birth of their gods, much less the actions or the laws of mortals" (*Jewish Antiquities* I. 16). Thus, returning to Tertullian's argument, Moses was "earlier than Saturn himself" (xix. 1). But he carries this argument even further, specifying the age of Moses in terms of specific dates common to Roman histories:

> If you chance . . . to have heard of one Moses, he is coeval with Argive Inachus, about four hundred years (to be exact, less seven) before Danaus who is *your* most ancient of men, a rough thousand years ahead of Priam's calamity. I might also say, fifteen hundred years before Homer, with authority for saying so. Then the rest of the [Hebrew] prophets—they, of course, come after Moses, but the very last of them are found not to be later than the early ones among your sages and lawgivers *and historians*. (xix. 3-4; cf. also xix. 1)

---

[48] Cited in Grant, *The Ancient Historians*, p. 268.

In the subsequent passage, Tertullian provides a brief but impressive foray into a project which he introduces without fully exploiting: namely, "an excursion into the histories and literatures of the world" (xix. 7). His extended introduction of this task is as daunting as it is ambitious. The apologist thus advances a direct assault upon Tacitus' claim that Jewish religious practices introduced by Moses were "new" (cf. *Histories* v. 4), an argument against this bias of Roman historiography which follows up the apologist's earlier refutation of Tacitus' "confused" discourse on the origin of the Jewish "name and religion" (cf. xvi. 1-2). Indeed, his vehement correction of Tacitus' erroneous notions regarding the origin of Judaism—and, consequently, of Christianity as well—leads him to slander this historian's name: "no, not 'tacit,' he, but a first class chatterbox when it comes to lies!" (*sane ille mendaciorum loquacissimus*; cf. xiv. 3). Writing with the Roman dictum in mind that "extreme antiquity gives books authority" (xix. 1), the Christian apologist draws Moses—and thus the full force of what we might call a comparative history—into his defense, since in his writings "is seen summed up the treasure of the whole Jewish religion, *and in consequence of ours as well*" (xix. 2).

If Wilken's thesis regarding the patristic attitude toward the Jews is correct when he generalizes that it "borders on the irrational,"[49] then we would suggest that Tertullian's careful historiographical treatment of Judaism, though by no means without harsh criticism, is an exception to the rule. His attitude toward Judaism is hardly magnanimous, of course, in that he portrayed the Judaeo-Christian history as one of a "transfer," in which Christians were the worshippers who were "far more faithful [than the Jews, who "at the last sinned against Christ cf. xxvi. 3], to whom *God would transfer his favor*, and that in fuller measure, because [the Christians] would be able to bear an ampler discipline" (xxi. 6). Yet this is no "irrational" attack: the apologist articulates this thesis by carefully developing a linear view of history, one which confirms the Jewish foundation upon which Christianity could claim antiquity, but one which at the same time highlighted the discontinuity by which Christianity subsequently became the sole bearer of that tradition. The precise historical point of this disjuncture is not without its significance. Precisely at the moment when the Roman-Jewish wars "tore asunder . . . the bond between Judaism and Graeco-Roman culture,"[50] Tertullian underscores the emergence of a new bond between the God of Moses and the Roman Empire, a "transfer" of another dimension altogether: namely, via Christianity which now established itself, according to Tertullian's peculiar revisionist

---

[49] Wilken, *Judaism* . . ., p. x.
[50] *Ibid.*, p. 43.

model of history, as the positive link between Jerusalem and Rome. While it was still true that Roman traditions and institutions—including "your laws and studies" (*iura vestra quam studia*; xix. 1)—borrowed from the Jewish legacy, following his dictum that "the earlier must be the seed" (*quod prius est, hoc sit semen necesse est*; xix. 1; cf. also xlvii. 1-2, *antiquior omnibus veritas* . . .), that line of continuity now had to be sought through Christianity, the representative of "the Jewish antiquities." That is, Roman law derived from a Jewish tradition which Christianity now represented! On this matter, therefore, we clearly see the subtlety of Tertullian's argument. As representative of this legal tradition, as the apologist is quick to point out, Christianity no longer bound itself to the Jewish law. This disavowal provides a crucial bridge between Christians and Romans which had not been possible for Judaism. Tertullian's careful discussion of the Christian relation to the Hebrew law, therefore, exonerates Christianity from the Roman attack against the Jews, a suspicion which Juvenal expressed with a venom when he condemned the Jews who "look down on Roman law, preferring instead to learn and honor and fear the Jewish commandments, whatever was handed down by Moses in that arcane tone of his."[51] In contrast, he sidesteps this criticism and offers instead a retorsion of characteristic irony: since Judaism itself antedates Roman history, and because "the earlier must be the seed," even Roman law must be derivative from the Jewish precedent (i.e., the *lex Moysis*; xix. 1). The "transfer" of God's favor from Judaism to Christianity, therefore, has wider sociological ramifications, since Christians now stand as heirs to this ancient law which had earlier "fertilized" (*concepisse*) Roman traditions.

Is Christianity a "novelty," according to Tertullian's reckoning of ancient history and the relationship in which Christianity stood to Judaism? Certainly not, following the logic of his argument. Yet he anticipates the direct criticism which Romans certainly raised in this regard. As he points out in the *Apology*, the apparent newness of Christianity as "this school which most people know to be rather modern, as dating from the reign of Tiberius" (xxi. 1) should not confuse the issue, since "this school . . . rests on the very ancient books of the Jews." Here, then, is the problem facing Tertullian: on the surface, it seems that Christianity is "but of yesterday" (*hesterni sumus*; xxxvii. 4), and thus he must underscore the manner in which Christianity claims a legitimate continuity with Judaism (i.e., *auctoritatem summa antiquitas vindicat*; xix. 1) while at the same time establishing the discrete identity of Christianity as the *vera religio*, the faithful representative of the house of Israel. In the succinct words of Fredouille, Tertullian

---

[51] Cited by Wilken, *Christians as the Romans Saw Them*, p. 51.

minimise, quand il s'adresse aux païens, la nouveauté du christianisme; ou, plus exactement, il prend soin de se montrer fort discret sur ce point . . . . Le mérite de Tertullien, son originalité aussi, ont été précisément de faire prendre conscience aux Romains du rôle et de l'importance des *nova* par rapport aux *vetera*, dans toute leur civilisation, mais d'abord dans le domaine juridique.[52]

Vetera et nova: Christianity, according to Tertullian's theory of history, represents something which is only superficially "new." Yet it is "new" in the manner in which it abandons Jewish law in favor of Roman standards of legality. At the same time, Tertullian applies a rhetorical principle which we have seen to be characteristic for his *Apology*: namely, that of "retorsion." By modulating—actually, inverting—the argument against Christians to one against Roman practice, he levels the charge of "novelty" against the Romans, concluding that not only do they "despise, neglect, and destroy that tradition, clean against the authority of your ancestors" (vi. 10) but their traditions are themselves a relative novelty when set against the broader spectrum of world history.[53]

III. FROM ORIGINS TO 'LAST THINGS': *History as Divine Trial* "*Nos ergo soli innocentes.*"[54]

"We, then, alone are innocent." With these bold words, Tertullian highlights his conviction that the concern with past history may not be the most urgent concern facing his audience, the "most religious protectors and maintainers of laws and ancestral usages":

> If they definitely are not gods, then definitely it is not a religion; if it is not a religion because they definitely are not gods, then we are definitely not guilty of injuring religion. On the contrary, the taunt has recoiled upon you, who, by your worship of a lie, by your neglect of the true religion of the true god [*veram religionem veri dei non modo neglegendo*]—and more than that—by your assault upon it, commit against the true God the crime of real irreligion [*in verum committitis crimen verae inreligiositatis*]. (xxiv. 2)

In this characteristic example of "retorsion," one of the classical methods of rhetoric which Tertullian applies with consummate skill throughout his *Apology*, the brunt of the Roman accusations against Christians falls back upon the authorities themselves. In this case, the "retorsion" does not depend in the first instance upon a theological but upon an historical argument. That is, even though Tertullian does ear-

---

[52] Fredouille, pp. 239, 242.
[53] *Ibid.*, pp. 241-2.
[54] Tertullian, *Apology*, xlv. 1.

lier (and insistently) invoke a Stoic conception of the deity which supports his case,[55] he is here bent on reinterpreting the scope of history, setting the specific Roman/Christian debate within the broader eschatological arena of divine judgment.

It is an unintentional irony of our own making that we end our study by speaking of eschatology. As we shall here suggest, Tertullian's eschatological revision of the scope of history finally modulates the level of discourse altogether. In turning from his insistent discussion of the past to redefine Roman (= world) history in broader terms, the apologist again invokes history in his defense of Christianity, but here he does so by translating the "judgment" facing Christians to that of God's judgment of all time:

> It is you, then, who are the danger to mankind, it is you who bring upon us public misfortunes—you, by your contempt of God and your worship of statues. In any case it ought to be more credible that God is angry, seeing that he is neglected rather than they who are worshipped . . . . For God who has ordained eternal judgment once for all after the end of the world does not hasten to make that separation (which is the essence of the judgment) before the end of the world. (xli. 1, 3)

This is retorsion at its best, one facilitated by the full weight of the apologist's eschatological reinterpretation of history. Tertullian's historiographical "revision" thus points beyond any argument from "tradition" which concerned itself only with the past. In this manner, he lifts his argument out of the "courtroom" of Roman law, entering the eschatological "forum," if we might call it that, in which the arena of forensic debate is nothing less than "the judgment seat of Christ" at the end of history (xxiii. 15). History here is a matter not of first, but of last things.

This apologetic treatise which had begun as an explanation of how Christians are to live under Roman law—or, variously, how Romans are to apply their laws to Christians living within their realm—now suggests that the more urgent question facing the *Romani imperii antistites* is the matter of how *Romans* are to live under God's judgment. Eschatology becomes much more than a vindication of Christian suffering at the hands of tyrannous authorities, since Tertullian reminds his reader at the close of his discourse that "there is a rivalry between God's ways and man's; we are condemned by you, but we are acquitted by God" (1. 16). Eschatology as the interpretation of the momentum of history finally defines the normative parameters of this case—

---

[55] See here Stephan Otto's suggestive study, *'Natura' und 'Dispositio': Untersuchung zum Natubegriff und zur Denkform Tertullians* (Muenchen: Max Hueber Verlag, 1960), esp. pp. 26ff., 74ff.

no longer do the Christians stand before the Romans, but all stand before the divine tribunal, answering to God's indictment of *inreligiositas*, the "neglect of the true religion of the true god." The *Apology* thus concludes with an indictment of Roman religion as "irreligion." Tertullian inverts Cicero's argument altogether, when the rhetor had claimed that "in all probability, disappearance of piety toward the gods will entail the disappearance of loyalty and social union among us as well, and of justice itself, the queen of all the virtues."[56] The proper understanding of the scope of history and the true nature of religion, Tertullian suggests, defines social stability and justice precisely on the basis of the necessary disappearance of such a misguided piety, or the "worship of a lie" (xxiv. 1). Rhetorical retorsion here reaches its limit: the "new" religion of the Romans becomes the affront to justice, the perversion of true worship, and ultimately a distortion of history itself. Eschatology finally dislocates the Roman attack upon Christianity by placing history along a different plane of orientation altogether.

Where, then, does this consideration of Tertullian's use of history bring us? In the first place, we have seen that Tertullian is not only interested in continuing the apologetic tradition developed in the east by Justin, Theophilus, and Athenagoras, even though the substance of many of his arguments echoes the approach found in their earlier writings. Rather, Tertullian's apology draws upon a broader array of arguments concerning the matter of origins—of Christianity itself, of course, but also of Judaism, Roman law, the "pagan" myths, etc. His wide-ranging and aggressive concern with origins fashions his apology into a broad canvas upon which he portrays Christianity as the "true religion of the true God," a proper "tradition" whose roots reach to the most ancient books of Judaism and thereby shame the "novelty" of Rome and her venerated institutions. At the heart of this *Apology*, therefore, we find a forensic argument containing a fully developed philosophy of history, one which borrowed freely from extant Roman historians in order to revise the condemnation of Christianity—and Judaism, as we have seen. Indeed, Tertullian redefines the argument regarding "novelty" by exposing the origins of Roman myths; he also marshalls Roman history to refute the Ciceronian contention that "reverence for the gods" was the cause of imperial success. Thus, we find this Christian apologist applying classical traditions of rhetoric with consummate skill, heeding Quintilian's advise above all else to state his case by calling upon historical evidence, arguments which were "above suspicion of prejudice or partiality." This treatise certainly demonstates the effective use of "the careful study of antiquity" to establish his argument on an authority intrinsic to his Roman audi-

[56] Cicero, cited in Wilken, *Christians* . . ., pp. 58-9.

ence. Such *auctores* could not be silenced by any proconsul, nor would they be ignored by a sophisticated Roman audience. Tertullian's argument proceeds with a persistent echo of such *auctoritates*.

"Nothing is so difficult to believe," claimed Cicero, "that oratory cannot make it acceptable, nothing so rough and uncultured as not to gain brilliance and refinement from eloquence."[57] Accepting this claim as the standard of his own rhetoric, Tertullian yet suggests that rhetoric as "mere dialectic" is not his aim, nor can a refutation of his argument avoid the claims of "truth" based on the historicity of his apology:

> "Who will undertake to refute this case,—not by dialectic, but in the same form in which we have established our proof, on the basis of truth?" (xlvi. 1)

The subsequent echo in Minucius Felix's *Octavius* (xiv. 2-7) is unmistakable. "Truth of the clearest kind," he argued in that treatise, "is affected by the talents of the disputants and the power of eloquence .... Fascination of words distracts [an audience] from attention to facts." Tertullian's insistent application of the arguments from history, which according to Cicero's analysis were "credible" because based on an assent shared by hearer and speaker, thus moves his *Apology* into what he felt was the undisputed realm of "facts." Hence, we come here upon an argument about truth which is by no means a flight into the speculative realm of metaphysics, but rather a sober and thorough examination of history.

Thus, the interior logic of Tertullian's argument might be understood by returning to his earlier admonition: "Consult your histories!" His argument tackles the task of justifying Christianity by entering the realm of historical interpretation, a universe of discourse which placed Roman religion under the same indictment applied against Christians—namely, that of "novelty." The Roman witness comes to offer testimony against its own cause. And, as we have suggested, he interprets the *vetera et nova*, the old and new things, according to a carefully worked out schema, one in which Christianity stands in an ambivalent relationship to Judaism and thereby acquires a venerable ancestry deserving of Roman respect. As bearer of the Jewish tradition (i.e., *vetera*), Christians inherit the status of representatives of the "discipline" which the decline of Judaism had forfeited (e.g., xxi. 5-7). At the same time, however, Christianity exhibits a necessary discontinuity with "the Jewish antiquities," a disjunction which enabled Tertullian to disavow what was still suspect in the legal heritage of Judaism and thereby affirm the proper respect which Roman law and culture (*nova*) should afford Christians.

---

[57] *Paradoxa Stoicorum*, "Prooemium," 3.

History in this treatise has thus become the very bedrock of apologetics. Indeed, the *Apology* can be read as an historiographical treatise, an extended consideration of "origins" and "ends" which applies the force of history squarely to the apologetic task. Tertullian's "audience," therefore, is not only that of the "magistrates of the Roman empire," as he claims at the outset. Rather, he is here entering into discourse with a diverse gathering of outstanding historians, encyclopedists, and rhetors of antiquity, including Varro and Tacitus, Cicero and Quintilian, and, of course, Josephus. Tertullian draws upon the rhetorical models of his Roman forebears, but he applies them to the task of Christian apologetics, defining the texture of that genre primarily in terms of its historiographical basis. For Tertullian, the Christian apologist is first and foremost an historian, a scholar of the past whose interests were by no means confined to Christian or even to Jewish origins. His field of study is broader, more inclusive: he launches his apology by interpreting the checkered and, according to his argument, previously distorted history of Rome itself. In this treatise, Rome has come to court on behalf of the Christians.

CHAPTER FIVE

EUSEBIUS: THE HISTORY OF SALVATION FROM THE
GARDEN OF EDEN TO THE RISE OF THE ROMAN
EMPIRE

Glenn F. Chesnut

Eusebius's *Church History* began its truly detailed historical narrative only with the birth of Christ, but his overall theory of history tried to accommodate all of world history, stretching as far back into the past as could be known to a Roman of his time. In order, therefore, to give a total picture of Eusebius's thought at the historical-theoretical level, this chapter is a prolegomenon of sorts, devoted in the main to exploring Eusebius's understanding of pre-Christian history: the creation and fall into superstition and savagery of the human race at the beginning of time, the period of the Old Testament patriarchs, the significance of Moses, and the implications of the rise of the Roman empire. Some of Eusebius's beliefs about the early Christian period itself and the church's relationship to the Roman emperors will also be noticed at one point.

Although Eusebius discusses pre-Christian history briefly in the introductory section of his *Church History* (1.1.7-1.4.15) in a sort of condensed summary, one must look elsewhere in his writings—including not only the *Chronicle* but also works like the *Praeparatio Evangelica* and the *Demonstratio Evangelica*—to obtain any detailed view of his picture of the pre-Christian world and the way this affected the later period about which he then wrote in such detail in his *Church History*. A Christian historian must always form some sort of opinion about Judaism and the world of the Old Testament in order to develop any overarching theory of history, and Eusebius was no exception here. Also, a historian living in the Roman empire at that time had to deal with the classical tradition as well, and the world that created the bright gods and goddesses who inhabited the pages of Homer, Hesiod, and Herodotus. If these beings did not truly exist as meaningful objects of worship, then one had to explain why so many people over so many centuries had thought so. A careful look at all of Eusebius's writings finds a coherent, comprehensive theory, affecting his understanding of the pre-Christian period and, as well, the early part of the subsequent era, when Christianity was an unlicensed sect dealing with often hostile emperors. Many of the ideas and presuppositions developed in that context affected Eusebius's thought through all the editions of his *Church History*, and even in the *Life of Constantine* that he wrote at the very end of his life, albeit with a conclusion to the story that the young Eusebius could never even have imagined.

The typical classical Greek or Roman historian did not have to contend, as Eusebius did, with a story whose overall historical sweep extended back to the very creation of the world. But Eusebius clearly felt that he had to do so, at least in outline, and in his own mind. From his Christian perspective, world history had had an overall pattern and design that had stretched over the centuries and that gave some explanation, in the process, to the historical role of the Christian religion whose story he then so carefully narrated in his *Church History*.

The history of the world, seen in this context, appeared to him as a sequence of stages: it had begun with a cosmic Fall into the world of history and temporality, then had come an era of superstition and savagery (broken only by the appearance of the Old Testament patriarchs), next had come the age dominated by the figure of Moses, and finally the period that began with the nearly simultaneous appearance of Christ and Augustus (the foundation of Church and Empire). Within the world thus created, the young Eusebius believed, Christianity was to carry out its missionary enterprise, until the Roman empire, the last of the great universal empires, became the complete agent of Satan in the last battles at the end of the world, and was destroyed in the second coming of Christ.

The whole story was a "salvation history" that set the Christian experience of grace and the Christian hope of the future into a context of historical knowledge shared by all educated people in the ancient world. In spite of the rather grim ending to the story, with apocalyptic destruction raining down as the history of this universe reached its final end, it was for most of its length a rather optimistic view of the world, seeing real, continuous progress in all areas—civilization, culture, morality, and religion. It was important not only to Eusebius's understanding of history, but also to his political thought. He used this theory of universal history both to justify the unique power of the Roman state over the Mediterranean world and to explain the proper function of the Roman emperor. When Eusebius was compelled, later on in his life, to insert the fully developed, post-Nicene figure of the Christian emperor Constantine into this story, it added some novel features that he had surely never even imagined in his youth, and it demanded that he reverse himself almost totally on the question of religious liberty, but it did not require him to alter the basic views of the structure and meaning of history, particularly in the pre-Christian period. Constantine gave him a triumphant conclusion to the story in the period that fell, Eusebius thought, just before the end of the world, but the clear success of Christian missionary efforts in the later third century would have given him a victory to proclaim whether there had been a Christian emperor or not.

In his basic understanding of pre-Christian history, one must not of course portray Eusebius as totally innovative by any means. The broad outlines of a Christian picture of world history had already been laid out by Christian theologians of the second and third centuries,[1] by writers such as Justin Martyr, Irenaeus, Clement of Alexandria and Origen. Eusebius took basic themes from them—the role of the daemons, the priority of Moses to Plato, Origen's theory of free will and the fall—and wove these traditional statements into a continuous account, bolstered by the best historical scholarship of the time (and in particular a detailed knowledge of the history of Graeco-Roman thought). He accompanied this with a full exposition of the theoretical consequences, for a practicing historian, of such a view of history. Eusebius was insightful and brilliant, a creator of new genres and a follower of the most radical philosophical theology of his time, but most of the pieces out of which he constructed his total picture of pre-Christian history had already been developed before his time.

Origen, the great radical theologian, gave Eusebius some of his most unusual ideas. Eusebius was a devoted follower of Origen's thought,[2] and his theology of history is colored by an especially rationalistic variety of Origenism from one end to the other. For Eusebius, following Origen, the "Garden" of Eden had been a realm outside this present space-time continuum, and "Adam" had been the totality of humankind. All our souls preexisted before this earth was ever created.[3] An act of disobedience on the part of some of those

---

[1] Anyone familiar with the second-century apologists, for example, will immediately recognize the elements in Eusebius's system that came originally from that source. Justin, for one, taught that at the beginning of history the daemons tricked human beings into regarding them as gods (*First Apology*, chapter 5), that Abraham and other Old Testament figures should be regarded as Christians before Christ (chapter 46), that Plato plagiarized his best ideas from Moses (chapters 44, 59-60), and that later on, in the Christian period itself, it was the daemons who were responsible for the rise of heresy (chapter 26). One could at length cite further references. On the general relationship of Eusebius to the second-century fathers, see Robert M. Grant, "The Appeal to the Early Fathers," *Journal of Theological Studies* new series 11 (1960): 13-24; and "The Uses of History in the Church before Nicaea," in F.L. Cross, ed., *Studia Patristica* 11 = *Texte und Untersuchungen* 108 (Berlin: Akademie-Verlag, 1972) 166-78.

[2] For the historical background of Eusebius's dependence on Origen, see Robert M. Grant, "Early Alexandrian Christianity," *Church History* 40 (1971): 133-44.

[3] Eus. Armen. *Chron.*, Karst edition, 36; *PE* 7.18.7-10(332cd).

unembodied noetic beings caused God to cast them into human bodies and imprison them on earth for a period of discipline, assailed by death and corruption.[4]

This cosmic Fall was a fall into *historical time*. Eusebius the historian was interpreting Origen's theological ideas here. Chronology—a necessary and integral part of historiography—could not begin until Adam had already fallen and been driven out of that hypercosmic realm, the "Garden," with its quite different temporality,[5] and had been cast down into the world τῶν πραγμάτων, of *history*, which was ceaselessly driving onwards towards its final eschatological destruction.[6]

But even after their souls had been cast down into bodies on this earth human beings still retained their freedom of will, which in fact was never lost even in the most fallen. The contrast with the Augustinian doctrine of original sin, developed a century afterwards, appears at every stage of Eusebius's doctrine of the first things. Due to this freedom of will, once humanity had entered this present worldtime a further, progressive Fall was able to take place. Most of those first human beings at the beginning of history soon fell into what Eusebius regarded as a subhuman, animal-like existence[7]—the life of desert nomads, he called it (his urban Palestinian prejudices showing up here), without πόλις or πολιτεία, without τέχνη or ἐπιστήμη, without legal system or any concept of ἀρετέ or philosophy (his thoroughly Greek prejudices appearing in his choice of words here).[8] This second fall was the fall of human society as such; the social structure of humankind, with all its social institutions, degenerated and disintegrated over a period of time.[9] The lack of real knowledge of God condemned them to the lowest sort of existence even on earth; conversely, any widespread growth of civilized human community would have to take place in company with the appearance of some sort of renewed knowledge of God.

To make matters more difficult, God and the members of the

---

[4] Eus. *PE* 7.18.7-10(332cd); *DE* 4.1.4(144d-145a). But also note *PE* 7.17.3(330d), where Eusebius used a different theory: humans were *created* as dwellers on earth, and for a positive function, that is, so that the universal worship service (the cosmic liturgy) would extend all the way down to the earth.

[5] Eus. Armen. *Chron.*, Karst edition, 36-37.

[6] Eus. *DE* 1.9.3-4(30d-31a).

[7] Eus. *DE* 4.6.6-10(155c-156a), see also 8. introd. 5-12(363c-365b).

[8] Eus. *HE* 1.2.18-19; *DE* 8. introd. 5-12(363c-365b).

[9] Compare Eus. *HE* 1.2.18-21. Eusebius was convinced that it took a span of generations for the historic Fall to work its way to the lowest depths. His historical investigations, for example, seemed to show that human beings in the earliest age had not worshiped man-made idols, so that this aspect of humanity's historic Fall had taken time to grow up—see Eus. *DE* 4.9.10(160bc); also *Theoph.* 1.42.

human race were not the only figures who were taking part in the history of events on earth. After humanity had fallen completely and human beings were living like animals, God divided the human race into nations and put one of the angels in charge of each nation as a shepherd.[10] But there were other incorporeal spirits also abroad in the world—the daemons—who promptly set to work to upset God's plan. These daemons lured men and women into wickedness and disrupted every human community, until they had obliterated the boundaries that God had set up for the nations. Most of the human race came into the power of the daemon-overlords, and remained under their control until Jesus' resurrection broke their power.[11]

The original religion designed by God for the majority of fallen humanity was a sort of astral piety. The angel-guardians were instructed by God to allow the nations they were caring for to worship the sun, moon, and stars. The human beings under their care were intellectually incapable of conceiving of anything that transcended the visible, material world.[12] It was therefore better for these early men and women to worship "the best of things visible in heaven" than to turn towards something daemonic.[13] Eusebius was here following an earlier tradition, but it also perhaps helps explain his unwillingness to write off astrology as totally nonsense. The prominence he gave to this theory suggests also that he may have sensed the value of the good feelings that had existed for a while between the sun-worshiping emperor Aurelian and the Christian church during his own adolescent years, and that he may have hoped for some possibility of restoring such a modus vivendi between Christianity and the more tolerant and enlightened Neoplatonic sun-worshipers. Clearly a bishop holding Eusebius's views would not have worried overmuch about the precise mixture of Christianity and sun worship that might still have existed in the emperor Constantine's mind immediately after the battle of the Milvian bridge. H. A. Drake has argued that, as late as his *Panegyric to Con-*

---

[10] The one exception was the Friends of God, who were put under the direct care of the Logos himself; Eus. *DE* 4.6.6-7.3(155c-157a). See G.B. Caird, *Principalities and Powers* (Oxford: Clarendon Press, 1956) 5. The idea is based on one reading of Deut. 32:8-9; the form quoted for example in Eus. *DE* 4.7.1(156bc). Compare also the story in Daniel 10:13 of the archangels Gabriel and Michael battling for twenty-one days against the angel who had been placed in charge of the nation of Persia.

[11] Eus. *DE* 4.9.1-9(158c-160b), 10.1(161a), 10.9-10(162d-163a); *Theoph.* 4.8.

[12] Eus. *DE* 4.8(157c-158b); *PE* 1.9.15(30ab). The one exception to this astral piety, of course, was the Hebrew nation, which worshiped the true transcendent God.

[13] Eus. *DE* 4.8(157c-158b). In Plato's *Timaeus* the heavenly bodies were regarded as alive, and in Eusebius's respected master Origen (*De principiis* 1.7) there was along discussion of this. Origen said that the sun, moon, and stars were preexistent souls clothed with their present visible bodies in order to give light to the human race. These lights above the earth were hence living, rational beings with the power of free will with respect to good and evil.

stantine in 336, Eusebius was still on occasion trying to bridge the gap between Christianity and the sort of Middle Platonic quasi-monotheism in which the supreme God was mediated to the rest of the universe through his Logos. The acceptance of the sun as a tolerated non-Christian symbol of the supreme God and his manifestation to us would have furthered this cause.[14]

Astral piety had therefore been God's original design, Eusebius said, for the majority of the human race. But the daemons were hard at work, and as the angel guardians lost control of the human beings under their charge, God's original plan for the fallen human race was to be disrupted here also. The first nations where the pure, primitive astral piety disappeared were Phoenicia and Egypt. This lapse into a more superstitious form of polytheism, Eusebius tells us, soon spread to other nations as well. Both the Phoenician and the Egyptian mysteries were brought to the Greeks, for example, the former by Cadmus and the latter by Orpheus.[15] Eusebius was here drawing on an important tradition within pagan Greek thought that held that the anthropomorphic gods and special cults of classical Greek religion had been of later and derivative origin.[16] It was a rationalizing approach to the Greek religious tradition, seen among the classical Greek historians, for example, in Herodotus.[17]

In spite of all the evils that had developed, however, even in the first primitive centuries of this earth's history the picture was not entirely without redeeming figures. Amidst the mass of fallen men and

---

[14] The idea that astral piety was better than idolatry could be found for example in Wisdom of Solomon 13-14, as G.B. Caird points out (*Principalities and Powers*, 13), "The author regards the worship of the heavenly bodies as misguided but pardonable, whereas 'the devising of idols was the beginning of fornication, and the invention of them the corruption of life.'" This general idea is very important for the light it throws on the problem of the "conversion" of Constantine. Many modern historians have been greatly puzzled by the confusing mixture of both solar monotheism and genuine Christianity in the historical data about Constantine. But it is clear that Eusebius, as one very influential church leader, would not have objected overmuch on principle to a slight admixture of solar monotheism in the imperial Christianity. Solar monotheism saw only the shadow, from his point of view, while Christianity saw the substance, but the sun worshipers were, nevertheless, quite literally "on the side of the angels" in the conflict with the daemons and their idolatrous human minions. On other attempts to build a bridge between Christianity and the more "enlightened" forms of paganism, see H.A. Drake, *In Praise of Constantine: A Historical Study and New Translation of Eusebius' Tricennial Orations* (Berkeley: University of California Press, 1976) chapter 4. Drake's book has a number of excellent insights from a classicist sensitive to what a non-Christian of the fourth century would have heard Eusebius saying, and can add something to the perspective of the more typically Christian-oriented patristics scholar.

[15] Eus. *PE* 1.6.4(17d-18a).

[16] Compare Eus. *PE* 1.9.13-14(29d-30a); see also *DE* 4.9.10(160bc). An account with slight differences is given in *PE* 1.6.1 and 3 (17b and d).

[17] Her. 2.49-58, 81; 5.57-61.

women were some of a quite different sort—Enosh, Enoch, Noah, Seth, Japheth, Abraham, Isaac, Jacob, Job, and Joseph—a whole series of figures from early biblical history.[18] These were the θεοφιλεῖς, the "Friends of God." They formed a small minority of good and virtuous human beings, worshipers of the true God. Their religion was based upon knowledge of the Logos, the rational structure of reality as a whole.[19] It was natural religion which they had—that is, one based on "natural concepts" (φυσικαῖς ἐννοίαις),[20] a piece of (originally) Stoic phraseology that Middle Platonism had taken over by Eusebius's time. Even though the Friends of God lived centuries before the coming of Jesus, and practiced a religion based on reason alone, Eusebius believed that they were properly to be described as "Christians in fact, if not in name."[21]

These Friends of God were called into being by a series of theophanies of the divine Logos. This distinct second person of the Trinity was the necessary intermediary between the world of history and the transcendent, unknowable Father. Through his "Word" or Logos, God the Father called out these great Old Testament figures and taught them those vital truths about God and human life that had been suppressed and forgotten by sinful men and women after the Fall. It was the Logos, in Eusebius's interpretation, who appeared to Abraham at the oak of Mamre, and to Jacob when he saw the ladder stretching up to heaven. The Old Testament recorded a whole series of such theophanies or divine manifestations.[22] In this way, the divine Logos became the agent through which the human race was to be lifted out of savagery and superstition and was to be led gradually, over the centuries, to civilization and a rational religion. This was God's way of helping humankind when the fallen race, at the beginning of history, had almost been completely swallowed up in evil.

The period of the great pre-Mosaic theophanies was followed by

---

[18] Eus. *PE* 7.8.4-36(306d-312b); *DE* 1.2.3-7(12-13) and 5.7(10b).
[19] Eus. *HE* 1.4.
[20] Eus. *HE* 1.4.4; *DE* 1.5.2-4(9cd).
[21] Eus. *HE* 1.4.6.
[22] Among the Old Testament theophanies Eusebius mentions are the two already cited—the appearance to Abraham at the oak of Mamre (Gen 18) and Jacob's ladder (Gen 28:10-15)—along with Jacob's dream (Gen 31:10-13), Jacob wrestling (Gen 32:24-30), Moses and the burning bush (Exod 3:1ff.), the pillar of smoke and the pillar of fire (Exod 13:21-22), the soldier with the drawn sword who appeared to Joshua (Jos 5:13ff.), and the Lord speaking to Job out of the whirlwind (Job 38ff.); see Eus. *HE* 1.2.6-16; *PE* 7.12.8(321d); *DE* 1.5.10-18(10d-11d); 5.19.4-5(246d-247a). The series finally culminated in the appearance of Jesus of Nazareth, when the Logos used an actual human life as the vehicle for revealing God to the human race. There were also postbiblical theophanies in Eusebius's system, namely to Constantine; this, of course, was not part of the traditional Logos theology that Eusebius had inherited from his predecessors; see Eus. *VC* 1.28-29, 32, 47; 2.12.

the period dominated by Moses himself. In order to justify Christianity's rejection of the law of Moses, Eusebius naturally had to portray this as in some way a step backwards. According to his explanation, when the Hebrew people took up residence in Egypt, they eventually found the Egyptian moral climate so enervating that they were no longer able to rise to the level of those virtues that had been practiced by the Friends of God among their foreparents. God therefore sent Moses to give the Hebrew people a different religious system—Judaism—that presented the truths of religion in riddles and symbols to this people grown too weak to face the naked reality.[23] This was a standard patristic argument. The law of Moses thereby became only an *Interimsethik*, so to speak, designed to care for the Hebrew people until the coming of Jesus, when it could be discarded.[24]

Eusebius then developed in greater detail another argument that had also already been used in earlier Christian apologetic—the claim that Plato had borrowed his best ideas from Moses. The Christians had the basic chronology on their side. The oldest books of the Old Testament antedated by several centuries the rise of classical Greek culture, and lack of knowledge of cuneiform and hieroglyphics kept educated people of Eusebius's period from any real knowledge of the magnificent sweep of Egyptian and Mesopotamian civilization in the second and third millennia B.C.E. So Eusebius adopted a diffusion theory of civilization and argued that all the world's knowledge of philosophy and ethics had spread outward from a Palestinian center by ordinary transcultural intellectual contacts during the millennium following Moses, that is, roughly the first millennium B.C.E.[25] This theory was presupposed in the important introductory section of his *Church History*. The law of the Hebrews, Eusebius said (1.2.23),

> became famous and spread among all human beings like a fragrant breeze. Beginning with them the arrogance of most of the nations was tamed by the lawgivers and philosophers who arose everywhere. Savage

---

[23] Eus. *PE* 7.8.37-40(312b-313a). See also *HE* 1.2.22—Moses' teaching contained "icons and symbols . . . but not clear and distinct initiations into the mysteries themselves." Compare *DE* 4.10.4-8(161c-162d).

[24] Eus. *DE* 1.6.31-32(16d-17a), compare 2.1-10(11-14).

[25] There was an important pagan countertheory that held that the city of Athens instead was the source and foster parent of all true civilization and all truly civilized human beings. It was this single city that had brought humanity out of the life of savagery. See James H. Oliver, *The Civilizing Power: A Study of the Panathenaic Discourse of Aelius Aristides*, in *Transactions of the American Philosophical Society* new series 58 (1968) Part 1. The Panathenaic discourse was composed shortly before 167, while Aristides was professor of rhetoric at Smyrna, an important Christian center in the second century (Oliver, 34-35). Oliver further states that Aristides was attacking both the Christian assertion that Plato had gotten his ideas from Moses, and also the Christian claim that Christians were the true possessors of the Logos (36).

and unbridled brutality was changed to mildness, so that deep peace, friendship, and mutual dealings with one another obtained.[26]

As civilization slowly spread over all the world through the course of the first millennium B.C.E. Eusebius pointed proudly to the savage and barbaric practices that were eradicated: murder, cannibalism, incest, killing aged parents after they became senile and burdensome, putting human corpses out to be eaten by dogs and carrion-eating birds, burning the living relatives of a dead person on his funeral pyre, and human sacrifice.[27] It can be noted that some of the items on Eusebius's list simply represented societal customs that normally differ from culture to culture—burial practices, for example, and the exact specification of the persons within the kinship system with whom sexual relations would be called incestuous. On the other hand, he never criticized accepted Roman customs such as, for example, the practice of judicial examination under torture, even though this went against Old Testament and rabbinic law. Eusebius's notions of "natural morality" were in fact very much conditioned by the standards of his own age and culture. What he was in fact celebrating was in large part simply the Hellenization and Romanization of the Mediterranean world over the preceding six centuries. But the historical myth made this the final triumphant reversal of a dreadful and long-lasting primeval fall that had occurred back at the beginning of history.

In Eusebius's theory, civilization was therefore spread from its Palestinian center over the entire inhabited world by the first century B.C.E. For the next era of history to dawn, this Palestinian center then had to be destroyed. Following the traditional Christian interpretation, Eusebius regarded the first-century Roman takeover as the end of Jewish Palestine. It was regarded as an act of God's hand, the necessary prelude to the appearance of the Messiah, who would then call in the Gentiles to the worship of the God of the Hebrews.[28]

History was now finally ready to receive the final and highest revelation of God, the incarnation. The Logos therefore entered human history once again, but in a new way, in the life of Jesus of Nazareth.[29]

---

[26] See also *DE* 8.introd.5-12(363c-365b). Eusebius makes the point repeatedly that Moses came earlier than any Greek thinker—*HE* 6.13.7; Armen. *Chron.*, Karst edition, 1. "The Greeks ... borrowed all their philosophy from barbarians," and therefore probably from Hebrew sources among others—*PE* 11.pref.1-2(507d-508a). "The philosophy of Plato in very many points contains a translation, as it were, of Moses"—*PE* 13.pref.(639ab).

[27] Eus. *HE* 1.2.19; *DE* 4.10.1-3(161bc); *De laud.* 13.6-8, 13.14; *Theoph.* 2.81-82.

[28] Eus. *DE* 7.introd.1(308).

[29] Eus. *HE* 1.2.23; *DE* 8.introd. 5-12(363c-365b); *De laud.* 13.15. Christ did not come to all the peoples of the earth until so late in the world's history, because the proper historical preparation had not yet been made—*DE* 8.introd. 5-12(363c-365b); *HE* 1.2.17.

Shortly afterwards, the priestly religion of Old Testament Judaism was brought to an end by the destruction of Jerusalem and the Temple in 70 C.E.[30] Like Josephus, Eusebius held that this had been the result of divine wrath, but in a Christian interpretation of the event said that the killing of Jesus and three of his apostles had been the culpable deed.[31] Eusebius was no ancient anti-Semite; he held that the responsibility had been placed completely upon the heads of that one particular generation that met death and ruin at Jerusalem in 70 C.E.[32] There was no notion in Eusebius's philosophy of history of any supposed "racial guilt" of the Jews.

With the coming of Christ came the creation of the Church. And closely connected with this in God's plan for history came another event that happened at roughly the same time: the final collapse of the Late Roman Republic and its conversion, under Augustus, into the Early Empire. In Eusebius's theology of history, Church and Empire shared a common birth and (ultimately) a common destiny, "two great Powers sprung fully up, as it were, out of one stream."[33] In Eusebius's *Chronicle*, the multiple columns displaying the parallel histories of the various nations of the world (Assyria, Egypt, the Hebrews, Athens, Sparta, and so on) were reduced to only two columns for the period after Christ—one for the history of the Roman empire and one for the parallel history of the growth of Christianity. For Eusebius, these two columns summed up all that was significant in the history of the centuries after the birth of Jesus.

With the final, firm establishment of the Roman empire at the time of Christ, the political history of the world entered a completely new phase according to Eusebius's scheme of history. Before the coming of Christ, the world was filled with "polyarchy." The inhabited world was split up into a number of states, some ruled by democracies, others by tyrannies. Egypt, Arabia, Idumaea, Phoenicia, Syria, and many other states were ruled by kings. People who belonged to one state had no mutual dealings with people from other states.[34] "Hence wars of all kinds naturally arose," Eusebius wrote, "nations clashing against nations, and constantly rising up against their neighbors, ravaging and being ravaged, and making war in their sieges one against another, so that from these causes the whole population, both of dwellers in the

---

[30] As Eusebius describes in gory detail in his *Church History*. See also *DE* 1.1.7(5-6); 8.introd. 2-3(363ab). By the fourth century there was little left even of the ancient ruins, *DE* 8.3.9-15(406b-407b).

[31] Eus. *DE* 1.1.7(5-6); *Theoph.* 4.14 and 16.

[32] Eus. *Theoph.* 4.17.

[33] Eus. *Theoph.* 3.2.

[34] Eus. *PE* 1.4.2-4(10ad); *DE* 7.2.20-22(344c-345a); *Theoph.* 2.67-68. See also *De laud.* 13.9-10, 16.1-5; *Theoph.* 2.69, 71-72, 78.

cities, and laborers in the fields, from mere childhood were taught warlike exercises, and always wore swords both in the highways and in villages and fields."[35] Eusebius suggested that those who wanted to see what life was like in that period of history should read the records of butchery and carnage contained in the classical Greek and Roman histories. It was this continual strife that Augustus ended when he made himself sole ruler of the Roman empire in 31 B.C.E. The "monarchy" of Augustus replaced the wartorn "polyarchy" of the ancient Mediterranean world with a new era of peace.

To Eusebius, it was not chance that made Christ and Augustus historical contemporaries—their lives were inextricably linked in God's providential plan for history.[36] Christ came to save human beings from the idolatry of polytheism and bring them to the true monotheistic worship of the one true Church in the same way that Augustus had come to save human beings from the strife of polyarchy and bring them to the true monarchical government of the universal human State. In Eusebius's thought *poly*theism and *poly*archy were linked together as necessarily as were *mono*theism and *mon*archy.[37] In good Platonic fashion, one level of reality was merely the icon or image of the next higher level: the organization of humanity's secular political life simply mirrored on a lower plane the organization of its spiritual life. The extreme monarchical nature of Eusebius's political ideas is discussed in almost every comprehensive history of the development of Western political thought; as can be seen here, it was linked in his own mind with a particular kind of philosophy of history that in fact used the defense of absolute monarchy in reverse as a sort of indirect, Platonizing argument in defense of Christian monotheism.

To Eusebius, polyarchy was linked with strife and warfare, while monarchy meant peace.[38] The primary example he gave of what would happen if the Roman imperial government broke down completely was drawn from the period before the triumph of Augustus in 31 B.C.E. But one cannot help wondering how much one is also hearing an echo here of more contemporary fears. The assassination of the emperor Severus Alexander in 235 C.E. had produced what is called the crisis of the third century. For nearly fifty years a string of barracks emperors reigned, each one rising briefly to power and then con-

---

[35] Eus. *PE* 1.4.2-4(10ad), perhaps an echo of Thucydides 1.6.1, "Indeed, all the Hellenes used to carry arms because the places where they dwelt were unprotected, and intercourse with each other was unsafe; and in their everyday life they regularly went armed just as the Barbarians did."

[36] Eus. *PE* 1.4.2-4(10ad); *DE* 3.7.30-31(139d); 7.2.20-22(344c-345a); *Theoph.* 3.1.

[37] Eus. *De laud.* 16.1-5; *Theoph.* 2.67-68, 76.

[38] "The deepest peace" (εἰρήνη) resulted when polyarchy and "piecemeal rule of the earth" was replaced by the rule of a single imperial authority, Eus. *DE* 8.3.9-15(406b-407b). Compare *DE* 9.17.14-15(457d-458a).

fronting mutiny and assassination as he strove to reassemble a disintegrating empire. At Palmyra in Syria and at Trier in Gaul, rival Roman empires were centered for part of this anarchic period. Real stability did not return until Diocletian was proclaimed emperor in 284 C.E. Eusebius had lived through some of the worst of this himself. Born around 260 C.E., he lived in an area that was under the control of Queen Zenobia of Palmyra when he was around ten years old.[39] When he was just beginning his adolescence, the emperor Aurelian was crushing the rival imperial power at Palmyra and returning the eastern Mediterranean world to Roman control. To Eusebius, a strong monarchy was the only alternative to a kind of suicidal civil warfare that he himself had experienced; the word "peace" (εἰρήνη) meant the stability of the reconstructed Late Empire, put together during his lifetime by the emperors Diocletian and Constantine. Even in the next century, Eusebius's successor church historians were still holding absence of civil strife as the central goal of both ecclesiastical and secular government,[40] a rather Byzantine attitude that placed "peace" of this kind above either personal liberties or freedom of self-expression.

Another important reason why the concept of εἰρήνη was given such importance in Eusebius's political thought was his equation of the Pax Romana with the eschatological Kingdom of Peace prophesied in Isaiah 2:4 and Micah 4:1-4,[41] when swords were to be beaten into plowshares, and spears into pruning hooks, and nation was not to lift up sword against nation any more.[42] To Eusebius, the fulfillment of those prophecies was not to be seen in the miraculous future kingdom of the millennialists, in which grapevines gave 225 gallons of wine from each grape,[43] but in the Roman rule he himself lived under. This claim was not mere rhetorical hyperbole on his part, but as will be

---

[39] Eusebius was probably born in Palestinian Caesarea; it is known that he developed his massive scholarship in the libraries of the presbyter Pamphilus in Caesarea and Bishop Alexander at Jerusalem (only fifty miles away), and that he spent all his later life in Caesarea. There is no suggestion in any ancient work that he originally came from elsewhere.

[40] Socrates, for example, at the conclusion of his history, *HE* 7.48: "But we shall here close our history, praying that the churches everywhere, with the cities and nations, may live in peace. For as long as peace continues, those who desire to write histories will find no materials for their purpose." As the chapter about Socrates will explain in more detail this historian also believed that the secular political sphere and the spiritual sphere were necessarily linked together. A disruption of "peace" in one area would produce, by a kind of cosmic "sympathy," a parallel disruption in the other (Socr. *HE* 5. introd.).

[41] Also, in Eusebius's interpretation, such passages as Micah 5:4-5a and Psalm 72(71):7, where the exegetical focal point was the word "peace."

[42] Eus. *PE* 1.4.2-4(10ad); *DE* 7.2.20-22(344c-345a); 8.3.9-15(406b-407b); *De laud.* 16.7-8; *Theoph.* 3.2.

[43] Irenaeus, *Adv. haer.* 5.33.3.

seen in chapter 7, a consistent part of his overall treatment of the problem of eschatology.

In the period after Christ, just as had been the case in the period before his coming, there was still, of course, a celestial dualism intruding as a disturbing force into the events of human history: the battle between the Logos and the daemons, a cosmic struggle between Good and Evil personified. In the Preface to Book Five of his *Church History*, Eusebius tells us that all church history was the history of a war against the invisible daemons.[44] The daemons were the Old Gods, the gods whom the pagan persecutors worshiped.[45] The evil daemon used these men as his agents. He had Licinius persecute Christianity in the East and start a war with Constantine, for example.[46] The evil daemon could "raise up" individual human beings as his personal agents,[47] and single out individual Christians for special attack,[48] or when God let him he could raise a wholesale persecution against the entire Church, as in the Great Persecution that Eusebius had lived through.[49] The evil daemon preferred to use persecutors to attack the Church, but when he was prevented from doing this he would use heretics instead:[50] Simon Magus, Menander, the Ebionites, Saturninus, Basilides, Carpocrates, the Montanists, Florinus, Blastus, Mani, the Donatists, and those who started the Arian controversy.[51] In fact, any kind of violent internal dispute in the Church, such as the turbulent Synod of Tyre in 335 that condemned Athanasius, was blamed on the evil daemon[52]—although one may wonder which people in particular Eusebius thought were daemon-inspired in that council!

The daemons were not always successful in turning Roman emperors against the Christians, so that the history of the first three centuries of Christianity was in fact marked by long periods of relative toleration. As a result, Eusebius in his young years divided all Roman emperors into two classes—those who had and those who had not persecuted the church. He believed that the history of the previous centuries proved that God gave success to the good emperors who were tolerant towards Christianity, whereas the bad, persecuting emperors always came to bad ends.[53]

---

[44] Eus. *HE* 5.pref. 3-4.
[45] Such as the persecutors of Eusebius's own time, Licinius and Maximin, Eus. *VC* 1.54, 58; 3.1.
[46] Eus. *VC* 1.49; *HE* 10.8.2.
[47] Eus. *HE* 5.21.1-2 (ἐγείρας).
[48] Eus. *HE* 6.39.5.
[49] Eus. *HE* 10.4.13-16.
[50] Eus. *HE* 4.7.1-3.
[51] Eus. *HE* 2.14.1-3; 3.26, 27.1; 4.7.1-3, 7.10-11, 5.14.1-16.1; 7.31.1. *VC* 1.45, 2.73.
[52] Eus. *VC* 4.41. Compare 3.1, 59.
[53] The phrase "the divine δίκη" was the standard term for divine retribution in Euse-

By the end of his life, by which time the Christian Constantine had gained total control over the entire empire, Eusebius had decided that the good emperor henceforward had to be more than simply a tolerant, liberal pagan. Sanction of polytheism and participation in pagan sacrifice in themselves made a bad emperor, whether the monarch persecuted Christians or not. Nevertheless, Eusebius made no changes in the nature of the this-worldly rewards promised the good emperor, or the character of the this-world punishments with which the bad emperor was threatened. He simply set higher requirements for gaining these rewards.

There were at least eight separate factors involved in the "success" granted the good emperor under Eusebius's theory, factors worth listing because of the insight they give into the ideas and values of the ancient world for which the church historian was writing. First, Eusebius believed that, in time of war, God gave success in battle to the good emperor,[54] and defeat to the bad.[55] Second, he believed that having a good emperor on the throne would result in general prosperity for the empire,[56] whereas having a bad emperor would produce hard times for the entire realm: civil war, famine, and pestilence.[57] Furthermore, "peace"—that ideal that so deeply affected the hopes and dreams of all the church historians investigated here—would reign everywhere when a good emperor was in command,[58] whereas war would be sent in divine retribution if a bad emperor gained control.[59] The good emperor himself was give a long reign,[60] and a happy end to his life, still in possession of his throne.[61] The bad emperor found his reign cut off short,[62] and went to an unhappy end, having lost all his power, or having been forced to resign the throne, or meeting death by violence or loathsome disease, or being defeated in battle and captured, or something else of this sort.[63] The good emperor was honored

---

bius's writings (he used the word even more often than Josephus). It was the "divine δίκη" that struck down the persecuting emperors, we are told continually: Eus. *HE* 7.30.20-21; 9.7.2, 9a.12; 10.4.29; *VC* 1.58 (Maximian), 58-59 (Maximin). Of course, the divine δίκη would strike down not only emperors, but other persecutors and enemies of Christianity as well; Eus. *HE* 2.6.8 and 3.5.6; 2.7.1, 10.1; 9.11.5-6. Compare *HE* 6.9.4-8; *VC* 1.12.

[54] Eus. *VC* 1.27.
[55] Eus. *HE* 7.13; 9.9.2-8; 9.10.
[56] Eus. *De laud.* 3.
[57] Eus. *HE* 8.14.18-15.2; 9.7.3-14 and 7.16-8.3
[58] Eus. *HE* 8.13.9. Compare Rudolph H. Storch, "The 'Eusebian Constantine,'" *Church History* 40(1971): 145-55.
[59] Eus. *HE* 8.14.18-15.2; 9.8.2.
[60] Eus. *HE* 8.13.9; *De laud.* 3, 9.18.
[61] Eus. *HE* 8.13.12-13; 8.appendix; *VC* 1.3, 17.
[62] Eus. *HE* 7.1, 30.20-22.
[63] Eus. *HE* 7.1, 10-13; 8.13.9-11, 13.15; 8.appendix; 9.9.2-8; 9.10 *VC* 1.27; *Theoph.* 5.52.

both during his life and after death.[64] The bad emperor's memory was dishonored after his death, his inscriptions and statutes torn down and mutilated[65]—surely a dire thought, given the nature of Roman emperors and their desire to become an "honored ancestor" to their posterity. The good emperor was given many children,[66] while the bad emperor would either be unable to beget children who would grow to maturity, or his children, relatives, and associates would all be put to death as soon as he himself was dead.[67] Furthermore, the good emperor would be permitted by God to leave the throne to his rightful heir,[68] whereas the bad emperor's line would come to an end with his own death.[69]

Hence the principle was asserted that the emperor's religious stance was the determinant of the course of imperial history. This same basic principle was taken over and enlarged upon, as shall be seen later, by Eusebius's fifth- and sixth-century successors. As the standards of Christian orthodoxy became more firmly set, and as the public's moral and personal expectations of a Christian monarch became progressively higher, these historians laid out more complicated requirements for becoming a "good emperor," but they promised essentially the same providential rewards to the emperors who fulfilled their standards: success in battle, prosperity and peace for the empire, a long reign, a happy end to his life, an honored memory, children, and a rightful heir as his successor on the throne. In the eastern half of the Roman empire there were to be no serious problems raised for this understanding of history until the rise of Islam in the early seventh century.[70]

The most important thing to note, however, is that implicit in Eusebius's whole treatment of the problem of Church and Empire, even in his younger years, was the assumption that the two were necessarily tied together at the deepest level: Christianity as the ultimate world religion and Rome as the ultimate world state. In his scheme of universal history, the nearly simultaneous appearance at the end of the first century B.C.E. of Christ and the emperor Augustus created these two forces, and both the Christian religion and the Roman empire were the culmination of all the millennia of history that had gone before. Even before Constantine's conversion to Christianity had be-

---

[64] Eus. *HE* 8.13.12; *VC* 1.27; 4.75.
[65] Eus. *HE* 8.13.15; 9.11.2; *VC* 1.27.
[66] Eus. *VC* 1.18; *De laud.* 3, 9.18.
[67] Eus. *HE* 7.1; 9.11.3-7; *VC* 1.27.
[68] Eus. *HE* 8.13.12-13; 8. appendix; *VC* 1.18.
[69] Eus. *HE* 7.1; *VC* 1.27.
[70] See Walter Emil Kaegi, Jr., "Initial Byzantine Reactions to the Arab Conquest," *Church History* 38 (1969): 139-49.

come a believable factor to be reckoned with, Eusebius seems to have understood that Rome's destiny and the Church's divine calling were somehow to be intertwined in any future he could foresee.

Eusebius therefore saw the major events of world history as a connected sequence, beginning with the creation itself and the original cosmic fall of the human race, and culminating in the emergence of early Christianity in the newly created Roman Principate. The remainder of this chapter must discuss the significance of a historian's seeing this kind of overall pattern in history. What kind of patterns had his pagan predecessors seen, or thought they saw? How did Eusebius's views fit into the historiographical traditions of the ancient world?

In attempting to discuss the long-term patterns of world history, the Graeco-Roman tradition before Eusebius had explored all three of the basic alternatives: theories of historical progress, theories of historical decline, and theories of repeating historical cycles.[71] The first to raise the issue had been Hesiod, around 700 B.C.E. with his famous account in the *Works and Days* of the Five Ages of Man.[72] He presented human history as one of decline, from a blessed Golden Age at the primordial beginning, to the fifth and present age, the Age of Iron, where "human beings never rest from labor and sorrow by day, and from perishing by night." Over against this there were also, from earliest times, Greek theories of historical progress. The pre-Socratic philosopher Xenophanes, for example, displayed the Ionian Enlightenment's obvious pride in its scientific discoveries.

> *Not from the beginning did the gods reveal everything to humanity,*
> *But in course of time by research human beings discover improvements.*[73]

On the other hand, both Hesiod and Xenophanes combined their theories of decline and progress, respectively, with cyclic views of history. It appears quite probable that Hesiod used a myth of eternal recurrence to set his theory of historical decline into a larger cyclic pattern, in which the destruction of the race of iron would allow a new golden age to emerge from the ruins. There seems to be no other way to explain the poet's cryptic remark at one point that he wished he had either "died before" the present dismal age of iron, which Zeus was going to destroy by abandoning it to an almost apocalyptic time of trib-

---

[71] One of the best recent studies of these themes is E.R. Dodds, "The Ancient Concept of Progress," in his *Ancient Concept of Progress and Other Essays* (Oxford: Clarendon Press, 1973) 1-24. Another important work is Ludwig Edelstein, *The Idea of Progress in Classical Antiquity* (Baltimore: Johns Hopkins University Press, 1967).

[72] Hesiod, *Works and Days*, 106-201.

[73] Diels, *Fragmente der Vorsokratiker*, fifth ed., frag. 18; trans. from E.R. Dodds, "The Ancient Concept of Progress."

ulation, "or been born *afterwards*" (174-175). Xenophanes thought that at long periodic intervals the sea rose and covered all the earth and destroyed all human life, thus introducing a cyclic element into his thought as well.

Cyclic elements of one sort or another appeared in most of the classical Greek historians. Herodotus, for example, emphasized the way the cyclic rise and fall of empires repeated itself incessantly through dreary centuries and millennia, and held that this was one of the basic structures of history. "For many states that were once great have now become small, and those that were great in my time were small formerly."[74] Characteristic Greek pessimism also made him certain in his heart that individual human prosperity would always be followed eventually by evil. "Men's fortunes are on a wheel, which in its turning suffers not the same man to prosper forever."[75] Thucydides said that he wrote his history in the belief that the sort of internal disintegration that the Athenian body politic suffered during the Peloponnesian war would be repeated again in some other nation in some later period of history.[76] To him, the historian's task was to study the pathologies of human societies, and like the Hippocratic school of Greek physicians, he thought of himself as cataloguing the progressive symptoms of a kind of political "disease" that would surely be met in human history again. In this sense he might be spoken of as thinking in cyclic terms, but only in a mild way.

In Polybius the cyclic element was much more important. He laid out an involved series of constitutional changes that in one tradition of Greek political thought (compare Plato) were supposed to take place in recurrent cycles in the history of an individual city-state. The force of nature (φύσις) kept a city-state from remaining for any long stable period in any one simple political system. Forces inherent in that system inevitably worked towards a degeneration or mutation into a different kind of government, in a perpetual repeating sequence: monarchy to kingship to tyranny to aristocracy to oligarchy to democracy to mob-rule to savagery and back around again.[77] This particular kind of cycle applied per se only to the individual city-state, and not to world history as a whole. But Polybius also believed in one version of that persistent Greek theme of the periodic world-destroying catastro-

---

[74] Her. 1.5. One sees an awareness of this inevitable cyclic pattern even in Polybius, who presented Rome's rise to power so triumphantly. The Persians had fallen, to be replaced by the Macedonians as rulers of the world. Then the Macedonians fell in their turn, to be replaced by the Romans (Polyb. 29.21). And the Carthaginians also fell, who were also replaced by the Romans. Some day, even Polybius admits, it would happen to Rome, too (38.21-22).
[75] Her. 1.207.
[76] Thuc. 1.22.4.
[77] Polyb. 6.3-9; Plato, *Republic* 8.1(544c)-9.6(580c).

phe, and so he was commited to a cyclic theory of history at the world-historical level on these grounds. "Floods, famines, failure of crops or other such causes" could produce "such a destruction of the human race as tradition tells us has more than once happened, and as we must believe will often happen again." In the catastrophe one had "all arts and crafts perishing at the same time," so that the pitifully few survivors had to build civilization and human society completely anew, out of savagery and total anarchy.[78]

Against this background of cyclic theories, the Greek historians (as opposed to the Roman historians later) generally believed strongly that the history of their own immediate past, extending back for several centuries even, had been one of continuous historical progress, and their viewpoint was basically cheerful and optimistic on these grounds. They developed this positive attitude by emphasizing the history of progress in technology, scientific knowledge, and the general civilized arts. Herodotus's history as a whole was a celebration of the military superiority of Greeks to barbarians, yet his experience in Egypt[79] gave him a vivid sense of how young Greek civilization was in comparison with other peoples. He knew quite well how important a role progress had played in recent Greek history. Thucydides, writing from a slightly later period of history, spoke with even more civilized amazement of "the weakness of olden times," when the soldiers of a Greek army had to row themselves across the sea in little undecked pirate boats in order to do battle with the enemy. Then came the invention of the trireme, which gave the technological basis for great ocean battles. But even the Athenian navy that triumphed at sea in the Persian war looked primitive from the viewpoint of his own time.[80] In Polybius, this sense of "modern superiority" was even more pronounced. He was extremely proud of the rapid technological progress that had taken place in his own day,[81] by which he meant the various sorts of modern inventions and developments discussed so much through the

---

[78] Polyb. 6.5.5. On the other hand, even Polybius did not teach the extreme Stoic view of time. Many modern writers have used as their primary example of the "Greek cyclic view of time" this early Stoic theory in which exactly the same sequence of historical events was supposed to occur again and again into infinity, with an identical Socrates drinking an identical draught of hemlock once every world-cycle, an identical wooden horse being brought within the walls of an identical Troy, and so on, down to the last detail of world history. The principal surviving Graeco-Roman historians certainly did not teach this sort of extreme theory. Even Polybius, though he spoke of natural catastrophes, nowhere taught of the great World-Conflagration in which, according to early Stoic theory, everything—earth, human beings, and even the gods (except for Zeus himself)—would be consumed in flames as each world-cycle came to an end. On the contrary, in 4.40.4-7, Polybius asserted the infinity of time.
[79] Her. 2.142-143.
[80] Thuc. 1.3.1, 10.4, 13.2-4, 14.3.
[81] Polyb. 9.2.5, the rapid progress in the ἐμπειρίαι and τέχναι.

course of his history: improvements in the design of hand weapons and armor, the replacement of the Macedonian phalanx by the Roman legion as the lord of the battlefield, the Roman development of the "crow" for use in sea-battles, Polybius's own invention of a long-distance signalling device, Archimedes' wonderful machines used in the defense of Syracuse, the increase in the number of banks of oars used on warships from three, as in the trireme (the classical warship of an earlier period), to five and even higher, and so on.[82]

Unlike these earlier Greek historians, the Roman historians who followed them were more apt to view the history of the immediately preceding period as one of decline. Sallust gave the classical account of this.[83] The early Roman republic had been filled with people of primitive virtue, who preferred hardship, discipline, and victory with honor, over all the lures of riches, revelry, and harlotry. But "by gradual changes" over the hundred years preceding his own time, Rome had "ceased to be the noblest and best" and had "become the worse and most vicious."[84] The final victory over her mortal enemy Carthage in 146 B.C.E. released all external pressure, and with that, self-discipline relaxed,[85] and the vice of *ambitio* sprang up.[86] The next step in Rome's moral downfall took place during the reign of the dictator Sulla. The license he gave his troops introduced the vice of *luxuria* into the Roman national spirit,[87] and the mass proscriptions that followed his complete takeover of the Roman state in 83 B.C.E. brought the further vice of *avaritia*, the "desire for money, which no wise person covets."[88] Forty years later, at the time Sallust was writing, Rome was fallen, he felt, into a permanent and irreparable state of decadence and moral corruption.

Tacitus also adopted a theory of historical decline from an original state of primitive perfection, but he pushed the golden age much further back into the past. "Mortals of the primeval age, untouched as yet by criminal passion, lived their lives without reproach or guilt," in

---

[82] See for example Polyb. 1.20.9-16; 1.22-23; 8.3-7; and 18.28-32.
[83] See especially the first thirteen chapters of his *Bellum Catilinae*.
[84] Sall. *Cat.* 5.9.
[85] "Those who had found it easy to bear hardship and dangers, anxiety and adversity, found leisure and wealth, desirable under other circumstances, a burden and a curse"—Sall. *Cat.* 10.2.
[86] A vice of "craft and deception," which found "one thought locked in the breast, another ready on the tongue"—Sall. *Cat.* 11.1-2; 10.5.
[87] When Sulla billeted his troops in the homes of private citizens in the reconquered province of Asia, "those charming and voluptuous lands . . . easily demoralized the warlike spirit of his soldiers," as they learned too great a love of women, drink, and classical Greek *objets d'art*—Sall. *Cat.* 11.5-6. Sallust does not say which of these three vices he considered the gravest sign of total moral degeneracy!
[88] Sall. *Cat.* 11.3.

a tribal society where the force of traditional custom meant that "good was sought instinctively."[89] Government was by the sort of primitive democracy typically found in the tribal stage.[90] The fall came when kings arose and destroyed the ancentral customs of that primitive social system with their despotism. Formal codes of law, like the laws of Lycurgus in Sparta or Solon in Athens, were attempts to curb the power of those kings and tyrants, and also attempts to replace vanished customs with new, consciously organized standards of behavior. Rome had followed this standard historical pattern; it had overthrown its kings and instituted government by law, but Tacitus dourly remarked that the Twelve Tables were "the last instance" in Roman history of truly "equitable legislation."[91] The lawmaking process became entangled in class warfare.[92] Then at the final desperate end of the Republic complete chaos resigned for twenty years during which there was neither law *nor* custom—"villainy was immune, decency not rarely a sentence of death."[93] Order was finally restored by Augustus, who gave Rome peace, but also the Principate.[94] He took complete control of the state, and all opposition quickly vanished. The surviving members of the senatorial aristocracy "found a cheerful acceptance of slavery the smoothest road to wealth and office."[95] The remainder of Tacitus's *Annals* and *Histories* was devoted to cataloguing the tyranny, cruelty, depravity, and paranoiac insanity of the line of emperors that followed. Tacitus's theory of Rome's decline and fall was joined to an antimonarchical zeal quite the opposite of Eusebius's glorification of the imperial power.

Tacitus's theories were based on a kind of romantic primitivism. Civilization was evil and corrupting. The *Annals* and the *Histories* used Rome as the example of this, while his *Germania* showed by the strongest possible contrast the virtues of the noble savage. The primitive Germanic tribesmen whom he described were still in the seminomadic stage, and he romanticized their bravery in battle, faithfulness in marriage, and simplicity in clothes and dwellings. There were many varieties of romantic primitivism in the ancient world—the philosophy of the wandering Cynic with his staff and single cloak and

---

[89] Tac. *Ann.* 3.26—behavior guided by *mos* (traditional custom) rather than by *ius* (formally enacted law).

[90] Tac. *Ger.* 11. This primitive democracy Tacitus called *aequalitas* (*Ann.* 3.26), that is, "political equality" in the sense of the Greek ἰσοτιμία.

[91] *Finis aequi iuris*—Tac. *Ann.* 3.27.

[92] *Dissensione ordinum*—Tac. *Ann.* 3.27. Each social class battled to distort the laws in its own favor, and as one might say today, class interest came to dictate the ideological structure of the state.

[93] Tac. *Ann.* 3.28.

[94] *Pace et principe*—ibid.

[95] Tac. *Ann.* 1.2.

knapsack, the bucolic poetry of writers like Theocritus, Ovid's theory of the Golden Age, Seneca's description of the noble savage—and as can be seen in Tacitus, it was quite possible to write history from this perspective.[96]

Eusebius's historical theories made an interesting contrast with these Greek and Roman ideas that had come before. The life of savages was never romanticized by him. The Edenic life was lifted by him to a nonphysicial, precosmic, spiritual realm. He had much more in common with positive Greek ideas of historical progress than he had with Latin ideas of corruption and decline, even though he placed a fall into immorality at the beginning of history. Although Hesiod's account of the end of the Age of Iron had had faintly apocalyptic overtones, and although orthodox Stoics believed that this present cosmos would end in a World Conflagration, Eusebius (as shall be seen in more detail in chapter 7) had a much keener sense, not only that this world would come to an early end some day, but that he himself was living well towards the end of historical time.[97] Although theories of historical cycles were fairly common in Greek speculation about history especially, there were clearly no important cyclical elements in Eusebius, at least as far as the this-worldly sequence of events was concerned. The history of this world for him was a line with a beginning and an

---

[96] An especially important study of the history of romantic primitivism in the Graeco-Roman period is Ragnar Höistad, *Cynic Hero and Cynic King: Studies in the Cynic Conception of Man* (Uppsala: C. Bloms, 1948). See also Donald R. Dudley, *A History of Cynicism, from Diogenes to the Sixth Century A.D.* (London: Methuen, 1937). Tacitus's description of primeval humanity is very similar to Ovid's account of the Golden Age at the beginning of his *Metamorphoses*. The human race's fall into corruption is attributed by the latter to the invention of the ship, and to the consequent beginning, not just of warfare abroad, but also of maritime commerce—surely an aristocratic senatorial bias at work! In Seneca, see the tragic hero's description of his earlier virtuous and idyllic life in *Hippolytus* 483-564, where again the development of shipbuilding and maritime commerce are said to have produced the fall of the human race.

[97] Eusebius seems to have believed, at all points in his life, that history would be brought to its final end with the full paraphernalia of apocalyptic horrors falling on earth. Christ would come for the second time, to battle the Antichrist and defeat him. The earth would be destroyed, all the stars extinguished, and then the Last Judgment would take place. Eus. *DE* 3.3.14-15(106ab), 3.17(106d); 9.15.6-8(453ac); 15 fragments 5 and 6. *De laud* 12.5. *Theoph.* 4.29. The total story of the world's history, for him, ran from the primordial fall into time and space at the beginning to this final cataclysmic termination of all earthly things at the end. Although I suggested the possibility of showing development in Eusebius's eschatological ideas in my article in *Religious Studies Review* 9 (1983): 118-23, I have subsequently rejected that hypothesis. Eusebius's writings seem to show a mixture of apocalyptic and Platonizing elements at all the stages of his life that can be reconstructed. This negative conclusion about any fundamental philosophical development in no way, of course, implies a rejection of Robert M. Grant's quite different observation, that Eusebius changed his mind about the book of Revelation and Papias. Grant is certainly correct on this point.

end, not a circle.⁹⁸

The question of whether Eusebius believed in some larger hypercosmic cycle still remains. He did reject that early Stoic cyclic theory of time that held that the historical events stretching from any one World-Conflagration to the next were exact duplicates of the events that had taken place in every previous cycle, and that would take place in every subsequent cycle.⁹⁹ On the other hand, he was an Origenist, and could easily have been influenced by the well-known theory of transmigration, espoused by some of the radical Origenists, which held that the soul was reincarnated in different bodies in different circumstances, in an endless series of existences.¹⁰⁰ Eusebius did not teach such a cyclic theory in the surviving parts of his writings,¹⁰¹ but on the other hand never condemned such an opinion either. Such an argument from silence is a weak one, but it is still difficult to avoid being suspicious when Eusebius condemns Plato's doctrine of transmigration of souls only because it asserted that human souls could be reborn in the bodies of *animals*—"dogs, hedgehogs, ants, horses, donkeys."¹⁰² Since the Origenistic theory spoke of transmigration only by ascent and descent up and down the great chain of rational being (daemons, human beings, sun, moon, planets, and angels), Eusebius's violent attack on Plato begged the important question too neatly.

Even if he did have some hidden sympathy with the radical Origenistic theory of multiple reincarnations, nevertheless Eusebius's basic view of temporality was linear and not cyclical. In his metaphysics, the basic ground of the universe itself was said to be pure, undifferentiated, unidirectional, linear temporal process.¹⁰³ His technical term for this was ὁ αἰών; in English, "aeon." This pure temporal flow, or better, this mysterious ground on which we construct our human concept of temporal sequence, was "stretched out in a straight line

---

⁹⁸ But see the warnings against the overenthusiastic speculations of many modern theologians on the "Greek mind's" understanding of time as a circle, and the "Hebrew mind's" understanding of time as a line, in Arnaldo Momigliano, "Time in Ancient Historiography," *History and Theory* Beiheft 6, *History and the Concept of Time (1966)*: 1-23.

⁹⁹ Eus. *Theoph.* 2.21. Augustine rejected Stoic cyclicism in similar fashion several generations later, in *De civ. Dei* 12.14(13).

¹⁰⁰ One must be careful about attributing this doctrine to Origen himself, as Henry Chadwick has warned in his chapter on "Origen" in *The Cambridge History of Later Greek and Early Medieval Philosophy*, ed. A.H. Armstrong (Cambridge: Cambridge University Press, 1967) 190-92.

¹⁰¹ Eus. *De laud.* 1 is ambiguous, and could have been intended to be read in an orthodox manner as simply a rather luxuriant liturgical hyperbole—"The timeless aeons before this heaven and earth, and others of these, infinite aeons of aeons, before all subsistence of visible things, acknowledge Him the sole and supreme sovereign and Lord." The passage about aeons in *De laud.* 2 is similarly ambiguous.

¹⁰² Eus. *Theoph.* 2.44.

¹⁰³ Eus. *De laud.* 6.4-5.

and stretches onward into infinity."[104] The Greek word αἰών is often translated into English as "eternity," but since the Platonic Ideas are also, in a different way, αἰώνιαι (eternal), the use of the word eternity can suggest a static view of the ground of the universe that is quite misleading. Eusebius used the word αἰών to mean eternity in the same sense as the famous passage from Marcus Aurelius: "As a river consisting of all things that come into being, aye, a rushing torrent, is eternity (ὁ αἰών). No sooner is a thing sighted than it is carried past, and lo, another is passing, and it too will be carried away."[105]

On the other hand, the aeon, for Eusebius, was not the same as χρόνος. The latter word is usually translated into English as "time," but frequently had a far narrower and more specific meaning in Greek philosophical language, so that this common translation also can be misleading to the average English reader. "Chronological time" might be a better translation of the word. When Eusebius speculated on the true meaning of χρόνος, he pointed out that what one meant by the present, that is, "the now," was always given its conceptual meaning by the human mind in the context of memory images of the past, and mental constructs embodying calculations and expectations for the future. But all the meaning was coming from purely mental constructs of what we imagined the past-present-future sequence to be, so that χρόνος, "chronological time," was a construct of the human mind that only interpreted what the mind thought the onward flow of the aeon to be at the moment. The aeon was what was truly real, chronological time (past, present, and future) was the human mind's interpretation of it.[106] So the aeon was not the same as time, but it also must be

---

[104] Eus. *De laud.* 6.4.
[105] Marcus Aurelius, *Meditations* 4.43.
[106] Eusebius had a well-developed metaphysical theory of χρόνος or "time." The temporal creature who was actually immersed in the flow of time could not, from his position *in medias res*, perceive any beginning to time or any other limitation to time's extent. And not only were the limits of time inaccessible to human thought, there were also epistemological and metaphysical problems attached to the simple division of time into past, present, and future. The past is not (οὐκ ἔστιν) because it is already gone, and the future also is not (οὐδ' ἔστιν) because it has not yet arrived. Although past and future therefore had the ontological status of nonbeing, this did not mean that one could fall back on the present (τὸ νῦν) to find true reality. There was a necessary time lag between the actual occurrence of the present and thinking about the present, such that the present could never be grasped by the mind while it was still present. Therefore one was thrown back on the unreality of the past or the unreality of the future if one attempted to grasp any object of thought, either in expectation of events in the future or in a synoptic view of events in the past. Therefore "the aeon," that is, pure temporal process itself, or one might say the ground on which we construct our human conception of "before" and "after," was totally resistant in all parts to any true comprehension by the human reason—Eus. *De laud.* 6.3. On the impossibility of conceptualizing the present tense as genuinely present reality, and its conceptual absorption into the nonbeing of the future and the past, one might compare the treatment of the distinction between past, present,

pointed out that it transcended the realm of unchanging formal knowledge in the same way that it transcended the realm of χρόνος, so to view it as static is also totally misleading.[107]

Eusebius said that God created the universe by hypostatizing it upon the fabric of this pure undifferentiated flow ("the aeon") like embroidery sewn on a long piece of ribbon.[108] First God created matter (ὕλη) and placed it in the already existing flow of the aeon, and then added form (εἶδος), and then created three-dimensional space by combining matter and form into body (σῶμα). Then came the four elements, and the numerical basis for the chronological division of time into days, months, and years.[109] But since the basic flow of the aeon on which this creation was grounded was linear and not cyclic, whatever Eusebius's position on any Origenistic ideas of possible multiple reincarnations of all the human souls in that universe, there was no idea in his thought of endless cycles simply going nowhere. The life of the universe moved forward and onward continuously with meaning and purpose.

Eusebius did not basically view time and history as cyclical. His view of the overall pattern of history in fact placed him closer to those Greek historians who had believed in progress in history than to the typical Latin historians. Unlike these Latin writers, he rejected any notion that the Roman empire was declining and falling into moral corruption and decadence. He rejected the basic premise of romantic primitivism, which held that civilization was necessarily evil and corrupting in itself. In opposition both to this and to the later view that Augustine was to take in his *City of God* roughly a century later, Eusebius held that the growth of civilization and the growth of true religion necessarily went hand in hand.[110] To Eusebius, the history of the pre-

---

and future in the Stoic idea of time; see S. Sambursky, *Physics of the Stoics* (London: Routledge and Kegan Paul, 1959) 103-104.

[107] See G.F. Chesnut, *Images of Christ: An Introduction to Christology* (Minneapolis: Seabury Press, 1984) 52-53. The popular interpretations of the modern philosopher and historian of philosophy, Charles Hartshorne, who argues that the ancients viewed eternity as static and refused to accept that temporal process was the truly concrete and real, can be very misleading if read back into the Greek patristic period; whether he is basically correct on Western medieval philosophy, the primary target of his attack, is a different question that I am less qualified to judge.

[108] Eus. *De laud.* 6.4.

[109] Eus. *De laud.* 6.5. Beyond this present aeon there will be another life or existence (ζωή, βίος) where the good will be rewarded and the wicked punished. This will be a realm of "nonchronological time (χρόνος ἄχρονος)" that is "not defined by intervals of days and months, the revolutions of years, or the recurrence of times and seasons" (Eus. *De laud.* 6.9, 6.19), but instead presumably some sort of pure noetic existence.

[110] In his *City of God* Augustine held that the Two Cities had always existed, since the beginning of life on earth. Whatever growth there had been in knowledge of the civilized arts, the tension between those two bodies of people had never been affected. At

ceding thousand years had been one of continual progress in both,[111] a position that he had held even before Constantine supplied him with a truly dramatic conclusion to that story.

The idea that real historical progress was possible, and the idea that true religion had the responsibility for creating civilized life itself, were among the most important things that Eusebius bequeathed to the middle ages. In spite of Augustine's attempt to provide a different understanding of history for the West at the time of the fifth-century collapse,[112] one of the forces that eventually gave Western Europe the courage to pull itself out of the dark age into which it began to fall was perhaps the implicit optimism of Eusebius's account of the possibilities of history. He gave the middle ages a positive vision of what humans could do to create civilization out of savagery.

---

the fundamental moral level, there had been neither progress nor decline. There had been as many people who truly loved God in primitive times as there were in his own time, while the opportunities for the subtler sins of pride and power in a sophisticated civilization made the Romans of his own day as liable to sin as any naked savage.

[111] Walter Goffart, "Zosimus, the First Historian of Rome's Fall," *American Historical Review* 76 (1971): 412-41, esp. 432, describes this "Christian theory of progress elaborated by Eusebius and expressed by the other Church historians," and then explains the pessimistic reaction to it that eventually came in the early sixth century.

[112] Eusebius may also of course have been partly responsible for creating one of the major problems that Augustine had to resolve in his *City of God*. For Eusebius, the Four Kingdoms in Daniel 2:31-45 were the Assyrian, Persian, Macedonian, and Roman empires (Eus. *DE* 15.fragment 1), which unfortunately implied that the inevitable collapse of the Roman government that Augustine saw coming after the sack of Rome by the Visigoths in 410 was the immediate precursor to the apocalyptic end of the world itself. This may well have been an important hidden agenda that Augustine had to accomplish in writing a "survival manual" for Christians caught in the fall of the Roman empire. For influences on Augustine's interpretation of biblical apocalyptic ideas, see also the Tyconius literature, for example, J. Haussleiter, "Die lateinische Apokalypse der alten Afrikanischen Kirche" in T. Zahn, *Forschungen zur Geschichte des neutestamentlichen Kanons und der altkirchlichen Literatur* (Erlangen: A. Deichert, 1891) 4:1-244; T. Hahn, *Tyconius-Studien*, Studien zur Geschichte der Theologie und der Kirche 6,2 (Aalen: Scientia Verlag, 1971); and E. Dinkler, "Ticonius," in Pauly-Wissowa, *Real-Encyclopädie*, Zweite Reihe 6, 1 (1936) cols. 849-56.

CHAPTER SIX

PAGAN AND CHRISTIAN HISTORIOGRAPHY IN THE FOURTH CENTURY A.D.[1]

Arnaldo Momigliano

I

On 28 October 312 the Christians suddenly and unexpectedly found themselves victorious.[2] The victory was a miracle—though opinions differed as to the nature of the sign vouchsafed to Constantine. The winners became conscious of their victory in a mood of resentment and vengeance. A voice shrill with implacable hatred announced to the world the victory of the Milvian Bridge: Lactantius' *De mortibus persecutorum*.[3] In this horrible pamphlet by the author of *De ira dei* there is something of the violence of the prophets without the redeeming sense of tragedy that inspires Nahum's song for the fall of Nineveh. 'His fury is poured out like fire and the rocks are broken asunder by him. The Lord is good, a strong hold in the day of trouble': this at least has an elementary simplicity which is very remote from the complacent and sophisticated prose of the fourth-century rhetorician. Lactantius was not alone. More soberly, but no less ruthlessly, Eusebius recounted the divine vengeance against those who had persecuted the Church. To us it naturally appears that there is something in common between the Jews who died in defending the old Jerusalem and the Christians who died in building up the new Jerusalem against the same Roman empire. Modern scholars have found it easy to prove that in form and substance the Jewish martyr is the prototype of the Christian martyr. Such scholarly discoveries have little relevance to

---

[1] The notes to this lecture are meant to provide no more than an introduction to the recent literature.
[2] Cf., however, P. Bruun, 'The Battle of the Milvian Bridge: The Date Reconsidered', *Hermes*, lxxxviii (1960), 361-70, which puts the battle in 311.
[3] The standard commentary is by J. Moreau, *Sources Chrétiennes* (Paris, 1954). Cf. W. Nestle, 'Die Legende vom Tode der Gottesverächter', *Arch. f. Religionsw.* xxxiii (1936), 246-69, reprinted in *Griechische Studien* (1948), p. 567. In general J. Stevenson, *Studia Patristica*, i (Berlin, 1957), 661-77. Not convincing S. Rossi, *Giorn. Ital. Filol.* xiv (1961), 193-213.

the realities of the fourth century. The pupils hated their masters, and were hated in their turn. With a cry of joy Eusebius, possibly a man of Jewish descent, retells from Josephus the story of the siege and capture of Jerusalem: thus may perish the enemies of Christ. Perhaps it is no chance that personally neither Lactantius nor Eusebius had suffered much from Diocletian's persecution. Like Tacitus in relation to Domitian, they voiced the resentment of the majority who had survived in fear rather than in physical pain. Eusebius had been near his master Pamphilus who had carried on his work on the Bible in prison while awaiting death.[4]

If there were men who recommended tolerance and peaceful coexistence of Christians and pagans, they were rapidly crowded out. The Christians were ready to take over the Roman empire, as Eusebius made clear in the introduction of the *Praeparatio evangelica* where he emphasizes the correlation between *pax romana* and the Christian message: the thought indeed was not even new. The Christians were also determined to make impossible a return to conditions of inferiority and persecution for the Church. The problems and the conflicts inside the Church which all this implied may be left aside for the moment. The revolution of the fourth century, carrying with it a new historiography, will not be understood if we underrate the determination, almost the fierceness, with which the Christians appreciated and exploited the miracle that had transformed Constantine into a supporter, a protector, and later a legislator of the Christian Church.

One fact is eloquent enough. All the pioneer works in the field of Christian historiography are earlier than what we may call their opposite numbers in pagan historiography. *De mortibus persecutorum* was written by Lactantius about 316. Eusebius' *Ecclesiastical History* probably appeared in a first edition about 312.[5] His life of Constantine—the authenticity of which can hardly be doubted—was written not long after 337.[6] Athanasius' life of St. Anthony belongs to the years around 360. Among the pagan works none can be dated with absolute

---

[4] The facts are gathered by H.J. Lawlor and J.E.L. Oulton, *Eusebius, The Ecclesiastical History and the Martyrs of Palestine*, translated with introduction and notes (London, 1928; reprint, 1954), ii, 332. Cf. S. Liebermann, *Ann. Inst. Phil. Hist. Orient.* vii (1939-44), 395-446.

[5] On the controversial question of the various editions of the *Ecclesiastical History* with which I do not intend to deal here, see especially E. Schwartz, introduction ot his *ed. maior* (Berlin, 1909), vol. iii, and article in Pauly-Wissowa, *Realencyclopädie*, s.v. Eusebius (now reprinted in *Griechische Geschichtschreiber*, 1957, pp. 540 ff.); R. Laqueur, *Eusebius als Historiker seiner Zeit* (Berlin and Leipzig, 1929); H.J. Lawlor and J.E.L. Oulton, introduction to their translation (1928); H. Edmonds, *Zweite Auflagen im Altertum* (Leipzig, 1941), pp. 25-45 (with bibliography).

[6] Bibliography until 1956 in B. Altaner, *Patrologie* (5th edn. Freiburg im Br., 1958), p. 209. Add J. Straub, *Studia Patristica*, i (Berlin, 1957), 679-95.

certainty before the death of Constantine. The *Historia Augusta* purports to have been written under Diocletian and Constantine, but the majority of modern scholars prefer—rightly or wrongly—a date later than 360.[7] The characteristic trilogy, to which the *Caesares* by Aurelius Victor belong, was put together later than 360.[8] The lives of the sophists by Eunapius—which are pagan hagiography—were published about 395.[9] Ammianus Marcellinus, too, finished his work about 395.[10] On the whole, the Christians come before the pagans in their creative writing. The Christians attack. The pagans are on the defensive.

Towards the end of the century the situation changed. Theodosius' death precipitated a political crisis, and the barbarians were soon taking advantage of it with invasions on an unprecedented scale. The intervention of the state in theological matters appeared less attractive to people who had witnessed the trials of the Priscillianists and the cruel executions that concluded them. Many Christians became less certain of themselves and went back to paganism. Many pagans became more aggressive and dared to say openly that the new religion was responsible for the collapse of the empire. In the pagan field resignation yielded to fury, and in the Christian field aggressiveness had to be turned into self-defence. This incidentally brought about a revival of pagan historical writing in Greek: pagan Greek historiography had been conspicuously absent from the ideological struggles of the fourth century. It thus becomes clear that the years between 395 and 410 saw new developments in historiography which are beyond the scope of this lecture. Though we shall not disregard them altogether, we shall confine our analysis to the years 312-95.

II

The clear-sighted determination of the Christians, which became suddenly apparent about 312, was the result of centuries of discipline and thought. In times of persecution and of uneasy tolerance the Church had developed its idea of orthodoxy and its conception of the providential economy of history. It emerged victorious to reassert with en-

---

[7] My essay reprinted in *Secondo Contributo alla storia degli studi classici* (Rome, 1960), pp. 105-43 gives the bibliography to which I wish to add W. Ensslin, *Studi Calderini-Paribeni*, i (1956), 313-23; J. Straub, *Bonner Jahrbücher*, clv-clvi (1955-6), 136-55, and more particularly E.M. Staerman, *Vestnik Drevnej Istorii*, 1957, 1, 233-45 translated in *Bibl. Class. Orient.* v (1960), 93-110, and A.I. Dovatur, *V.D.I.* quoted, pp. 245-56. I am not moved by the arguments of J. Schwartz, *Bull. Fac. Lettres Strasbourg*, xl (1961), 169-76.

[8] The problem is discussed in my *Secondo Contributo alla storia degli studi classici*, pp. 145-89. A later date is suggested by G. Puccioni, *Studi Ital. Fil. Class.* xxx (1958), 207-54 and *Ann. Scuola Normale Pisa*, xxvii (1958), 211-23.

[9] Cf. also W.R. Chalmers, *Class. Quart.*, N.S., iii (1953), 165-70.

[10] Cf., however, O.J. Maenchen-Helfen, *A.J. Ph.* lxxvi (1955), 384-400.

hanced authority the unmistakable pattern of divine intervention in history, the ruthless elimination of deviations. The foundations of Chrsitian historiography had been laid long before the time of the battle of the Milvian Bridge.

We all know the story of the man who went into a London bookshop and asked for a New Testament in Greek. The assistant retired to a back room and after ten minutes came back with a grave look: 'Strange, Sir, but Greek seems to be the only language into which the New Testament has not yet been translated'. The story may remind us of two facts. The first is that there was a time in which the New Testament was only available in Greek. The second and more important is that at that time it was as difficult as it is now to find a bookshop with a New, or for that matter an Old, Testament in Greek. About A.D. 180 a man like Galen could walk into a bookshop only to discover that they were selling an unauthorized edition of his own lectures. But though he was interested in the Christians, Galen would hardly have found a Bible. The Bible was no literature for the pagan. Its Greek was not elegant enough. Lactantius noted: 'apud sapientes et doctos et principles huius saeculi scriptura sancta fide care(a)t' (*Inst.* v. i. 15). If we find a pagan who had a slight acquaintance with the Bible, such as the anonymous author of *On the Sublime*, we suspect direct Jewish influence: justifiedly so, because the author of the *Sublime* was a student of Caecilius of Calacte, who, to all appearances, was a Jew.[11] Normally the educated pagans of the Roman empire knew nothing about either Jewish or Christian history. If they wanted some information about the Jews, they picked up second-hand distortions such as we read in Tacitus. The consequence was that a direct acquaintance with Jewish or Christian history normally came together with conversion of Judaism or to Christianity. People learnt a new history because they acquired a new religion. Conversion meant literally the discovery of a new history from Adam and Eve to contemporary events.[12]

The new history could not suppress the old. Adam and Eve and what follows had in some way to be presented in a world populated by Deucalion, Cadmus, Romulus, and Alexander the Great. This created all sorts of new problems. First, the pagans had to be introduced to the

---

[11] Cf. A. Rostagni, *Anonimo-Del Sublime* (Milan, 1947); E. Norden, 'Das Genesiszitat in der Schrift vom Erhabenen', *Abh. Berlin. Akad.* (1954), p. 1.

[12] On the implications of the Christian vision of history see, for instance, L. Tondelli, *Il disegno divino nella storia* (Turin, 1947); O. Cullmann, *Christus und die Zeit* (2nd edn., Zdurich, 1948); W. Kamlah, *Christentum und Geschichtlichkeit* (2nd edn., Stuttgart, 1951); R.L.P. Milburn, *Early Christian Interpretations of History* (London, 1954); K. Ldowith, *Weltgeschichte und Heilgeschehen*, (Stuttgart, 1953); C. Schneider, *Geistesgeschichte des antiken Christentums* (Munich, 1956). See also H. Rahner, *Griechische Mythen in christlicher Deutung* (Zdurich, 1945), and the studies by S.G.F. Brandon and K. Ldowith in *Nemen*, ii (1955).

Jewish version of history. Secondly, the Chrisitian historians were expected to silence the objection that Christianity was new, and therefore not respectable. Thirdly, the pagan facts of life had to get into the Jewish-Christian scheme of redemption. It soon became imperative for the Christians to produce a chronology which would satisfy both the needs of elementary teaching and the purposes of higher historical interpretation. The Christian chronographers had to summarize the history which the converts were now supposed to consider their own; they had also to show the antiquity of the Jewish-Christian doctrine, and they had to present a model of providential history. The result was that, unlike pagan chronology, Christian chronology was also a philosophy of history. Unlike pagan elementary teaching, Christian elementary teaching of history could not avoid touching upon the essentials of the destiny of man. The convert, in abandoning paganism, was compelled to enlarge his historical horizon: he was likely to think for the first time in terms of universal history.

The spade-work in Christian chronology was done long before the fourth century.[13] The greatest names involved in this work, Clemens Alexandrinus, Julius Africanus, and Hippolytus of Rome, belong to the second and third centuries. They created the frame for the divine administration of the world; they transformed Hellenistic chronography into a Christian science and added the lists of the bishops of the most important sees to the lists of kings and magistrates of the pagan world. They presented history in such a way that the scheme of redemption was easy to perceive. They showed with particular care the priority of the Jews over the pagans—in which point their debt to Jewish apologetic is obvious. They established criteria of orthodoxy by the simple device of introducing lists of bishops who represented the apostolic succession. Calculations about the return of Christ and the ultimate end had never been extraneous to the Church. Since the Apocalypse attributed to St. John established itself as authoritative in the Church, millennial reckonings had multiplied. Universal chronology in the Christian sense was bound to take into account not only the beginning, but also the end; it had either to accept or else to fight the belief in the millennium. Chronology and eschatology were conflated. Both Julius Africanus and Hippolytus were firm believers in the millennium, with-

---

[13] Besides the fundamental H. Gelzer, *Sextus Julius Africanus und die byzant. Chronographie* (Leipzig, 1880-98), I shall only mention A. Hamel, *Kirche bei Hippolyt von Rom* (Gütersloh, 1951); M. Richard, *Mél. Sciences Religieuses* vii (1950), 237, and viii (1951), 19 (on Hippolytus); B. Kötting, 'Endzeitprognosen zwischen Lactantius und Augustinus', *Hist. Jahrb.* lxxvii (1957), 125-39; P. Courcelle, 'Les Exégèses chrétiennes de la quartriéme 'eglogue', *Rev. Etud. Anc.* lix (1957), 294-319; A.-D. Van Den Brincken, *Studien zur Lateinischen Weltchronistik bis in das Zeitalter Ottos von Freising* (Düsseldorf, 1957; with bibliography).

out, however, believing in its imminence. But the higher purpose of philosophy of history was never separated from the immediate task of informing and edifying the faithful. Hippolytus' introduction to his *Chronicon* is explicit. To quote a sentence from one of its Latin translations (another was incorporated in the Chronographer of 354), it was his purpose to show 'quae divisio et quae perditio facta sit, quo autem modo generatio seminis Israel de patribus in Christo completa sit'.

At the beginning of the fourth century Christian chronology had already passed its creative stage. What Eusebius did was to correct and to improve the work of his predecessors, among whom he relied especially on Julius Africanus.[14] He corrected details which seemed to him wrong even to the extent of reducing the priority of the Biblical heroes over the pagan ones. Moses, a contemporary of Ogyges according to Julius Africanus, was made a contemporary of Kekrops with a loss of 300 years. Eusebius was not afraid of attacking St. Paul's guesses about the chronology of the Book of Judges. He freely used Jewish and anti-Christian sources such as Porphyrios. He introduced a reckoning from Abraham which allowed him to avoid the pitfalls of a chronology according to the first chapters of Genesis. He seems to have been the first to use the convenient method of presenting the chronology of the various nations in parallel columns. None of the earlier chronographers seems to have used this scheme, though it has often been attributed to Castor or to Julius Africanus. He made many mistakes, but they do not surprise us any longer. Fifty years ago Eduard Schwartz, to save Eusebius' reputation as a competent chronographer, conjectured that the two extant representatives of the lost original of Eusebius' *Chronicon*—the Latin adaptation by St. Jerome and the anonymous Armenian translation—were based on an interpolated text which passed for pure Eusebius. This conjecture is perhaps unnecessary; nor are we certain that the Armenian version is closer to the original than St. Jerome's Latin translation. Both versions reflect the inevitable vagaries of Eusebius' mind to whom chronology was something between an exact science and an instrument of propaganda.

But we recognize the shrewd and worldly adviser of the Emperor Constantine in the absence of millenarian dreams. Eusebius, and St. Jerome who followed him, had an essential part is discrediting them. Of course, they did not stamp them out. Millenarian reckonings reappear in the *De cursu temporum* which Bishop Hilarian wrote at the

---

[14] The essential work after E. Schwartz is R. Helm, 'Eusebios' Chronik und ihre Tabellenform', *Abh. Berl. Akad.* (1923), p. 4. Cf. also R. Helm, *Eranos*, xxii (1924), I-40, and A. Schöne, *Die Weltchronik des Eusebius in ihrer Bearbeitung durch Hieronymus* (Berlin, 1900). D.S. Wallace-Hadrill, 'The Eusebian Chronicle: the extent and date of composition of its early editions', *J.T.S.*, N.S. vi (1955), 248-53.

end of the fourth century.[15] They also played a part in the thought of Sulpicius Severus about that time.[16] As we have already said, the disasters of the end of the century made a difference to dreams, as they made a difference to the other realities.

Thanks to Eusebius, chronography remained the typical form of Christian instruction in the fourth century. It showed concern with the pattern of history rather than with the detail.

The Christians indeed were not alone in having a problem of historical education. The pagans had their own problem. But we can state immediately the difference between pagans and Christians in the teaching of history. The pagans were not concerned with ultimate values in their elementary teaching. Their main concern was to keep alive a knowledge of the Roman past. After the social and political earthquakes of the third century a new leading class had emerged which clearly had some difficulty in remembering the simple facts of Roman history.[17] This explains why Eutropius and (Rufius?) Festus were both commissioned by the Emperor Valens to prepare a brief summary of Roman history. Eutropius was the first to obey the royal command. But the seventy-seven pages of his Teubner text must have proved too many for Valens. Festus, who followed, restricted himself to about twenty pages. He was not modest, but literal, when he commended his work to the 'gloriosissimus princeps' as being even shorter than a summary—a mere enumeration of facts. The new men who, coming from the provincial armies or from Germany, acquired power and wealth, wanted some knowledge of the Roman past. They had to mix with the surviving members of the senatorial aristocracy in which knowledge of Roman history and antiquities was *de rigueur*. The establishment of a new senate in Constantinople, by adding another privileged class, complicated this educational problem. The senators of Constantinople, picked as they were from the municipal upper class of the East, were not likely to be uneducated, but they were not particularly strong either in the Latin language or in Roman history. These people too needed *breviaria*. Eutropius was soon translated into Greek by a friend of Libanius and began his momentous career in the Byzantine world. There can be few other Latin authors able to boast of at least three successive translations into Greek.

In their characteristic neutrality, the pagan *breviaria* presented no danger to the Christians. They were so devoid of religious content that they could not give offence. On the contrary, the Christians could easily exploit them for their own purposes. Eutropius was very successful in Constantinople where the aristocracy soon became predomi-

---

[15] The text is edited in C. Frick, *Chronica Minora*, i (1892).
[16] S. Prete, *I chronica di Sulpicio Severo* (Città del Vaticano, 1955).
[17] E. Malcovati, *I Breviari del IV secolo*, in Annali Università Cagliari, xii, 1942.

nantly Christian. The Christian compiler known as the Chronographer of 354 incorporated in his own work a pagan recapitulation of the history of Rome—the so-called *Chronica urbis Romae*.[18] When St. Jerome decided to continue Eusebius' *Chronicon* to 378 he used pagan writers such as Aurelius Victory and Eutropius, not to mention the *Chronica urbis Romae* which he probably knew as a part of the Christian chronography of 354. All this, however, only emphasized the fact that the Christians had no compilation comparable to Eutropius and Festus. If *breviaria* were not needed during the fourth century when the Christians felt very sure of themselves, they appeared less superfluous towards the end of the century when the pagan version of Roman history gained in authority. Sulpicius Severus, who had absorbed pagan culture in Gaul, was the first to realize the deficiency and to fill the gap just about A.D. 400. He combined Christian chronographers and the Bible with *historici mundiales*, the pagan historians. His purpose was still the dual one of the earlier Christian chronography: 'ut et imperitos docerem et litteratos convincerem.' Later, about 417, Orosius followed his example when he was requested by St. Augustine to produce a summary of the history of Rome in support of his *Civitas dei*. Orosius gave what from a medieval point of view can be called the final Christian twist to the pagan epitome of Roman history.[19]

III

Epitomes are only on the threshold of history. So far we have considered books which were meant to remind the reader of the events rather than to tell them afresh. But an important fact has already emerged. Whether in the form of chronographies or, later, in the form of *breviaria*, the Christian compilations were explicit in conveying a message: one can doubt whether the majority of the pagan compilations conveyed any message at all. Sulpicius Severus and Orosius fought for a cause, and it is to be remembered that Sulpicious Severus expressed the indignation felt by Ambrosius and Martin of Tours against the appeal to the secular arm in the Priscillianist controversy. Consequently, it was very easy to transform a pagan handbook into a Christian one, but almost impossible to make pagan what had been Christian. Later on we shall consider one possible exception to the rule that the Christians assimilate pagan ideas, while the pagans do not appropriate Christian ones. The rule, however, stands: it is enough to

---

[18] Mommsen, *Über den Chronographen vom J. 354* (1850), partially reprinted in *Ges. Schriften*, vii, is still the standard work. Text in Mommsen, *Chronica Minora*, i (1892).
[19] Among the recent literature see K.A. Schöndorf, *Die Geschichtstheologie des Orosius* (Munich, 1952). Cf. also J. Straub, 'Christliche Geschichtsapologetik in der Krisis des römischen Reiches,' *Historia*, i (1950), 52-81.

indicate the trend of the century—and, incidentally, to explain why the Chrisitians were so easily victorious. Just because the trend is so clear, we can perhaps conjecturally add yet another case of the easy transformation of pagan historical *breviaria* into Christian ones. All is in doubt about the first part of the *Anonymus Valesianus*—which is a brief life of Constantine under the name of *Origo Constantini imperatoris*. But a fourth-century date seems highly probable; and it also seems clear that the few Christian passages are later interpolations from Orosius. If so, the *Origo Constantini imperatoris* is a beautiful example of a short pagan work which was made Christian by the simple addition of a few passages.[20] The Christians could easily take it over because of the relatively neutral character of the original text. The pagans for their part kept away from Christian explosives.

Christian initiative was such that it did not hesitate to appropriate Jewish goods also. Pseudo-Philo's *Liber antiquitatum Biblicarum* was originally a Jewish handbook of Biblical history. It seems to have been written in Hebrew for Jews in the first century A.D., it was later done into Greek, and, to all appearances, in the fourth century it was changed into a Christian handbook and translated into Latin.[21]

The question then arises whether the Christians became the masters of the field also on the higher level of original historical writing and whether here, too, they confirmed their capacity for assimilating without being assimilated.

If the question were simply to be answered by a yes, it would not be worth asking. The traditional forms of higher historiography did not attract the Christians. They invented new ones. These inventions are the most important contributions made to historiography after the fifth century B.C. and before the sixteenth century A.D. Yet the pagans are allowed by the Christians to remain the masters of traditional historiographical forms. To put it briefly, the Christians invented ecclesiastical history and the biography of the saints, but did not try to christianize ordinary political history; and they influenced ordinary biography less than we would expect. In the fourth century A.D. there was no serious attempt to provide a Christian version of, say, Thucydides or Tacitus—to mention two writers who were still being seriously studied. A reinterpretation or ordinary military, political, or diplomatic history in Christian terms was neither achieved nor even attempted. Lactantius in the *De Mortibus persecutorum* is perhaps the only Christian writer to touch upon social and political events. He

---

[20] Text and discussion by R. Cessi in his ed. of the *Anonymus Valesianus* (Rer. Ital. Scrip., 1913), but his conclusions are not accepted here. The Groningen dissertation by D.J.A. Westerhuis, 1906, is still very valuable. New edition by J. Moreau (Leipzig, 1961).
[21] See the edition by G. Kisch, *Pseudo-Philo's Liber. Antiquitatum Biblicarum* (Notre Dame, Indiana, 1949).

does so in a conservative and senatorial spirit which must be embarrassing to those who identify the Christians with the lower middle class, but he never seriously develops his political interpretation: he is not to be compared as an analyst with Ammianus Marcellinus or even with the *Scriptores historiae Augustae*.

The consequence is plain. No real Christian historiography founded upon the political experience of Herodotus, Thucydides, Livy, and Tacitus was transmitted to the Middle Ages. This is already apparent in the sixth century when a military and political historian like Procopius was basically pagan in outlook and technique. When in the fifteenth and sixteenth centuries the humanists rediscovered their Herodotus, Thucydides, Livy, and Tacitus, they rediscovered something for which there was no plain Christian alternative. It is not for me to say whether an alternative was possible: whether an earlier 'Tacitus christianus' would have been less foolish than the post-Reformation one. What I must point out is that the conditions which made Machiavelli and Guicciardini possible originated in the fourth century A.D. The models for political and military history remained irretrievably pagan. In the higher historiography there was nothing comparable with the easy christianizing of the pagan *breviaria*.

Here again Eusebius was the decisive influence. How much he owed to predecessors, and especially to the shadowy Hegesippus, we shall never know, unless new evidence is discovered.[22] But it is fairly clear that Hegesippus wrote apologetic, not history, Apart from him, there is no other name that can seriously compete with Eusebius' for the invention of ecclesiastical history. He was not vainly boasting when he asserted that he was the 'first to enter on the undertaking, as travellers do on some desolate and untrodden way'.[23]

Eusebius, like any other educated man, knew what proper history was. He knew that it was a rhetorical work with a maximum of invented speeches and a minimum of authentic documents. Since he chose to give plenty of documents and refrained from inventing speeches, he must have intended to produce something different from ordinary history. Did he then intend to produce a preparatory work to history, an ὑπόμνημα? This is hardly credible. First of all, historical ὑπομνήματα were normally confined to contemporary events. Sec-

---

[22] Among the recent literature see K. Mras, *Anz. Oesterr. Akad.* (1958), pp. 143-45; W. Telfer, *Harv. Theol. Rev.* liii (1960), 143-54.
[23] Cf., among many, H. Berkhof, *Die Theologie Eusebius' von Caesarea* (Amsterdam, 1939); Id. *Kirche und Kaiser* (Zürich, 1947); F.E. Cranz, *Harv. Theol. Rev.* xlv (1952), 47-66; K. Heussi, *Wissenschaftl. Zeitschr. Univ. Jena* vii (1957-8), 89-92; F. Scheidweiler, *Zeitschr. f. d. Neut. Wissenschaft* xlix (1958), 123-9; D.S. Wallace-Hadrill, *Eusebius of Caesarea* (London, 1960).

ondly, Eusebius speaks as if he were writing history, and not collecting materials for a future history.

It was Eduard Schwartz who in one of his most whimsical moments suggested that German professors of *Kirchengeschichte* had been the victims of their poor Greek. They had not understood that Ἐκκλησιαδτική ἱστορία did not mean *Kirchengeschichte*, but *Materialien zur Kirchengeschichte*. Eduard Schwartz, of course, was fighting his great battle against the isolation of ecclesiastical history in German universities, and we who share his beliefs can hardly blame him for this paradox. But a paradox it was.[24]

Eusebius knew only too well that he was writing a new kind of history. The Christians were a nation in his view. Thus he was writing national history. But his nation had a transcendental origin. Though it had appeared on earth in Augustus' time, it was born in Heaven 'with the first dispensation concerning the Christ himself' (I. i. 8). Such a nation was not fighting ordinary wars. Its struggles were persecutions and heresies. Behind the Christian nation there was Christ, just as the devil was behind its enemies. The ecclesiastical history was bound to be different from ordinary history because it was a history of the struggle against the devil, who tried to pollute the purity of the Christian Church as guaranteed by the apostolic succession.

Having started to collect his materials during Diocletian's persecutions, Eusebius never forgot his original purpose which was to produce factual evidence about the past and about the character of the persecuted Church. He piled up his evidence of quotations from reputable authorities and records in the form that was natural to any ancient controversialist. As he was dealing with a Church that represented a school of thought, there was much he could learn in the matter of presentation from the histories of philosophic schools which he knew well. These dealty with doctrinal controversies, questions of authenticity, successions of *scholarchs*. But he did away with all that was anecdotal and worldly in the pagan biographies of philosophers. This is why we shall never know whether Clemens Alexandrinus was fond of eating green figs and of basking in the sun; which are established points in the biography of Zeno the Stoic. At the same time Eusebius certainly had in mind Jewish-Hellenistic historiography, as exemplified for him and for us by Flavius Josephus. In Josephus he found the emphasis on the past, the apologetic tone, the doctrinal digression, the display (though not so lavish) of documents: above all there was the idea of a nation which is different from ordinary pagan nations. Jewish historiography emphatically underlined the importance of the remote past in com-

---

[24] Über Kirchengeschichte' (1908) in *Gesammelte Schriften*, i (1938), 110-30.

parison with recent times and the importance of cult in comparison with politics.

The suggestion that Eusebius combined the methods of philosophic historiography with the approach of Jewish-Hellenistic historiography has at least the merit of being a guide to the sources of his thought. Yet it is far from accounting for all the main features of his work. There were obviousl differences between the history of the Church and that of any other institution. Persecution had been an all-pervading factor of Christianity. Heresy was a new conception which (whatever its origins) had hardly the same importance in any other school of thought, even in Judaism. An account of the Christian Church based on the notion of orthodoxy and on its relations with a persecuting power was bound to be something different from any other historical account. The new type of exposition chosen by Eusebius proved to be adequate to the new type of institution represented by the Christian Church. It was founded upon authority and not upon the free judgement of which the pagan historians were proud. His contemporaries felt that he had made a new start. Continuators, imitators, and translators multiplied. Some of them (most particularly Sozomen) tried to be more conventional in their historiographical style, more obedient to rhetorical traditions. None departed from the main structure of Eusebius' creation with its emphasis on the struggle against persecutors and heretics and therefore on the purity and continuity of the doctrinal tradition.

Eusebius introduced a new type of historical exposition which was characterized by the importance attributed to the more remote past, by the central position of doctrinal controversies and by the lavish use of documents.

I am not yet able to answer two questions which are very much on my mind: whether in the Middle Ages there was a school of pure ecclesiastical history from Cassiodorus to Bede, to Adam and Bremen and to John of Salisbury; and whether this school, if any, was characterized by a special interest in documents. What is certain is that from the sixteenth to the eighteenth century ecclesiastical history (especially of the early Church) was treated with a much greater display of erudition, with much more care for minute analysis of the evidence than any other type of history. There is no work in profane history comparable with the Magdeburg Centuriators and with Baronius. Naturally this is the expression of the fiercely controversial character which ecclesiastical history assumed with the Reformation. But we may well wonder whether the ecclesiastical historians of the Renaissance would have entered upon the path of erudition and documentation—and incidentally of illegibility—without the powerful precedent of Eusebius and his immediate pupils. Conversely, we may well wonder whether modern political historiography would ever have changed from rhetoric and pragmatism to footnotes and appendixes without the example of ecclesiastical history. The first man who applied careful scrutiny of the evidence to the history of the Roman empire was Le Nain de Tillemont, who came from ecclesiastical history and worked in both fields. Among the Maurists of St. Germain-des-Prés erudition spread from ecclesiastical to profane, even to literary history. Perhaps we have all underestimated the impact of ecclesiastical history on the development of historical method. A new chapter of historiography begins with Eusebius not only because he invented ecclesiastical history, but because he wrote it with a documentation which is utterly different from that of the pagan historians.[25]

Thus we are brought back to our main point. Eusebius made history positively and negatively by creating ecclesiastical history and by leaving political history alone. In a comparable manner another Christian invented the biography of the saints and left the biography of generals and politicians to the pagans. The inventor was Athanasius, whose life of St. Anthony was promptly made available in Latin by Evagrius. The complicated pattern of suggestions which lies behind the rise of hagiography—*exitus illustrium virorum*, Jewish legends, lives of philosophers, 'aretalogies', & c.—cannot detain us here. The studies by K. Hoil and R. Reitzenstein seem to have established that Athanasius was more directly inspired by the Pythagorean type of the θεῖος ἀνήρ, such as we find in the life of Apollonius of Tyana by Philostratus and in the life of Pythagoras himself by Iamblichus.[26] Athanasius intended to oppose the Christian saint who works his way to God with the help of God to the pagan philosopher who is practically a god himself. By imparting a mortal blow to the ideal of the pagan philosopher, he managed to produce an ideal type which became extremely popular among ordinary Christians. Only small groups of pagans believed that Pythagoras or Diogenes was the best possible man. The great majority of pagans was more interested in Hercules, Achilles, and Alexander the Great. But in Christian society the saint was soon recognized as the only perfect type of man. This gives hagiography, as begun by Athanasius, its unique place. It outclassed all other types of biography because all the other types of men became inferior to that of the saint. In comparison, the ordinary biography of kings and politi-

---

[25] W. Nigg, *Die Kirchengeschichtsschreibung* (Munich, 1934). Cf. H. Zimmerman, 'Ecclesia als Objekt der Historiographie', Sitzungsb. Akad. Wien, ccxxxv (1960).
[26] Cf. R. Reitzenstein, *Sitzungsb. Heidelberg. Akad.* I, 1914, n.8; K. Holl, *Ges. Aufsätze* ii (1928), 249-69; K. Heussi, *Ursprung des Mönchtums* (Tübingen, 1936); A.-J. Festugière, *Rev. Et. Grecques*, I (1937), 470-94; H. Dörries, *Nachr. Ges. Wiss. Göttingen*, xiv (1949), 359-410. Cf. also the English translation of the life of St. Anthony by JR.T. Meyer (Ancient Christian Writers, x, 1950).

cians became insignificant. One of the most important features of the lives of saints is to give a new dimension to historiography by registering the activity of devils in the plural. It is no exaggeration to say that a mass invasion of devils into historiography preceded and accompanied the mass invasion of barbarians into the Roman empire. A full treatment of 'Devils in historiography' must be reserved for a future course at the Warburg Institute on 'Devils and the Classical Tradition'. But so much can be said here: the devils seems to have respected the classical distinction of literary genres. They established themselves in biography, but made only occasional irruptions into the field of *annales*.

The difficulty of writing a Christian biography of a king as distinct from the life of a saint is already apparent in the life of Constantine by Eusebius, though it was produced perhaps twenty years before the composition of the life of St. Anthony by Athanasius. Eusebius had no other choice but to present the life of Constantine as a model of a pious life—παράδειγμα θεοσεβοῦς βίου, as he himself says. The task was certainly not beyond Eusebius' ingenuity, but it flouted anybody's respect for the truth. Moreover, it implied neglect of all that counts in a life of a general and a politician: military glory, political success, concern for ordinary human affairs, and the rest of the passions power carries with it. No wonder that this life of Constantine was never a success, had hardly any influence on later biographies, and found some modern shcolars ready to deny the Eusebian authorship even at the risk of being contradicted by papyrological evidence. It continued to be easier for a Christian to work on the life of a saint than to write the life of an emperor. We may sympathize with Eginhard when he decided to go back to Suetonius for his life of Charlemagne.

IV

We can thus see that a direct conflict between Christians and pagans is not to be expected on the higher level of the historiography of the fourth century. The Christians, with all their aggressiveness, kept to their own new types of history and biography. Eusebius' life of Constantine was an experiment not to be repeated—historiographically a blind alley. The pagans were left to cultivate their own fields. This perhaps reinforced their tendency to avoid any direct discussion with their formidable neighbours in the field of historiography. The opposition to Christianity can be guessed rather than demonstrated in the majority of the pagan students of history. It shows itself in the care with which pagan historians of the past—such as Sallust, Livy, and Tacitus—were read and imitated. It is also apparent in the implicit rejection of the most characteristic Christian values, such as humility and poverty. But it seldom takes the form of direct critical remarks.

There are two or three sentences in the *Historia Augusta* which sound like a criticism of the Christians. One is the good-humoured remark that in Egypt 'those who worship Serapis are, in fact, Christians and those who call themselves bishops of Christ are in fact devotees of Serapis' (Firmus, viii. 2). In the last sentence of Aurelius Victor's *De Caesaribus* there is perhaps a criticism of Constantius II's Christian ministers: 'ut imperratore ipso praeclarius, ita apparitorum plerisque magis atrox nihil'. But notice with what care the emperor is declared blameless. Finally, there are the well-known criticisms of Ammianus Marcellinus against the Roman clergy and other bishops, such as Bishop George of Alexandria. But here again notice that the same Ammianus praises Christian martyrdom, and respects the blameless life of provincial bishops. The pagans were bound to be prudent—and their mood was altogether that of a generous and fair-minded liberalism. The *Historia Augusta* is by no means the big anti-Christian pamphlet which some scholars have seen in it. On the contrary, the ideal emperor Severus Alexander worships Jesus with Abraham in his private chapel. Ammianus Marcellinus makes an effort to disentangle what is *absoluta* and *simplex religio* and what is *anilis superstitio* in Christianity (XXI. XV. 18). According to him what matters is *virtus*, not paganism or Christianity. As we all know, this attitude is also to be found in Symmachus, in some of the pagan correspondents of St. Augustine and in the Panegyricus by Nazarius (IV. vii. 3). Rufius Festus, who was an unbeliever, but whose pagan sympathies are shown by the disproportionate amount of space he devotes to Julian, is full of deference towards the Christian god of his master Valens: 'Maneat modo concessa dei nutu et ab amico cui credis et creditus es numine indulta felicitas.' 'May long last the happiness that was granted to you by the friendly god whom you trust and to whom you are entrusted.' This is a very decent way of saving one's conscience without offending one's master.

The only exception is Eunapius, whose history of the fourth century was so anti-Chrisitian that, according to Photius, it had to be re-edited in a less offensive form. The greater part of this history is lost, but Eunapius' attitude is clear enough from the extant fragments and even more so from his lives of the Sophists, where Julian is the hero and the apology for Neoplatonic paganism is unbridled. If Julian won victories it was because the right gods helped him. We can still read in the margins of the *Codex Laurentianus* of Eunapius' lives of the Sophists the indignant remarks of one of his Byzantine readers. Eunapius clearly meant his lives of the Sophists to compete with the lives of the Christian saints whose cult he despised (*Vit. soph.* 472). But Eunapius reflects the changed mood of the end of the century when even the most optimistic pagan could no longer nurture illusions about Christian tolerance.[27] Furthermore, his particular type of reaction is that of a professor who wrote for Greek *literati* rather than for the pagan aristocracy of the West. As we observed, the Greek pagans of the East seem to have become vocal only at the end of the century. During the century itself Latin was the main language of pagan historiography.

In the West, among the Latin historians, the resistance to Christianity showed itself in a mixture of silence and condescension; Christianity is rarely mentioned. It it is mentioned, kindness and good humour prevail. What counts is the vast zone of silence, the ambiguity which gives Latin pagan historiography of the fourth century its strange imprint of reticence and mystery. Seldom are historians of historiography faced by works so difficult to date, to analyse in their composite nature and to attribute to a definite background. For the first time we come across historical work done in collaboration—which adds to its elusiveness.

The *Historia Augusta* is the classic example of historiographic mystery. The work purports to have been written by six authors at various moments of the reigns of Diocletian and Constantine. Some at least of the alleged authors claim to have written in collaboration. This very claim of team-work is baffling: co-operative 'Cambridge histories' were not common in antiquity. The writing is sensational and unscrupulous, and the forged documents included in this work serve no obvious purpose. One or two passages may point to a post-Constantinian date either for the whole collection or at least for the passages themselves. But the date and the purpose of the *Scriptores historiae Augustae* remain an unsolved problem.

A less famous, but no less remarkable, mystery is the tripartite corpus under the title *Origo gentis Romanae*—a title which incidentally must be translated as 'History of the Roman people'. It includes a history of Roman origins from Saturnus to the murder of Remus, a collection of short biographies from Romulus to Augustus (the so-called *De viris illustribus*), and, finally, short and accomplished biographies of Roman emperors to A.D. 360. The imperial biographies were written by Aurelius Victor whom we know to have been a friend of Julian and a *praefectus urbi* under Theodosius. The other two sections of the trilogy are anonymous: they were wirtten by two different authors, neither of whom can be identical with Aurelius Victor. A fourth man acted as editor and put together the three pamphlets to form the present triology. All these people were pagan. I have elsewhere suggested that the editor of the triology may have tried to produce a complete pagan history of Rome at the time of the emperor Julian. But this is a pure guess, though not an unreasonable one I trust. The compiler

---

[27] The *Vitae sophistarum* are now to be read in the ed. by G. Giangrande (Rome, 1956).

himself does not say anything about the precise meaning and date of his compilation. He may have known the Christian Chronographer of 354: he has certainly adopted a compositional scheme which reminds us of the *Chronica urbis Romae* included in the Chronographer of 354. What is extraordinary and, to my mind, important in this trilogy is the absence of any direct allusion to Christianity. The author is pagan: there is no reference to the Christians.

Ammianus Marcellinus is not a mystery in the sense in which the *Historia Augusta* and the tripartite *Origo gentis Romanae* are mysteries.[28] He speaks about himself more than the majority of the ancient historians ever did. His keen eye is constantly on the look-out for individual features. He is a man full of delightful curiosity. Yet what we do we ultimately know about Ammianus? He does not even tell us why he, a Greek from Antioch, chose Latin as his literary language. He says very little about the theological controversies of his time and almost nothing about the religious feelings of the people he must have known best. Magic seems to interest him more than theology. Yet theology counted most. He was a soldier. Yet he is apparently not interested in military organization. He has an uncanny ability to describe a character without defining a situation. He never gives himself away. His histories might have for motto his own words: 'quis-quis igitur dicta considerat, perpendat etiam cetera quae tacentur' (XXIX. iii. 1). It is symbolic that the greatest feat of his military career was to escape unnoticed from besieged Amida while the Persians were breaking into the city. He may have become more reticent about religion in the books XXVI-XXXI which he wrote after 392 when Theodosius hardened against the pagans. But even the earlier books, written as they were in more tolerant years, are not much more explicit. He dislikes the Germans, yet his unwillingness to analyse the causes of the barbarian successes is notorious. He deplores the greed and avarice of some Roman aristocrats, especially of the Anicii who were just then turning to Christianity. But he cannot have had any general objection against the senatorial class among which he had his pagan friends, Praetextatus, Eupraxius, and Symmachus. An acute and passionate judge of individuals, he avoids our direct questions and leaves us wondering. His master Tacitus is a paragon of directness by comparison.

---

[28] It will be enough to refer to the two well-known monographs on Ammianus by W. Ensslin (*Kli*, Beiheft xvi, 1923) and E.A. Thompson (Cambridge, 1947). Full bibliography will be found in Ch. P. Th. Naudé, *Am. M. in die lig van die antieke Geskiedskrywing* (diss. Leiden, 1956). V.S. Sokolov, *Vestnik Dreunej Istorii*, 1959, 4, 43-62. Cf. also S. Mazzarino, 'La propaganda senatoriale nel tardo impero', *Doxa*, iv (1951), 121-48. Id. 'La democratizzazione della cultura nel Basso Impero', *Rapports XI Congrés Intern. Sciences Historiques*, ii (Stockholm, 1960), 35-54. L. Dillemann, *Syria*, xxxviii (1961), 87-158.

If reticence, love of the pagan past, moderation, and erudition were the prominent features of these Latin historians, the Christians did not have much to fear from their work. Historians of this kind could please other historians. Ammianus Marcellinus, the *Historia Augusta*, and the now lost histories by Nicomachus Flavianus, were read in the sixth century in the circle of Symmachus and Cassiodorus, when there was a revival of interst in Roman history.[29] But Ammianus, the *Historia Augusta*, and Aurelius Victor were never popular for all we know. The fact that at least one of these historical works, the *Historia Augusta*, is guilty of professional dishonesty is not a sign of strength for historiography of this kind. It would be unfair to generalize when so much of the fourth-century historical production is lost. Within the limits of our knowledge we are constantly reminded of the fact that the true pagans of the fourth century found their most profound satisfaction not in writing new history, but in copying existing histories, trying to solve problems of antiquarianism, commenting on Virgil and other classics, reading and writing poetry in a pagan spirit. The real passion was in those who tired to revive the past by direct religious worship, by discussion of ancient customs, by the study of ancient writers. Our instinct is right, I think, when we consider Macrobius, Symmachus, Servius, and Donatus more typically pagan than Ammianus Marcellinus. Festus who wrote the historical *breviarium* has sometimes been identified with Festus Avienus, the translator of Aratus. The identification is not to be maintained. The historian Festus was even accused of atheism by Eunapius (p. 481). The poet Festus Avienus, a friend of the Nicomachi Flaviani, was warmly devoted to Jupiter and to the Etruscan goddess Nortia of his native country.[30] When he died, his son wrote on his tomb that Jupiter was opening the skies to him—the son echoing in his lines his father's lines:

>   nam Iuppiter aethram
> pandit, Feste, tibi candidus ut venias
> Iamque venis (*I.L.S.* 2944)

This seems to have been the driving spirit of dying paganism in the West. Therefore, St. Augustine, who knew where to look for the real enemy, was not worried by contemporary pagan historians in the Latin tongue, such as Ammianus Marcellinus. Greek historians, such as Eunapius, worried him even less because he probably did not know them: his command of Greek was modest. But he was disturbed by the idealization of the Roman past which he found in fourth-century Latin antiquarians, poets, and commentators of poets. He saw in them

---

[29] See my *Secondo Contributo alla storia degli studi classici* (1960), p. 198.
[30] Cf. A. Garroni, *Bull. Comm. Arch. Com.* (1915), pp. 123-35.

the roots of the new resistance against Christianity which became evident towards the end of the century. He went back to the sources of their antiquarianism, and primarily to Varro, in order to undermine the foundations of their work. He fought the antiquarians, the sentimental and emotional pagans, of his time—not the contemporary historians. The latter might be left to die from natural causes. But the former had to be fought. The result is to be seen in the *De civitate dei*. It is also to be seen in the work of St. Augusutine's pupil Orosius who was induced by him to write against the readers of Livy, not against the readers of the *Historia Augusta* or of Ammianus. All went according to plan, except that the pagan historians of the fourth century were not really going to die. They were only going to sleep for some centuries. They belonged to that classical tradition in historiography for which ecclesiastical history, whatever its merits, was no substitute. Though we may have learnt to check our references from Eusebius—and this was no small gain—we are still the disciples of Herodotus and Thucydides: we still learn our history of the late empire from Ammianus Marcellinus.[31]

---

[31] Cf. also J. Sirinelli, *Les Vues historiques d'Eusèbe de Césarée durant la période prénicéenne*, thèse (Paris, 1961), and W. Lammers (ed.), *Geschichtsdenken und Geschichtsbild im Mittelalter* (Darmstadt, 1961) with bibl.

PART TWO

THE JUDAIC INVENTION OF HISTORY

CHAPTER SEVEN

THE TANNAIM AND HISTORY

Nahum N. Glatzer

I. *THE TRADITIONAL HISTORICAL TEACHINGS AND THE APPROACH OF THE TANNAITES*

1. The Historical Teaching of the Old Testament

After briefly and clearly surveying the peoples of antiquity, including those who shaped history but failed to record it, George Foot Moore concludes that the Israelites and the Greeks were the only two peoples of antiquity to produce a historical literature.[1] He contends that the reason for this phenomenon lies "in the particular disposition of these two peoples."[2] But I believe that the "mighty raising of the national consciousness which followed after the struggle and the shaking off of the Philistine yoke, the establishment of the Kingdom and the victories of David against neighboring nations" was in fact only the "superficial cause" for history writing.[3] It could not have been merely the above events, the "thrilling material" of history, since this "material" was also available to other nations. Rather than the events themselves, it was the religious experience that led the observer to perceive the Rule of God in history and to recognize a purpose within history itself.[4] This recognition of a purpose within history was contingent upon the view of a progression in history (although this thought surfaced only later). Before this belief of a purpose within history existed, there were accounts and narratives of events, but there was no recording of history. It was only through this belief that the writing of history was established.

The belief that a plan was being realized within history also encompassed belief in primeval history, original sin, the account of the Del-

---

[1] *Die Eigenart der hebräischen Geschichtsschreibung im alttestamentlichen Zeitalter* (Berlin: 1910).
[2] Ibid., p. 66.
[3] Ibid., p. 67.
[4] In the course of his exposition (p. 70) G.F. Moore supplements his earlier writing and suggests the "honest belief."

uge and the building of the Tower of Babel. The origins of these accounts were considered inconsequential, for the accounts were not perceived as "myths and legends," nor as the "entry" of history, but as important factors that shaped history.[5] Only when Creation was placed in its sequential order within the context of history, namely as its beginning, was there a sufficient opportunity for events to be interpreted as history.

A "pragmatic framing"—that is, a fatalistic viewpoint expressed in the attitude of the nation toward God—may be recognized, for example, in the Book of Judges or in the recording of history during the 7th-6th century, B.C.E., which was dominated by Deuteronomistic thinking.[6] It is important to note the connection between this pragmatism and that which Moore calls "the onset of a philosophical view of history." This latter view comprised the idea of a just world-order and the unity of history, which is correlative to God's unity. Furthermore, it included the belief that through all events the direction toward world fulfillment, which is God's aim in history, would be maintained. It seems to me that "pragmatic framing" is itself framed by this higher interpretation of history. If this philosophical view were absent, the pragmatism would have to be judged differently. The existence of this pragmatism can only be understood within the context of this relationship.

The comprehensiveness of this interpretation of events is evident in the historical view held in the year 586 B.C.E. Here we find no consciousness of a catastrophic end of times. The year 586 stood as a confirmation of the concept of Divine Judgment, and so it meant the end of the biblical recording of history. In contrast, the apocalyptic writers in the year 70 C.E. regarded their era as a catastrophe, as the end of history itself.

The relationship to the present was particularly determined by the relationship with the past. This was defined by Ezra, as will be presently discussed, and must also have affected the recording of history. If at a later time only the Maccabean uprising became an object of historical writing, the reason has to be found in religious experience as described above. Through it, the Rule of God, which was revealed in history, could again be ascertained. However, in the course of the Hasmonaean policies this historical interpretation was questioned. Consequently, the schools which were historically oriented discarded the interpretation of the Rule of God. This led to the doctrine's disappearance.

---

[5] Ibid., p. 68.
[6] Ibid., p. 72.

2. The Historical Teaching of Ezra

The importance accorded historical teaching within the religious views of the Tannaites dates back to Ezra, although not the views themselves but rather in the way these views were formulated into a composite picture. The most noteworthy fact—that Ezra based his new communal organization upon history rather than on a legal system—has been recognized by H.H. Schaeder.[7] The law itself, which from then on gained a decisive importance concerning the regulation of life, was subsumed in the interpretation of history. Thus, although life at that time emphasized the fulfillment of the law, life itself was based upon a deep relationship with the past.[8]

Even if Ezra's concept of history is essentially similar to the concept one finds in tradition, its importance is nevertheless remarkable for Ezra's time and for the institutions of that era. In his relation to history, Ezra differs from the great founders of religions whose work denies history (although their work may attempt to establish a connection with it).[9] During these extremely difficult times Ezra recalls the history of Israel to make his community aware of the Rule of God and ask for His care. This history traced the Election of Israel to sin, its defeat, repentance and reconciliation.[10] History for Ezra thus reveals God's judgment and His mercy. It enables one to understand the present and to provide answers to one's questions.

It is impossible to explain the connection between the historical teaching of Ezra and that of the Tannaites. But we may suppose that Ezra's recollection of history, which we find to be the preferable expression to "Ezra's relationship with history," lost some of its immediacy in successive generations. Later, during the time of the Maccabean uprising, there was an apparent revival of Ezra's approach to history. Subsequently, it was again rejected in favor of a different approach. But it was revived once more after the year 70 C.E. when a situation arose that was much more difficult than Ezra's but was comparable with it in its necessity for a new beginning. This recollection of history took shape in its new, historically visible form, namely the utilization of history to gain perspective on the present. This will be discussed at a later point.

In the first two centuries of the Common Era another circumstance added to the religious problems which were already complicated by the current historical situation: the most successful religious movements were rooted in a devaluation of history. Thus, teachings which

---

[7] *Esra der Schreiber* (Beiträge zur historischen Theologie 5), (Tübingen 1930).
[8] Compare p. 70.
[9] Compare p. 73.
[10] Neh. 9.

privileged history would have to take on a more radicalized form. The historical thinking in Ezra was restricted to the acceptance of conceptualizations of history found in the Old Testament. These concepts were the basis of historical works and the concepts themselves were thought to be real history, when in fact this historicist thinking could be expected to produce only recollections of events. It was inevitable that this historical thinking would lead to a Tannaitic reinterpretation of the historical material based upon faith in order to accomplish the utilization of history for religion.

The difference in the above forms of historical thinking is apparent in the position taken by the religious law in the system within the context of human action. The recollection of history in Ezra led to an acceptance of events, whereas in the Tannaitic interpretation of history human action is a factor that effects events. Thus in Ezra's thoughts the law is based upon history, while in the Tannaitic mindset the law is interpreted into history. Furthermore, the messianic hope (which was not yet included in Ezra's concept of history), during the course of time established a position within historical teaching. It was completely drawn into the notion of history by the Tannaites because in their view the appearance of the Eternal would be most clearly revealed in the aim of history itself. For them, the aim of history when it is realized as the end of history is part of its concreteness.

The Palestinian schools reacted against the establishment of messianism since it again and again endangered those of their teachings which had a positive attitude towards history. They used not only their laws but also used, in a more decisive manner, their teachings which held that history in its real form was a necessary prerequisite to the end of times.

II. THE DENIAL OF HISTORY IN APOCALYPTIC TEACHING (THE FOURTH BOOK OF EZRA)

The Apocalpytic writers and the Tannaites were affected in the same way by their contemporary political events. ("Political" in this context should be interpreted in the broadest sense of that word.) The similarity of this starting point is significant for us, since it emphasizes different reactions to the same events and different solutions to the same problems.

The presentation of history in the Old Testament follows the presumed order of events: salvation, sin, evil, repentance and salvation. The history of the nation is perceived in this way, as is the history of the world. The inner-worldly messianism of the prophets represents the completion of the last stage in this sequence. It can be only briefly mentioned that on occasion man's salvation is derived from God's mercy or His fulfillment of the Covenant with the Fathers rather than from man's own repentance.

The historical teachings of the Apocalypse lies between the biblical and the Tannaitic teachings. The suffering of the righteous, the oppression of the Chosen People by the "wicked kingdom" (this was the dominant mood of the times) led the Apocalyptic writers to despair that God's plan would ever be realized through history. As the Apocalyptic writer looked upon the history of his people, his perspective yielded a picture of continuing decay. His view was that repentance and mercy do not follow upon salvation and sin. Rather the world has adhered to sin until it is ripe for decay. God's judgment will not restore to order this world of apostasy but instead will establish a new aeon. As my example of this depiction of history as decay, I take the Fourth book of Ezra.*

1. Zion and Babylon-Rome

The picture of the contemporary scene can be sketched with a few strokes: "Zion is desolate, and those who live in Babylon are wealthy" (3:2); "the seal of Zion—for she has now lost the seal of her glory, and has been given over into the hands of those that hate us" (10:23). This state of affairs was first attributed to sin (3:25 f.), but the realization that the inhabitants of Babylon did not act in a better way (3:28) led to an incomprehensible situation. It seemed as if God supported sinners and left the godless unharmed, but destroyed His people (3:30). The foundation of the world order was severely shaken by the following events: the enemies of Israel lived in happiness, although they rejected the commandments (3:33); those who contradicted God's promises were allowed to tread down on those who believed in His covenants (5:29); the nations which were "said to be nothing" (6:56) destroyed the people on whose account the world had been created (6:55).

It became impossible for the Apocalyptic writer to visualize salvation for this world in such disarray. He himself allowed it to decay. He interpreted the past as one of decay which had reached its nadir in his own time. His hope was directed at a future which could only commence after the destruction of the present era.

The same contemporary conditions led the Tannaites to an opposite solution. They did not abandon the concept of the unity of history; for them, the Rule of God had been effective because of its illuminated plan in the past. In the present, however, the purpose of the Rule of

---

* To a great extent, the translations from passages from the Fourth Book of Ezra rely upon *The Old Testament Pseudepigrapha*, Vol. 1, Apocalyptic Literature and Testaments, edited by James H. Charlesworth (Garden City, N.Y.: Doubleday & Co., 1983).

God was barely visible, but it nevertheless still worked according to the plan. In a later time the future would illuminate that plan within the framework of history. Thus the future would be comprehensible.

2. The Decay

Right at the beginning of the Fourth Ezra (3:4-28) the author provides a retrospective upon the time from Adam until the destruction of the Temple. Ezra accepts as a reliable tradition that God again and again chooses the righteous one and protects him (Noah, Abraham, Isaac, Jacob and David). However he thinks it important that the "law," the revelation of the Divine Will, does not prevail. Instead the "evil root," which exists side by side with the law in the heart of the people, necessarily results in that "what was good departed, and the evil remained" (3:22). If the purpose of this observation is to demonstrate that "the deeds of Babylon are not better than those of Zion" (3:31), then in Chapter 7 this mood of decay becomes clear. This chapter deals with the world in its transition to a better world. Although God has created this age for the sake of Israel, that "what had been made was judged" by the sin of Adam (7:11), this world has ceased to be the place in which the realization of the plan is enacted and its paths have become "narrow, sorrowful, toilsome, miserable and bad, full of dangers and involved in great hardships" (7:12). Ezra's review at the end of his speeches asserts that the law is being transgressed (14:31) and that this creates an interruption within history. Consequently, neither repentance nor mercy will follow. Rather, God will "take away what He gave" (14:32).

This idea is repeated in different ways. God "explains to human beings what they should do" (7:21), but humans scorn this law (7:24). The result is that "empty things are for the empty."[11] In 7:129-131, apostasy produces a similar result: "Therefore, there shall not be grief at their damnation."[12]new fn 12 In 8:60 f., the deteriorating nature of history is due to ingratitude towards "the name of Him who made them," and history shouts for judgment. In The Vision Of Zion this consciousness of man's decay is condensed into a great lament, while the law remains "in its glory" (9:37). However, the answer to the lament omits the possibility of repentance, which might sustain this world.

This mood of decay becomes evident in the image of aging: "Creation is already aging" (5:55). The religious consciousness of the eternal possibility of a new beginning cannot arise in a world "that has lost its

---

[11] "Full things for the full" does not speak of the penitent or the one who received mercy.
[12] "Those to whom salvation is assured" is not considered in its dynamic sense.

youth" (14:10). Man cannot maintain hope that meaningful events will occur since the world is "becoming weaker through old age" (14:16). Hope is centered on a new age because the first one and its history is decaying.

3. The Devaluation and End of the Age

The Devaluation of Creation and of History. The parable of the sea which could only be reached through a narrow river (7:1-5) depicts the world's place: it is only a passageway for the world to come. "Therefore, unless the living pass through the difficult and vain experiences, they can never receive those things that have been reserved for them" (7:14). Gunkel is correct in indicating that for the Apocalyptic writer the optimistic world view is limited only to Creation itself.[13] In contrast, the present times are controlled by the dogma of the "Decline of Creation." Gunkel calls this view the "modern, Jewish pessimistic one"; this, however, pertains only to the Apocalyptic writer. The question presented here is whether Creation can be separated from history. The Apocalyptic writer can either regard history as decay, or he can dispense with it because he makes this distinction. For the Tannaite, the God of Creation is the God of History. That which was part of the original Plan of Creation subsequently unfolds during the development of history. Thus, for the Tannaite, the renunciation of history would be a renunciation of Creation. This furthermore would constitute a rejection of the acknowledgment of Divine Rule.

The world has only a relative importance as a passageway to the new age. This is the reason why Ezra must not consider the present but only the future (7:16). The righteous can bear their difficult circumstances only because they "hope for easier ones" (7:18). Among the privileges of the righteous will be that they "have now escaped what is mortal" (7:96). The deepest longing of man "to behold the face of Him whom they served in life" (7:98) will be given to the righteous only in the hereafter as the seventh and last of their rejoicings.

In the Tannaitic teaching of history, by contrast, the above longing of man is thought to be fulfilled in this world. This is the reason why, for the Apocalyptic writer, the expectation that the people will be restored can only be fulfilled in the Hereafter, while for the Tannaite, the restoration can take effect within history itself. In The Vision Of Zion, God shows Ezra the "brightness of her glory and the loveliness of her beauty" (10:50). The Zion that receives this beauty is no longer an earthly place since "no work of man's building could endure in a place where the City of The Most High was to be revealed" (10:54).

The separation of Creation from history on the one hand and the

---

[13] "Das vierte Buch Esra," in Kautzsch' *Apokryphen*, Vol. II. p. 369, n. a.

separation of the end of time from history on the other, is the reason for the twofold devaluation of history—from the point of Creation and from the end of time. Furthermore, by the end of time the causal agents that were established in Creation and that have been effective throughout history will have lost their potency. Ezra illustrates this with examples from Abraham to Hezekiah (7:106-110) in which the strong help the weak and the righteous intercede on behalf of the godless. However, this is depicted a something that is possible only in this world, since it is not the end of time (7:112).

The devaluation of history is particularly obvious in the assumption that not every man is entitled to a meaningful existence and to productive work.[14] Nature has produced many worthless things; only a few human beings should be redeemed.[15] Since sin is considered to have a destructive impact upon history, since Creation has decayed, and, furthermore, since Creation can only be recommenced at the end of time, it became possible to say about the reality that had come into place between Creation and salvation, "So let the multitude perish which has been born in vain" (9:22).

Teachings that are positive toward history attempt to find the Eternal—which would be evidence of the Divine Rule over events; the apocalypse has to negate this possibility. "The ways of The Most High have been created to be eternal; but you who were created as a mortal human being that lives in an impermanent aeon, how can you grasp the eternal?" (4:11). "Those who dwell upon earth can understand only what is on earth, and he who is above the heavens can understand what is above the height of the heavens" (4:21). There is no entry leading from the earthly to the Eternal.

This terrible boundary, this curse of not being able to recognize the Eternal within history is negated by the Tannaites in their teaching of history. The emphasize God's actions of the past, which also serve to point to the future. The greatness of the future is assured by what has transpired in the past. Ezra, however, laments that "no one knows the things which have been done or will be done by You" (14:21).

The Devaluation of Life. The devaluation of history corresponds to the devaluation of the life of the individual. Since the reason for suffering is concealed and since the sinful life has a quality of cruel finality, "it would be better for us not to be here" (4:12). Life and sin appear as contradictions: "It would have been better if the earth had not produced Adam, or else, when it had produced him, had restrained him from sinning" (7:16). And since "Jacob's travail" cannot

---

[14] Compare here the Tannaites' basic, positive attitude towards every individual human life.
[15] Compare the parable of the earthenware and the gold (8:2), of the planter (8:42) and of the berry (9:21).

be conceived as having been purposeful and since a better future cannot be ascertained, there is the question "Why then was I born?" (5:35), or the wish if only "we also had been consumed in the burning of Zion" (12:44). The belief that the "soul cannot escape," since "all who have been born are involved in iniquities" (7:68), leads to the condemnation of reason, for it can only produce the certain knowledge that one will perish (7:64). Therefore, it would have been better "if the dust itself had not been born, so that the mind might not have been made from it" (7:63). Nothing can be expected from such a life. Consequently, "the life that is corruptible" is renounced and men hasten to escape from "these times" (14:13f.).

The End of the Age. For the Apocalyptic writer, history is rejected as the place where all questions can be resolved; only in the coming age will the answers become apparent. Almost all of the events in this world hasten towards this new age (4:26). The Apocalyptic writer thinks he is at that point in time in which The Most High has looked upon his times and concluded that they are ended (11:44). He longs for the judgment, saying, "Could you not have created at one time those who have been and those who are and those who will be, so that you might show your judgment the sooner?" (5:43). Although the Apocalyptic writer receives an answer which contains an allusion to a woman's womb—the womb brings forth each child only at its appointed time (5:46)—this time sequence is meaningless if the present is not worthy of being considered (7:16) and only the end of times appear to be of value.[16] The messiah is "to deliver the Creation and create a new order" (13:26). However, this new order of history has not been gained as a result of purification nor has it been created as a continuation of history.

4. The Plan

Even if the work of man and the life of the righteous may be considered to be meaningful in the Apocalypse of Ezra, the preponderance of sin is decisive in the consideration of the world order. As I have tried to point out, it is sin that has given history a stigma of decay which the small number of righteous cannot overcome. From this viewpoint, the Plan of God, which is mentioned again and again, is conducted by blind necessity and administered by God. The kindness which emanates from God cannot arise in Apocalyptic literature. This kindness, in the Tannaitic teaching of history, has the capacity to alter history from being merely the necessity of events to being providential.

Ezra receives a hint concerning the end of times and its established

---

[16] Compare also 14:13f.

order in response to his critical question concerning the end. Having asked why all human beings were not created at the same time, Ezra receives the answer, "Creation cannot make more haste than the Creator" (5:44). This present age is divided into twelve parts and the Apocalyptic writer is told the exact course of events (14:11f.). The end comes when the predicted "measure is fulfilled," "for he has weighed the age in the balance, and measured the times by measure, and numbered the times by number" (4:37). God, the strict guardian of this order, "will not move or arouse them." The Kingdom of Evil can end and the Kingdom of God can commence since The Most High has looked upon his times "and behold, they are ended, and His ages are completed" (11:44). Wherever a hint of God's patience is given concerning the inhabitants of the world, Ezra stresses that His patience cannot interrupt His rigid plan. "For how long the time is that The Most High has been patient with those who inhabit the world, and not for their sake, but because of the times which he has foreordained!" (7:74). Consolation is therefore beyond the reach of human understanding: "For you come far short of being able to love my Creation more than I love it" (8:47). This is a love which the Apocalyptic writer is able to recognize as being true as he confronts the decay of this age and the horror of the inevitable judgment. He cannot experience this love nor can he reciprocate it. The notion "Let many perish who are now living, rather than that the law of God which is set before them be disregarded," illustrates the adherence to a strict order (7:20).

To the notion of the plan, described above, Ezra adds the idea of predetermination. God prepared the world as a dwelling place before humanity even existed (9:18). Ezra describes the magnificence and the splendor of Creation in order to demonstrate that the idea of Creation preceded the act of Creation (6:1-5). However, "When The Most High made the world and Adam and all who have come from him, he first prepared the judgment" and the end (7:70). The signs of the end of time have been decided upon "from the days that were of old" (9:4). And God revealed to Moses "the secrets of the times and declared to him the end of the times" (14:5).

In order to clarify this notion of a plan, Ezra makes use of examples from nature. The onset of the end appears in the image of the pregnant woman whose womb cannot retain the child after the nine months have been completed (4:40). And as no womb can give birth to ten children simultaneously, but only to one at a time, a certain sequence has thus been established in the world (5:46).[17] The devaluation of this world (which was "made for the sake of many" [8:1]), by the world to come (which was made for the sake of a few), is illustrated in

---

[17] Gunkel has: to beget.

the parable of the earth producing more clay than gold (8:2)—and on this same earth all that is planted will not take root (8:41). And, since no human being can be ill on someone else's behalf or sleep in his stead, "everyone shall bear his own righteousness or unrighteousness" (7:104f).

This comparison between the Rule of God and the events in nature produces an awareness of one's own impotence and does not leave room for the concept of intercession by God. Consequently, the Apocalyptic writer refers to himself as a creature and also founds his requests for mercy from God upon examples from nature. He seeks justification for his existence from the necessities of nature. Nature, which surrounds her creatures with care, is juxtaposed with the Creator, who "destroys His creatures with a swift word" (8:6-14). The earth will be preserved, while the seed that was received will perish. To the Apocalyptic writer, the earth is contrasted with humanity, into which the law was sown, but which will perish while the seed—that is, the law—"does not perish but remains in its glory" (9:34-37). In one instance, however, the sameness of events in nature and in human fate is declared to be unjust. Another law is demanded for man who has been made in God's image "for whose sake all things were created." Mercy is insisted upon, since it is an expression of the relationship between creature and Creator (8:42-45).[18]

5. The Relationship To History

The difference between Apocalyptic and Tannaitic teaching is particularly apparent in their relationship to the past. Principally, the Tannaites make use of history in order to answer questions that originate from the present. The Apocalypse of Ezra, which is based on partially the same traditions as the Tannaitic teachings, uses historical memory. The purpose of this usage is to provide a basis for certain kinds of questions and justifications for their solutions. Our perception of the relationship of the Apocalypse to history is based upon our consideration of the choices it makes from history. We ask whether the Apocalypse's questions concerning a historical event serve only as proof of already existing answers or, alternatively, whether the historical event itself is the cause for particular answers.

Before we inquire into the usage of history, I would like to present a survey of the existing material. Ezra is most intensely interested in Creation. Chapter 6 verses 1-5 describe the vast extent of things that came into being as a result of Creation. Chapter 6 verses 38-54 set forth the development of Creation according to the sequence of the days of Creation. The creation of Adam is mentioned in 7:70 and

---

[18] Compare 8:7.

10:14. The creation of Adam is also mentioned in 3:4 at the beginning of a larger survey and his sin is talked about in 7:11 and 7:118. Abraham appears in the same survey, also in 7:106; he is referred to in 6:8 in connection with Jacob and Esau. Moses is conceived in 7:106, presented as a prophet in 7:129, shown the revelation in the bush in 14:3. The exodus from Egypt and Sinai appears in 3:17, 9:29 and 14:3. The exodus and the conquest of the land is found in 14:29. The captivity of the Ten Tribes is mentioned in 13:40. Daniel is referred to 12:11.

Furthermore, the compilations in certain aspects of historical events should be mentioned. Chapter 3 verses 4-27 recount history from Adam through the Deluge, the Fathers, Egypt and Revelation to the Sanctuary and its destruction. The men "who have not tasted death" are found in 6:26. The men who prayed on behalf of their age, Abraham, Moses, Joshua, Samuel, David, Solomon and Hezekiah, are listed in 7:106-110. In the Vision of Zion the entire history of Zion is summarized (10:45-48). The time period from the Egyptian bondage until the entry into the Land is mentioned again in 14:29.

In what sense was this historical material utilized? On the one hand, the Apocalyptic writer utilizes hints of historical events as catalysts for points of departure for historical teachings which are important to him. On the other hand, this approach is not the same as using historical examples only after their meaning has been reinterpreted for the Apocalypse, or after a new line of thought has been introduced which makes them significant for the Apocalypse. The description of the work of Creation (6:38-53) from which Ezra concludes that God "created the world for us" (6:55) belongs to the first category above. The enumerated men who intervened with God on behalf of their evil contemporaries (7:106-110) teach Ezra that human intercession may be possible even on the last day of judgment. The memory of the creation of man (10:14) and the historical memory of Jerusalem and its destruction (10:45-48) serve a dual purpose. They serve first as a simile for the pain of the Apocalyptic writer, and secondly as a conceptual source of consolation.

We find that history is being used in the same way by the Tannaites. However the second approach to the utilization of historical material, described in the above paragraph, has inherent tendencies which basically devalue history. In contrast, the reinterpretation of history by the Tannaites is based upon a religious motivation that matured in their contemporary era. Nevertheless, it had an essentially positive attitude toward history.

The absence of meaning in contemporary events leads to the consideration of history as a process of decay from its beginning. In the historical account (3:4-28), the apostasy almost appears to be inserted into history as a necessity. This is because the evil mind of man was not eliminated, and thus the law could not possibly bear its fruit.[19] In the end, it is Adam's sin which is the basis for this decay (7:11), for since then "the ways in this aeon have become narrow" (7:12). Adam's sin effected not only his decline but ours as well (7:18). For the Tannaites, the stories of the Exodus and the sojourns in the desert appear as the great encounter of God and His people. In contrast, for the Apocalyptic writer, this story is one of decay. This is because the law which is "being glorified forever" is offered to the people, but the people failed (9:29-32).[20]

For the Apocalyptic writer, in the new age which will be established after the destruction of this era, everything will be fulfilled that history could not achieve: Divine Justice shall prevail; the Divine Plan of Salvation shall be victorious; good shall vanquish evil. Events in the Fourth Book of Ezra are thus related to or interpreted within the context of the end of time. In chapter 6 verses 1-5, Creation is described in order to draw a comparison between the uniqueness of the Creator and the uniqueness of the Judge at the end of time.[21] The birth of Jacob and Esau is retold as an allegory for the overthrow of Roman rule by the Kingdom of Israel (6:8f). "The men who from their births have not tasted death" appear among the omens of the end of time (6:26). The story of the captivity of the Ten Tribes is told in the vision of a man. It is related to their return at the end of time (13:39-47). The Exodus from Egypt and the sojourn to the Sinai are recounted because of "the secrets of time and the end of times" which are revealed to Moses (14:3-5).

Ezra asks for God's mercy in order to write down "everything that has happened in the world from the beginning" (14:22) because "no one knows the things which have been done" (14:21). This explicitly expresses the kind of division that the Apocalyptic writer thought existed between the Work of God and the history of man. The Apocalyptic writer could receive little assistance from history. After noting the deeds of the past, Ezra adds the future things that "will be done by You". The history of the past and of the future belong together, and they are the subject of a unified plan. This originates from the ancient consciousness of the Jew, Ezra.[22] For the Apocalyptic writer there is a

---

[19] Compare 3:20.
[20] Similarly in 14:28-32: God, who "is a righteous judge," must take away what he has given; compare in Tannaites the interrelationship of sin and mercy as well as the interrelationship of good deeds and *Zakhut*.
[21] Compare 7:70, in which it is nooted that the Judgment was prepared prior to Creation.
[22] For Gunkel this is a critical passage since he concludes from it that the contents of the Holy Scriptures have historical and escathological implications. If this is true, then es-

dichotomy between history and the end of time. This is because it is impossible to comprehend contemporary history from a religious viewpoint. However, we shall see how the Tannaites attempted to gain a basically different solution from the same situation and set of problems.

III. THE AFFIRMATION OF HISTORY IN TANNAITIC TEACHING

1. The Decay

In the last chapter I maintained that contemporary events had a similar impact upon the Apocalyptic writer and on the Tannaites. Some evidence concerning the Tannaites' position towards decay in their era will be presented here. Admittedly, their era is of greater duration than the Apocalyptical period of the Fourth Book of Ezra.

R. Eliezer ben Hyrkanos reports on the gradual decline of certain groups of the people as follows: the Sages have become like Bible teachers; the Bible teachers like teaching proctors, the teaching proctors like the common people and the common people become more and more destitute.[23] All the sayings which commence with "from the day when the Sanctuary was destroyed" and which lament the increasing violence, cursing, decay of spiritual values and the decay of the "men of action" extend up until the time of R. Pinehas ben Yair—that is, until the end of the era under consideration. The tension is so great during this period that "an iron wall divides Israel from its heavenly Father."[24] The sorrows of this time are so extensive that it is impossible to record them.[25] "If we wanted to write it down, we could not describe it." One could willingly accept the sorrows and record them only by severely restraining oneself. This was how R. Hananya ben Hiskiya could write his scroll of fasting. However, usually the above course of action did not provide enough strength to continue these recordings.[26] A look at the past indicates that the despondency of that age has deeper causes than those of all prior times.[27]

The disaster appears to be of such finality that God Himself can only lament about it. It seems that He does not intervene in the course of history. R. Zadok, who looks at the ruins of the Temple and complains about God, is shown in a nightly vision that God is in mourn-

---

chatology must be related to history in the same degree that history is related to its own completion at the end of time.
[23] b Sota 49a f.
[24] Cf. further b Ber. 32b.
[25] R. Simon ben Gamliel II, b Shab. 13b.
[26] Anonymous, ibid.
[27] R. Simon ben Gamliel II, CantR on 3:1 commencing with Num 21:4; Ekha 5:9; Dan 7:15; Isa 21:3.

ing over Zion.[28] At the beginning of every night's watch God cries out in a lion's voice and laments the destruction of His house.[29] R. Yose ben Halafta hears the Divine Voice behind a ruin in Jerusalem saying: "Woe unto me that I have destroyed my House, burnt my Sanctuary and exiled my children among the nations of the world."[30] Later versions try to avoid the "Woe unto me" and they substitute instead "Woe unto the sons whose failures...." The age itself, however, gives proof to the consciousness of a lamenting God. When he appears, the prophet Elijah reports that the voice "of the One whose children are in exile can be heard every day." In the time of the Hadrianic edicts it is again Elijah who explains to R. Nehoray the following: the reason for the earthquakes, which this Sage believes to be due to the transgressions of the commandments, is in reality an expression of God's displeasure about the destruction of the Sanctuary while the theaters and the circuses of the heathens remain.[31]

These events appear to reverse all the laws. The righteous individual becomes a prey of the wicked.[32] For example, R. Akiba's judge is the tyrant Rufus. According to a midrash this is a cruel realization of the scriptural saying: God judges the righteous through the wicked. All the rules of judging the righteous life versus the evil life are proved to be inadequate: "There is nothing concerning the recklessness of the evil ones nor the suffering of the righteous ones that is within our jurisdiction."[33]

2. The Question Concerning Reason and Meaning

The fault of human beings. Typically these disastrous events are explained as being punishment for the errors of human beings. However, it is implicit within these explanations that the actual reasons for these events are unknown. After the destruction of the Temple the following saying of R. Yohanan ben Zakkai is related: "You did not want to serve Heaven, thus you must serve the nations; you did not want to pay the half-shekel to God, thus you must pay fifteen shekels to the government of your enemies; you did not want to prepare the pathways for the attendants at the Festivals, thus you must prepare the towers and castles for those who go to the King's vineyards."[34] Gamaliel II also perceives the rule of the wicked despot as a punishment for

---

[28] Seder Eliahu Rabbah 28 (p. 149).
[29] R. Eliezer ben Hyrkanos, b Ber 3a.
[30] b Ber 3a; the correct reading according to *Dikduke Sofrim*.
[31] Shokher Tov on Ps 18:8 (p. 141f.).
[32] R. Yehuda Hanassi, on Koh 3:17; KohR on this verse.
[33] R. Yannai; as a Tannaite in the Post-Hadrianic time: according to Bacher, II, 385 n.1; against Graetz and Strack. See also Avot IV:15.
[34] Mekh on 19:1; 61a f.

Israel, which has left "her father in Heaven."[35]

It is significant that in explaining the reason for the destruction of Betar, fault is attributed to the killing of the righteous R. Eleazar of Modiim by Bar Kokhba, whereupon the Divine Voice announces the defeat of the heroes.[36] R. Simon ben Yohai perceives the decay of the Palestinian towns, "which were uprooted from their places," as the punishment for not having paid the instructors of the youth.[37] R. Yose ben Halafta has Isaac say in his blessing over Esau: "When you see that your brother has shaken off the Yoke of Torah, then implement decrees to persecute him. You may then deal with him as you wish."[38] Since Rome was referred to as Esau in the language of the age, the Tannaite thus saw that the curse had become real in his time.

God's Justice. R. Eleazar ben Azarya opposes such self-accusations. He wants to "free the whole world from judgment" since the "bent down—the drunken one from wine" could not be held responsible.[39] Instead of attempting to conclude that fate controls their own actions, a consciousness develops that an unpredictable but nevertheless Divine Justice is in effect. The "Elders" in Rome at the time of the destruction of the Temple answer the question of what God has been doing since the completion of Creation in the following manner: "Hell is being heated for the wicked ones. Woe to the world that will bear the brunt of His judgment."[40] And R. Simon ben Yohai interprets the sacrilege that the Roman Emperor committed against the Sanctuary as an affront to God; such misconduct must be punished.[41] In the Post-Hadrianic epoch, one's act is supposed to be preserved "if it is directed toward the Name of God."[42] This thought seems to be evident from the above contemporaneous saying.

R. Akiba had in particular a belief that Justice was in effect, although unknowable.[43] In response to the masters who cry at the ruins of the Sanctuary, R. Akiba refers to the prophecy of the rebuilding of Jerusalem. This prophecy will be fulfilled with the same certainty as the previous prophecy of disaster. When R. Akiba visits Rome with his friends, the sight of happy Rome elicits mourning within them over the destruction of the Temple. However, R. Akiba reacts differently since he is certain that the world will be rearranged pursuant to

---

[35] EstR Petihta.
[36] EkhaR on 2:2.
[37] Pes. ed. Buber 120b.
[38] GenR 67.
[39] b Eruv 64b f.; interpretation of Isa 51:21.
[40] GenR 10; the partner in the dialogue is "King Ptolemy."
[41] Tanh on Ex 38:21.
[42] R. Yohanan the Sandalmaker, Avot IV:11.
[43] Sifré on Deut § 43; EkhaR on 5:18 (p. 159f.) commencing with Zach 8:4 and Jer 26:18 (Micha 3:12).

Justice.⁴⁴

There was intense hope to see the end of Roman rule. R. Yose ben Kisma construes the repeated cycle of "construction and decay" as signaling a time in which "the son of David will come."⁴⁵ R. Meir says in a midrash about Rome "that once again the rule will be restored to its owner."⁴⁶ R. Simeon ben Yohai perceives the Parthians as the forebearers of a political change, which would result "in the coming of the Messiah."⁴⁷ In his interpretation of Isaiah 49:14, R. Yehuda Hanassi has God lament over the discontent of Israel. However, among God's charitable acts there is already in store the future elimination "of the Kingdom of Edom" which will take place after the disposal of Babylon, Media and Greece.⁴⁸ In his interpretation of Jeremiah 49:20 he has the "destroyers of the second Temple fall into the hands of the Persians."⁴⁹

3. The Relationship to One's Immediate Environment and to History

The Tannaitic teaching of history presents us with distinctions between two realms: one's immediate environment and history. How the negative relationship to one realm determines the positive relationship to the other will be shown to us later. Here it should only be pointed in the following evidence.

The Relationship to One's Immediate Environment. The rejection of "one's immediate environment" is most explicitly expressed in the rejection of the alien teaching and alien religion. In a dialogue with a heathen, R. Gamliel II calls his gods "dead and dogs" in contrast to the Kingdom of God which comprises everything and thus does not deem it necessary to destroy idols.⁵⁰ It is related that R. Akiba has a dialogue "between Israel and the nations" in which the nations are surprised at Israel's strong faith; they are ready to follow Israel.⁵¹ However Israel rejects them with the words of the Song of Songs: "I am my lover's and my lover is mine."⁵² This rejection is exacerbated and turns into contempt. In a prayer of R. Nehunya ben Hakana, those who "sit in the house of study" are differentiated from those who idly "sit at the corners." He says: "I run and they run; I run toward the life of the

---

⁴⁴ b Makk 24a f.; EkhaR ibid.
⁴⁵ b San 98a.
⁴⁶ KohR on 1:9; *Hazir* is read as *lehahzir.*
⁴⁷ CantR on 8:8.
⁴⁸ Pes. ed. Buber 130b f.
⁴⁹ b Yom 10a.
⁵⁰ b Avod Zar 54b.
⁵¹ Mekh on 15:2; 37a.
⁵² Cant 6:2.

world to come and they run towards ruin."[53] R. Yose ben Halafta says that in the messianic age the nations with their gifts of homage are accepted, however Rome is rejected upon God's command.[54]

The Relationship to History. The descriptions of decay which we cited above conclude with the following question and answer: "But to whom can we cling? To our Heavenly Father." This belief saw its highest act of devotion in martyrdom.[55] Its connection to history and its expressions are illustrated in a midrash about Jacob's dream, which is traced back to R. Meir. God shows Jacob how the princes of Babylon, Media, Greece and Rome rise and fall. God commands Jacob to rise as the others; he, however, is afraid this ascent may result in a descent. Jacob was promised another fate but he lacks trust in God.[56]

Trust in God would require a trust in the course of history; distrust of history results in one becoming an apostate in the sight of God. Subsequent to this apostasy, God responds in history: "Your children shall be enslaved by the four Kingdoms." And the reversal of this situation will happen at the end of times within the framework of history, as a final homecoming. This relationship to history is positive in comparison to that relationship which rejects contemporaneous events.

---

[53] b Ber 28b.
[54] b Pes 118b, commencing with Ps 68:31 f.
[55] Cf. the interpretation of Ps. 50:5 by R. Yoshua ben Karha of the Post-Hadrianic period in which "covenant" is established in martyrdom and the "slaughtering" is understood as a presentation of one's life; Tos San 13:11.
[56] Pes. ed. Buber 151a on Gen 28:12.

CHAPTER EIGHT

HISTORY FABRICATED: THE SOCIAL USES OF NARRATIVE
IN EARLY RABBINIC JUDAISM

William Scott Green

Whatever else we think we know about ancient rabbis, we certainly know that some of them, at different times, produced texts. Virtually all our information about these figures comes from documents formulated, written, and redacted within the rabbinic movement. With few exceptions, these texts, fashioned and molded by rabbis, constitute the material remains of rabbinic Judaism; they are the primary evidence for its existence. Since a precise understanding of rabbinic textual constructions provides the foundation and justification for all other inferences from the texts, a prerequisite to any historical reconstruction of ancient rabbis is a delineation of the textual facts of the literature they made.

Rabbinic literature is made up of documents dated from the third century to early medieval times that treat two broad subjects: *halakhah* (rabbinic praxis, the way of doing things) and the interpretation of Scripture. The documents consist of large numbers of distinct, usually self-contained passages of varying length and character grouped in patterns of thematic, topical, or scriptural arrangement. These pericopae may be brief halakhic or exegetical dicta, somewhat elaborated discourses composed of the arguments and opinions of several rabbis on a halakhic problem, or narratives about rabbis or, less often, about biblical characters. The stories about rabbis are always about unrelated events; the literature is devoid of biography or hagiography.

Most rabbinic documents are unattributed works; all in fact are anonymous; and all comprise significant numbers of unassigned pericopae. Rabbinic literature has no authors. No document claims to be the writing of an individual rabbi in his own words, and all contain the ostensible sayings of, and stories about, many rabbis, usually of several generations. Selected to suit the purposes of compilers and redactors, the documents' components are not pristine and natural. They have been revised and reformulated in the processes of transmission and redaction, with the consequence that the *ipsissima verba* of any rabbi are beyond recovery. Rabbinic literature is severely edited, anonymous, and collective.

Rabbinic documents do not introduce or explain themselves to their readers, and they provide no easy access for tyros and noninitiates. The literature as a whole, especially its halakhic content, presupposes not only considerable information but also codes for interpretation. Its terse and formulaic syntactic constructions and its lean and disciplined vocabulary constitute a scholastic shorthand. Even the most elementary halakhic statement presumes a tacit dimension of rabbinic knowledge, attitudes, behaviors, and motivations. Rabbinic literature virtually ignores the world beyond its own preoccupations. Its documents obscure their origins by neglecting the events that led to their formation, and they report remarkably little about ordinary Jews or non-Jews. This insularity is reinforced by the nearly total absence of external witness to rabbinic religion, culture, and society. The documents present the restricted discourse of a small number of men who appear primarily engaged in observing, discussing, and analysing ideas, opinions, and behaviors, sometimes those recounted in Scripture, but most often those of one another. Rabbinic writing addresses rabbinic specialists; it is a parochial literature wholly obsessed with itself.

The work before us is to develop a strategy of reading these faceless and self-enclosed texts that will yield a critical description of the men they claim to represent, to devise a mode of inquiry that will sunder their seemingly impenetrable facade. This labor requires reflection on the activity of text-making and on the materiality of the texts themselves.

Groups and individuals constitute themselves in society not only through their speech and behavior but also through the production of material works. In the case of literate groups, this means the making of texts. The texts establish the group's identity, objectify its existence, consolidate its picture of reality, and codify the discourse that gives the group its distinctive character. The priestly and Pharisaic struggles to control the form and content of what has become "Scripture" in Judaism, the obsession with the production and protection of texts at Qumran, and the Marcionite controversy, for instance, testify to the importance of text-making in the histories of early Judaism and Christianity. The production of a text, like that of any cultural artifact, is a social activity. Producers of texts draw on socially acquired linguistic, literate, and literary skills ai.d are informed by a tacit awareness of the socially embedded behavioral conventions, cognitive capacities, and aesthetic traits and preferences of their actual or expected audience.

The texts produced by literate groups are intricate cultural constructions, and the elements and syntactical frameworks of textual constructions lend whatever significance to their substance a controlled analysis can discern. The form of such texts governs and constrains the presentation of their substance and is as much a part of their production as is their content.

The technical knowledge presupposed by most of rabbinic literature shows that rabbis produced their texts not for the world at large, nor for strangers and outsiders (and, therefore, certainly not for us), but for themselves. In the texts, selected reports of the opinions, arguments, and activities of generations of rabbis are encased in anonymous, synchronic, and rhetorically disciplined frameworks. It follows that the documents' picture of the world and of the rabbis themselves necessarily is over-determined, manipulated, and incomplete. Rabbinic editors offer no comprehensive and nuanced report, no mirror image of their colleagues and precursors. They produce instead a vision of their world as they understood it, their world as they construed it, and, therefore, their world as they imagined it and described it to themselves. With language as their principal representational tool, the producers of rabbinic documents create the world they reveal. Rabbinic literature thus emerges not, as so many have assumed, as an arcane, unsystematic, yet essentially neutral and inerrant record of "what actually happened" in rabbinic antiquity, but rather as an enormous labor of intellect and imagination that codifies a particular Jewish conception of reality in a distinctive mode of discourse that both derives from and generates that conception.

Rabbinic documents are formally discontinuous with, not imitative of, earlier Jewish writing, and they exhibit all the signs of deliberately and consciously wrought literary products, of strategic and willful literary choice. No mere vehicles for the passive receipt and transmission of what precedes them, these texts manifest rabbinism's cultural vitality and sense of originality. Since rabbis are their intended audience, they emerge as a principal mode of rabbinic self-representation. The construction of rabbinic documents, their genre(s), their discursive style and practice, and their rhetorical tropes constitute the primary data we know rabbis made in their own way and for themselves. Rabbinic discourse, the way of talking, thinking, and knowing delimited by the material forms rabbis devised for their literature, is palpable evidence of their culture. Attention to the rabbinic literary strategy for mapping the world and representing rabbis to themselves can open a path to understanding the men whose experience made such writing plausible.

The enormous and variegated rabbinic literary output and our still primitive knowledge of most documents reduce to folly attempts to characterize all of rabbinic literature with a single adjective. Nevertheless, the documents from which any description of ancient rabbis must be drawn—the Mishnah, the Tosefta, the earlier nonhomiletical midrashic collections, and the two *gemarot*—do share some common formal traits. These are most easily identified in the Mishnah, rabbinism's first documents,[1] but they have broader applicability.

Like most rabbinic literature, the Mishnah is an anonymous document composed of brief, discrete passages or cognitive units that address halakhic topics. These units have been arranged into series, each of which treats and elaborates a particular halakhic theme. The largest of these thematic catalogues, the tractates of the Mishnah, contain subtractates, smaller series of passages on subtopics of the tractate's larger subject. Throughout the Mishnah, the discrete units of the tractates and subtractates are neither chronologically nor biographically aligned, nor, in general, are they formally linked to one another. The Mishnah exemplifies the list genre, and the absence of formal links among units suggests a rhetorical strategy of parataxis. That is, although the subtractates and intermediary units of the Mishnah do develop particular themes or problems, each cognitive unit is formally independent and isolated. Each can be known and studied by itself, independent of its position in the present list. An internal Mishnaic witness, the measurable, if not excessive, number of units that appear in more than one tractates, makes this conclusion plausible.[2]

These same traits are evident, mutatis mutandis, in the other documents from which our information about ancient rabbis derives. To be sure, the argumentation characteristic of the pericopae (*sugyot*) in the Babylonian and Palestinian *gemarot* is more elaborated and sustained than anything in the Mishnah or the Tosefta, and the study of the formation of these pericopae poses a special and interesting problem in the study of Talmudic literature.[3] But the two Talmuds follow the Mishnah's arrangement, and the relations among their *sugyot* resembles that among the Mishnah's cognitive units. The intra-Talmudic index (*masoret ha-shas*) along the outer side of each page of *gemara* reveals a sizable number of independent units, or parts of them, that have been used in different tractates, *sugyot*, and halakhic contexts. The midrashic collections consist largely of lists of autonomous exegeti-

---

[1] See Jacob Neusner, *Judaism: The Evidence of the Mishnah* (Chicago, 1981).

[2] This description is based on ibid., and is abbreviated from my "Reading the Writing of Rabbinism: Toward an Interpretation of Rabbinic Literature," *Journal of the American Academy of Religion* L1/2:2191-206.

[3] See David Goodblatt, "The Babylonian Talmud," in J. Neusner, ed., *The Study of Ancient Judaism* (new York, 1981), 2:120-99. In the same volume, see Baruch M. Bokser, "An Annotated Bibliographical Guide to the Study of the Palestinian Talmud," pp. 1-119.

cal comments attached to and arranged in the order of the verses of the biblical book being interpreted. The ubiquitous use in these texts of the disjunctive device *davar'a hher* ("another thing") to distinguish one comment from another, provides palpable evidence of parataxis. Even the later, homiletic *midrashim*, alleged to be coherent compositions, exhibit in their prologues the rabbinic penchant for paratactic lists.[4]

The configuration of rabbinic documents thus places each cognitive unit in a formal relation of equivalence to all others. No single halakhic dictum, exegesis, or idea (or document, for that matter) dominates all others. None is subordinate, none formally set off as the epitome of all wisdom and truth. Rather, all stand, as it were, next to one another in a relation of mutuality and exquisite tension. For this reason rabbinic documents read as if suspended in space, moving towards no literary or cognitive conclusion. Many of them even lack formal beginnings and endings. The paratactic construction of rabbinic documents makes their generative conceptions and foundational principles seem recondite and rabbinism's structure of ideas seem intractable and elusive. Even such devotees as E. E. Urbach point to the literature's failure to provide "a systematic treatment of . . . beliefs and opinions" and its "lack of consistency and system."[5] This claim for the prevalence of paratactic construction in rabbinic literature does not condemn its documents as chaotic, inchoate, or unsystematic. Rather, it calls attention to the absence of explicit formal hierarchy and documentary hypotaxis as a deliberate literary and rhetorical strategy that both reflects and shapes the way rabbinic Judaism sees, knows about, and experiences the world.

These substantive and literary traits all inform the presentation of persons in rabbinic documents and make the construction of portraits of ancient rabbis extremely problematic. The sources at best provide the barest hint of the relations between rabbis and the nonrabbinic social and economic world, and they thus block our perception of the rabbis at work in society. A truly critical analysis of rabbinic religious leadership becomes difficult, for without evidence of followers little of certainty can be said about leaders. The absence of biography obscures evidence of family lineage, local origin, economic status, and other marks of social identification. Indeed, rabbinic masters are never introduced, and their patronymic surnames, though known in most cases, are sparingly applied. In the documents rabbis simply appear from nowhere, speaking and arguing as if everyone knows who

---

[4] Martin Jaffee. "The Midrashic Proem," in W. S. Green, ed., *Approaches to Ancient Judaism* IV (Chico, 1983), pp. 95-112.

[5] E. E. Urbach, *The Sages: Their Concepts and Beliefs*, trans. Israel Abrahams (Jerusalem, 1975), p. 4.

they are. The absence of biography, however, hardly exhausts the problem. The picture of rabbis offered by their texts is exceedingly fragmented. The dicta and opinions assigned to, and the stories told about, any given master are nowhere collected under his name but are scattered throughout the documents, often in different versions that serve the varied purposes of compilers and redactors. In the texts rabbis routinely appear in disagreement with one another, but the tradents (those who transmit sayings) and editors who report the disputes tend not to resolve them. The conflicting opinions remain in endless juxtaposition. This strategy of representation leaves the relative importance of the opinions uninflected. It thereby suppresses evidence of authority, domination, and power among the disputants and makes all rabbis appear as equals.

Rabbinic literature is largely indifferent to the presentation of distinctive individuality. No document pays homage to a particular rabbi; none celebrates one man's virtue, reflects his thoughts, or recounts his deeds. The sources offer no museum of well-rounded rabbinic portraits, only a gallery of partial sketches and disjointed images. Rabbinic literature presents its protagonists paratactically, in pieces. It is a literature of contention without victors, in which the sense of separate existences is minimal. This massive labor of homogeneity suggests that devotion to individual masters played little role in the motivations of the men who made up the texts. In all of the literature no rabbi emerges as central, dominant, or determinative; none appears to symbolize, guide, or shape rabbinic destiny. No rabbinic text claims to be the product of the life, career, or inner struggle of a single great man. Rather, the men appear as products of the sources.

No doubt, individual rabbis achieved importance, decisively shaped rabbinic culture, and affected the lives of their contemporaries. No doubt, stories about rabbis are not wholly fabrications and falsehoods, literary inventions grounded in no historical reality. But, whatever their origin, the segments of rabbinic lives thought worthy of narration and transmission appear in their present form for purposes other than hero worship, dedication to a particular master, or a desire to recount and preserve the past.

A representative narrative illustrates these problems. The story, which appears in the Mishnah, Tractate Rosh HaShanah 2:8-9, reads:

A. Rabban Gamaliel had pictures of the shapes of the moon on a tablet and on the wall of his upper chamber, which he would show to untrained observers and say, "Did you see it like this or like that?"
B. It happened that two came and said, "We saw it in the east in the morning and in the west in the evening."
C. Said R. Yohanan b. Nuri, "They are false witnesses."
D. When they came to Yavneh, Rabban Gamaliel accepted them.

E. And again two came and said, "We saw it at its [expected] time, but on the next night it did not appear."
F. And Rabban Gamaliel accepted them.
G. Said R. Dosa b. Harkinas, "They are false witnesses."
H. "How can they testify that a woman has given birth when the next day her belly is between her teeth?"
I. R. Joshua said to him, "I approve your words."
J. Rabban Gamaliel sent a message to him: "I decree that you shall come before me with your staff and your money on the day that falls as the Day of Atonement according to your reckoning."
K. R. Aqiba went and found him upset.
L. He said to him, "I am able to learn that whatever Rabban Gamaliel has done is done,
M. "as it is written, *These are the appointed seasons of the Lord, the holy assemblies which you shall proclaim* (Leviticus 23:4), Whether in their time or not in their time, I have no other appointed seasons but these."
N. He came to R. Dosa b. Harkinas.
O. He said to him, "If we come to judge the court of Rabban Gamaliel, we will have to judge each and every court that has stood from the days of Moses until now,
P. "as it is written, *Moses went up with Aaron, Nadav, and seventy of the elders of Israel* (Exodus 24:9). And why were the names of the elders not made explicit? Rather, it is to teach that each and every [group of] three who stood as a court over Israel, lo, they are like the court of Moses."
Q. And he took his staff and his money in his hand and went to Yavneh on the day that fell as the Day of Atonement according to his reckoning.
R. Rabban Gamaliel stood up and kissed him on the head.
S. He said to him, "Come in peace, my master and my disciple—my master in wisdom, and my disciple, since you have accepted my words."

This account is particularly useful since it reports an alleged historical event with political consequences for the rabbinic movement. It also treats an issue crucial in the history of Judaism, the determination of the sacred calendar after the destruction of the Jerusalem temple.

In Judaism the yearly calendar is calculated according to the sun, but the months, and therefore the dates of the annual holy days, are determined by the appearance of the moon. Before the fall of the Jerusalem temple in A.D. 70, the priests proclaimed the sacred times of the year. In the aftermath of the temple's destruction, the new rabbinic movement appropriated that priestly task to itself. This story reports a conflict on this issue between Gamaliel II, the patriarch and ostensible leader of the rabbis at Yavneh, and two other Yavnean masters, Dosa b. Harkinas and Joshua b. Hananiah.

The story, as well edited as any in rabbinic literature, can be divided into three substantively related but formally unintegrated segments, A, B-D, and E-S. A sets the stage and supplies the halakhic topic of the pericope, the examination of witnesses about the appearance of the nem moon. B-D is a brief prelude to the longer account at E-S. In B-D Gamaliel examines two witnesses and accepts their testimony, presumably for the beginning of a new month, despite the objection of Yohanan b. Nuri. In the barrenness of B-D, so typical of rabbinic narratives, we are told the rationale neither for Yohanan b. Nuri's judgment nor for Gamaliel's rejection of it. The opinions simply are juxtaposed without being brought into explicit interaction.

At issue in both B-D and E-I is the correct evaluation of testimony about the new moon. Gamaliel accepts even irregular testimony. Yohanan b. Nuri and Dosa b. Harkinas oppose such practice and are supplied with identical language. At no point in either B-D or E-I does anyone deny or even question the patriarch's authority to proclaim the dates of festivals. The addition of Joshua's comment at I does not change matters; the issue still is not who decides but how one decides. At J this matter is dropped, never to be resolved, and the focus of concern abruptly shifts to the question of patriarchal authority. The issue is not who is right but who is in charge. Gamaliel commands Joshua to violate what the latter regards as the correct Day of Atonement.

Aqiba's appearance at K-M is a surprise. He plays no role in the disagreement, and his apparent support of the patriarch on this matter conflicts with the testimony of Mishnah Rosh HaShanah 1:6, in which he attempts to prevent witnesses from testifying before him. K-M obviously is an intrusion into the narrative.

According to N, Joshua goes to Dosa. The identity of the speaker at O-P is unclear, but H. Albeck supposes it to be Dosa.[6] This reading is questionable since the ruling against Gamaliel is attributed to Dosa, not Joshua. Q-S complete the narrative. The actor at Q must be Joshua, for the language at Q is identical to that of J. At R-S Gamaliel appears the magnanimous victor.

The uncertain identity of the speaker at O calls attention to Joshua's place in the story. His name and words appear only once, at I, where he affirms Dosa's judgment. After that, he becomes an invisible figure whose presence is never made explicit. Talmudic literature contains many accounts of Joshua's opposition to Gamaliel, the most famous of which tells of Gamaliel's deposition from the patriarchate. In such cases Joshua typically propounds his own opinion, which is reported in his own name. His role here, then, is highly unusual, and this suggests that his name has been inserted into an earlier account of a

---

[6] H. Albeck, *Shishah Sidré Mishnah. Seder Mo'ed* (Jerusalem-Tel-Aviv, 1958), p. 317.

Gamaliel-Dosa dispute. Dosa b. Harkinas is an obscure figure who appears only eleven times in the Mishnah. At Mishnah Ketuvot 13:1-2, however, he sides with priestly authority in civil matters, and after A.D. 70 he may have represented priestly claims in religious matter as well. If so, then the earlier account on which this version is based, something like E-G, J, and Q, would have been a straightforward story about Gamaliel's dominance of the priestly party after 70. If this be the case, then the addition of Joshua and Aqiba to the account has preserved the plot of the original, something difficult to alter if the earlier version were well known, but the addition has dramatically redirected the implications of the plot. This analysis, which is necessarily speculative because of the nature of the sources, shows the difficulty of constructing the historical background of rabbinic texts. Even if accurate, it does not explain what the narrative is about. Let us return to the story in its present form and read it as a whole.

In a conventional narrative about Gamaliel, G would precede F, on the model of B-D. The reversal of those elements here establishes that the point at issue is Gamaliel's ruling. At G Dosa demurs, and the graphic imagery supplied at H, a common rabbinic expression, adds bite to his judgment. Gamaliel cannot be right. At I Joshua endorses Dosa's view, to be made the object of Gamaliel's displeasure at J. The point of J is clear; Gamaliel's decree is a blatant exercise of authority. At K Aqiba enters to find Joshua "upset." Rabbinic stories normally eschew such nonessential detail, so the description of Joshua's mood is uncharacteristic. Its presence here highlights the dispute and fixes the context for Joshua's action at the end of the story. Aqiba supports Gamaliel at L-M with the exegesis of Leviticus 23:4, but he endorses Gamaliel's position as patriarch, not his opinion. Indeed, the exegesis at M makes clear that Gamaliel is wrong. If the appointed seasons were observed "in their time," that is, properly, there would be no reason to apply the verse. Aqiba takes the verse to mean that Israel's appointed seasons are only those proclaimed by human agency, and since Gamaliel is the recognized leader of the rabbis what he "has done is done," whether or not it conforms to the times revealed by nature. Aqiba's conclusion is presented as the result of intellection; it is something he has been "able to learn."

N-P contains the exchange between Joshua and Dosa, but the identity of the speaker is unclear. In the flow of the narrative the words at O-P make better sense if said by Joshua than to him. Since at K-L Aqiba "went" and "said," N-O ought to read likewise. Joshua, therefore, goes to Dosa to withdraw his support and offer his reasons. His rationale and the exegesis of Exodus 24:9 assume the existence of a line of rabbinic courts that extends back to Moses. If the decision of one court can be held open to question, then so can the decisions of all courts—a procedure that would undermine the coherence and credibility of rabbinic (self-)government. The issue in O-P, then, is the welfare of the rabbinic movement not the correctness of Gamaliel's opinion.

At Q-S Joshua goes to Gamaliel in apparent submission and is received with generosity. Gamaliel rises to greet him, a gesture of respect, and welcomes him warmly. But the words of greeting assigned to him blunt the effect of his victory. Joshua is both "master" and "disciple," at best an ambiguous status. By calling Joshua his "master in wisdom" (in the story's context a clear reference only to the halakhic conflict between them), Gamaliel implicitly acknowledges the error of his own decision. Joshua is Gamaliel's "disciple" by virtue of his acceptance of the latter's words, but the exegesis at O-P leaves no doubt that Joshua's "discipleship" is voluntary, motivated neither by fear of nor personal devotion to Gamaliel, nor by regard for his halakhic acumen, but by a concern for the solidarity of rabbinic collectivity.

In the end it is not clear who has won. Joshua and Gamaliel are both "master" and "disciple" to one another, a relation that blurs any hierarchy. Gamaliel's position remains intact, but his authority results from Joshua's refusal to judge his court, not from Gamaliel's qualities of intellect, charisma, or power. Indeed, it could be argued that the real hero of the narrative is Joshua, and secondarily Aqiba. It is Joshua who is able to suppress his correct opinion for the sake of the collective welfare, and it is Aqiba who calls the matter to his attention.[7]

Although doubtless grounded in some event of conflict between the new Yavnean patriarch and other rabbis, the story actually says little about it. We do not know where or when the conflict took place, and we are told nothing of its broader social, religious, or political ramifications. Indeed, its very presence in the Mishnah, in the midst of legal rulings and disputations, suggests that rabbinic authorities did not want such consequences as part of their record. The protagonists appear in a skeletal and paratactic narrative framework that allows characters to be added to the story without altering the plot. They speak in clipped, truncated phrases that may indicate what they think but expose nothing of why they think it. The motives, passions, reasons, and principles that make the conflict possible are wholly obscured. Finally, from J onwards the protagonists are identified by pronouns whose antecedents are not clear. As readers we cannot be certain who speaks and who listens, but this ambiguity obstructs neither the story's progress nor its intelligibility. At one level, then, although the narrative includes the names of Gamaliel, Dosa, Aqiba and Joshua, it really is

---

[7] For somewhat different analyses of this passage, see Shamai Kanter, *Rabban Gamaliel II: The Legal Traditions* (Chico, 1980), pp. 107-11, and my *The Traditions of* (copy illegible).

about no one in particular. Its images consequently tell us less about life as lived than abOut life as imagined.

But if this story tells us little about history as we would like to know it, it does reveal much abOut the contours and values of rabbinic culture and religion. It portrays rabbis as heirs and, for their own time, equivalents of Moses. To judge one of their courts is, of necessity, to judge the court of Moses. Rabbis, not God, fix the boundaries of sacred time, and he has "no other appointed seasons but these." The story exposes a powerful recognition that the rabbis are creating something new in their culture, something they, not God, are responsible to maintain. The persistence of that creation depends on the voluntary cooperation and mutuality of numbers of rabbis and can be destroyed by contrary attitudes and behaviors. In such a context no rabbi can appear to dominate others, and disputes among rabbis must be resolved without humiliation to any party. In this narrative, the medium for such resolution is the exercise of intellect. Joshua changes his mind neither because he fears Gamaliel's power nor because he respects the person of Aqiba. He does so because of the exegesis Aqiba has "learned." In idealized rabbinic life it is through the discipline of "learning" that the sharp and projecting edges of individuality and ego are blunted, controlled, and directed in pursuit of some larger goal.

The attempt to describe the rabbis of antiquity yields a result disappointing for conventional history but fruitful for the study of culture. The virtual anonymity of persons in rabbinic literature reveals a powerful cultural disinclination, perhaps an incapacity, to construe rabbinic culture and religion as the work of powerful individuals. It is as if, when they came to put their story down on paper, rabbis could not bring themselves to tell it, and therefore were unable to imagine it, in terms of themselves. In rabbinic documents there is no place for the expression of private ego, no room for the imposing, charismatic personality, and no occasion for the emergence of any single, great man who represents the fate and destiny of the many in his own life and person.

As we have seen, the content of rabbinic documents virtually certifies that they were produced for an internal audience. They are of rabbis, by rabbis, and for rabbis; they constitute a rabbinic conception of rabbinic culture, composed for itself and addressed to itself. Rabbinic texts present their contents, whether halakhic teaching or images of persons, in pieces, in fluid paratactic literary frameworks that exhibit little temporal dimension. Rabbinic discourse shields itself from intellectual penetration by others; it is the work of a group bounded and set apart. It would be derelict to claim that these texts existed in precisely their present form throughout rabbinic antiquity. The diachronic range of most documents indicates that their production is not contemporary with the events described and the persons depicted in their pages. But it also is gratuitous to argue that the present form of the texts is unrelated to or at variance with the ways their contents initially were composed, received, transmitted, and redacted. Rather, the generations of rabbis who produced, preserved, accepted, and believed the materials contained in rabbinic documents apparently found this mode of depicting reality credible. Unless we suppose all of rabbinic writing to be one massive literary artifice, we must assume that to some degree the texts reflect and conform to rabbinic experience of and in the world.

This proposition can be tested by a consideration of some aspects of rabbinic social life. Unfortunately, because of the character of the sources, our knowledge of the inner workings of rabbinic society is likely always to be fairly schematic. Rabbinic social life in Palestine after 200 remains substantially unexplored. But the data about Sasanian Babylonia and Roman Palestine before 200 have been critically analyzed, and some conclusions are possible. In a meticulous philological examination of academic terminology in the Babylonian Talmud, David Goodblatt has shown that Babylonian rabbinic instruction was effected through disciple-circles rather than schools.[8] Rabbinic disciples apparently did not attend institutions with corporate identities but clustered around individual masters whom they served, at least in part, as apprentice lawyers. Rabbinic disciples could change teachers either for intellectual or personal reasons. Masters could be abusive and demanding, and some had acquired special expertise in particular subjects. Martin Goodman's work on Roman Palestine suggests that the model of disciple-circles applies there as well.[9]

The picture of a network of relatively autonomous disciple-circles suggests that in order to attract students rabbis had to be figures of forceful personality and distinctive individuality. But the very possibility that students could change teachers at will, the apparent movement of disciples among masters, implies a system of social relations in which all rabbis theoretically were equivalent to one another. In a world of face-to-face relationships in which rabbis had to compete with one another for students, no master could fail to be aware of his colleagues' skills, and none could escape public scrutiny within the movement. In such a system individual claims to special power and authority are easily refuted and rendered fragile.

Hints that the realities of rabbinic social life restrained rabbinic claims to special power and encouraged the literary suppression of individuality also appear in the rabbis' treatment of themselves as mira-

---

[8] David M. Goodblatt, *Rabbinic Instruction in Sasanian Babylonia* (Leiden, 1975).
[9] Martin Goodman, *State and Society in Roman Palestine: 120-200* (Totowa, N.J., 1983).

cle-workers. During the first two centuries, charismatic types who claimed miraculous powers were antithetical to and played little role in rabbinism. God could perform miracles, but rabbis could not. By the middle of the third century that picture had changed, and miracle-power became a conventional component in the rabbinical dossier.[10] This shift corresponds to a general development among religious virtuosi in the late Roman world. The third century is witness to the emergence of a class of charismatic individuals, holy men, "friends of God," who claim a special power, an intimate relation with the divine, that definitively sets them off from other men.[11] In late antique Christianity and paganism this claim accompanies a vigorous expression of individuality and is recounted in individual lives, in the literary portraiture of hagiography. In rabbinism, however, miracle-working does not generate hagiography and appears not to have had the socially disruptive effects it did in pagan and Christian manifestations.

This difference, rabbinism's failure to adopt the pagan and Christian model and portray itself to itself in terms of great and powerful individuals, is partly a function of the social system sketched above. But it also is a consequence of the distinctly intellectual character of the rabbinic enterprise. Whatever personal traits, whatever magnetism or charisma, a rabbi possessed, his standing and credibility within the rabbinic movement initially depended on his learning. Rabbinical status derived not from the exercise of mysterious and arbitrary divine favor but from the result of intellectual labor. Whatever else being a rabbi meant, it meant the publicly demonstrable mastery of a considerable body of Scripture and halakhic material. Rabbis did not hide from one another in the desert, nor did they seclude themselves behind cloister walls. The evidence of the sources suggests that they lived in a world of persistent mutual scrutiny, a world of continual evaluation and judgment. In such a world rabbis could not help but be aware of their mortality and could not possibly maintain the illusion of special power, at least, and especially, among themselves.

The rabbis of antiquity constituted a recognized group of intellectual specialists in ancient Jewish society. But despite their claims to control Israel's destiny, they lacked the political power to direct their society or to enforce the myriad *halakot* and scriptural interpretations they believed held the key to its redemption. Their literature's manifest lack of interest in that society suggests its reciprocal lack of interest in them. In the absence of real power, rabbis exerted what

---

[10] See Jacob Neusner, *A History of the Jews in Babylonia* (Leiden, 1969), 4:344-69, and my "Palestinian Holy Men: Charismatic Leadership and Rabbinic Tradition," in W. Haase and H. Temporini, eds., *Aufstieg und Niedergang der Römischen Welt* (Berlin, 1979), 19.2, pp. 619-47.

[11] Peter Brown, *The Making of Late Antiquity* (Cambridge and London, 1978).

influence they could but devoted themselves primarily to forging their own collective identity. The bulk of their literature is recondite and insular, bespeaking the shared privacy of the initiated. Its obsession with detailed scriptural exegesis and halakhic disputation means that rabbis needed each other as an audience. Their sense of social credibility and group membership, therefore, in large measure depended on how they treated one another. To alienate a colleague by arrogance, humiliation, or claims to special power was to risk losing an audience and consigning the work of collective identity to failure. Peter Brown's observations about the *philotimia* of Antonine city life could apply with equal force to the rabbis of antiquity.

> Elites tend to maintain a set of strong invisible boundaries, which mark firm upward limits to the aspirations of individuals, and to direct the aspirations of their members to forms of achievement that could potentially be shared by all other members of the peer group. In a peer group, therefore, forms of individual achievement, like wealth, are there to be spent, not hoarded. Those who accumulate too much to themselves are cut down to size in no uncertain manner, if not by the envy of their fellows, then, at least by the ineluctable envy of death . . . Men committed to constant competition within a "model of parity" are not likely to allow any one of their peers to draw heavily on sources of power and prestige over which they have no control. Appeals to the other world as a source of special status had to be kept within strictly conventional limits if they were to be acceptable.[12]

All these values are manifested in the formal traits of rabbinic literature and in the narrative we examined above. That story is neither a report of a historical event "as it actually happened" nor an account about Gamaliel, Mishnah, Dosa, or Aqiba as individuals. Rather, it is an idealized model of rabbinic behavior, a culturally determined construction of how rabbinic society ought to operate. The search for the rabbis of antiquity, then, suggests a degree of conformity among the ways rabbis lived with one another, imagined one another, and represented one another in their literature. It leads not into the lives and careers of great men but into a self-absorbed community of intellectuals who competed with each other but needed each other and strove to maintain at least the illusion of each other's dignity.[13]

---

[12] Ibid., p. 35.
[13] My thanks are due to Professors Fitz John Porter Poole. Gary G. Porton, Eugene D. Genovese, Elizabeth Fox-Genovese, Geza Vermes, and Martin Goodman for insights I could not have gained on my own and for helping to develop the theoretical aspects of this problem.

CHAPTER NINE

History Transcended: The Mishnaic Uses of the Past

Jacob Neusner

Often called "the talmudic age," because of one of the paramount documents of Judaism that emerged in ca. A.D. 700, the period from the first through the seventh centuries, while rich in historical crises, produced for Judaism an essentially ahistorical canon. The traits of that canon tell us the conception of history of those who wrote it and perhaps also suggest ideas concerning history that were broadly familiar to those who received it, obeyed its laws, and adopted its theology. There are two ways of describing traits of historical sense characteristic of the authoritative writings of Judaism that emerged in the period at hand. The first is to ask whether and how the canonical writings contain historically useful information. What kind of history can we locate within the principal writings of the age? The answer to that question will provide perspective on the historical perspectives and doctrines of the authorships of those writings themselves. The sorts of information they chose to preserve, the ways in which through historical reflection and consequent narrative they represented and explained the world as they knew it—these will be contained to begin within the way things that happened are represented. And one effective way for us accurately to assess the historical interest and perspective of a writing is to attempt to use that writing for historical purposes ourselves. That is why we shall begin with an account of the type of historical data the canonical writings of talmudic times present, only then turning to the modes of historical thought and reflection revealed in the more important of those same sources.

We read the canonical books first as historical sources of their own time, then as accounts of how history was written at that time, for a simple reason. Keen interest in things that have happened and what they mean, an effort to tell in a reasonably careful and accurate way what happened in their own day or in times past—these evidences of a powerful historical sense, such as we find in the Old Testament, will then point toward one set of conclusions. The absence will suggest a different set. The second is to assess the role of the past in indicative documents of the system of Judaism and of the age at hand, finding out how events are understood and interpreted, how considerable a role (if any) is assigned to history and the lessons of history in major writings. For that purpose we consider two principal documents, the Mishnah, ca. A.D. 200, an essentially ahistorical philosophical system in the form of a law-code, and the Talmud of the Land of Israel, the first of the two Talmuds of ancient times, ca. A.D. 400, a profoundly historical statement presented as a commentary to the Mishnah. We first treat the Talmud[1] as a historical source, with attention, also, to how the document is used today for that purpose, and then, in the second and third parts that follow, we move to the doctrine of history in principal talmudic writings.

I. The Talmudic Sense for History and the Talmud as a Source for History

A subdivision of the vast realm of historical learning marked off solely by information contained in a particular book finds the definition of its program and tasks in the pages of that book. The field of historical study bearing the adjective "talmudic" covers the age in which the talmudic canon took shape and to which it refers. That field of history attends to the places in which the people of that document flourished. So the time and place conform to the limits set by the principal source of historical study. The boundaries of topics, too, fall within the bindings of one book. Now to those who study other realms of historical learning, the one at hand must appear artificial, merely theological. In general people define a range of historical inquiry through limits posed by geography, political change to denote beginnings and endings, surely in addition national or ethnic traits that include some and exclude others. More to the point, the pertinent historical information will derive from many different sources, not from a single book. Accordingly, anyone opening a book of history will find puzzling the particular sort of historical study under way here.

---

[1] By "the Talmud" therefore it is clear I mean not merely the second Talmud, the one called the Bavli or Talmud of Babylonia, ca. A.D. 600, but the entire canon of writings of the Jewish sages of Babylonia and the Land of Israel ("Palestine"), a canonical corpus beginning with the Mishnah, closed at ca. A.D. 200, and ending with the Talmud of Babylonia, completed at ca. A.D. 600. These documents to be sure refer to events spread over a longer period of time, specifically from the creation of the world onward to the end of history. They cover, in their scope of commentary, things that are supposed to have happened through much of the known world of their day. But in chronology, the account becomes particular to the first-hand knowledge of its authors and editors at ca. A.D. 70 or so, and, in geographical area, it covers the affairs of the Jews in the specified provinces, the one under Iranian, the other under Roman, rule.

Specifically, such a person will ask what sort of history may bear the adjective "talmudic," as distinct from "American," "medieval," or "African," thus national, chronological, or regional, not to mention economic, social, or political. Indeed, who has ever heard of a field of historical study defined by a particular book, unless it is what is in said book that is studied, e.g., Constitutional history or the history of New England seen through Cotton Mather's sermons!

Talmudic history—that is to say, the kind of historical perspective found within the canonical writings of Judaism in late antiquity—cannot be said to deal with great affairs, vast territories, movements of men and nations, much that really mattered then. Even the bulk of the women and men of Israel, the Jewish nation wherever they lived, in the time of the composition of the canonical writings at hand, by the testimony of the authors themselves fall outside of the frame of reference. Most Jews appeared to the sages at hand to ignore—in the active sense of willfully not knowing—exactly those teachings that seemed to the authors critical. To use the mythic language, when God revealed the Torah to Moses at Mount Sinai, he wrote down part, which we now have in the Hebrew Scripture ("the Old Testament"), and he repeated the other part in oral form, so that Moses memorized it and handed it on to Joshua, and then, generation by generation, to the contemporary sages. The contemporaries of the sages did not know the oral half of the Torah, only sages did, and that by definition. Only sages knew the whole of the Torah of Moses. So, it follows, the talmudic corpus preserves the perspective of a rather modest component of the nation under discussion. How could we define a subject less likely to attract broad interest than the opinions of a tiny minority of a nation, about the affairs of an unimportant national group living in two frontier provinces on either side of a contested frontier? Apart from learning from these modest folk, some facts about life on the contested frontier of the ancient world—and that was only the one that separated Rome from Iran, the others being scarcely frontiers in any political sense—what is to be learned here that anyone would want to know must prove puzzling.

Self-evidently, we cannot expect to find stories of great events, a continuous narrative of things that happened to a nation in war and in politics. The Jews, as it happens, both constituted a nation and sustained a vigorous political life. But the documents of the age under discussion treat these matters only tangentially and as part of the periphery of a vision of quite other things. But if *manifest* history scarcely passes before us, a rich and complex world of *latent* history—the long-term trends and issues of a society and its life in imagination and emotion—does lie ready at hand. For the talmudic canon reports to us a great deal about what a distinctive group of people were thinking about issues that turn out to prove perennial and universal, and, still more inviting, the documents tell us not only what people thought but how they reasoned. That is something to which few historians gain access, I mean, the philosophical processes behind political and social and religious policy, class struggle, and popular contention. For people do think things out and reach conclusions, and for the most part, long after the fact, we know only the decisions they made. Here, by contrast, we hear extended discussions, of a most rigorous and philosophical character, on issues of theory and of thought. In these same discussions, at the end, we discover how people decided what to do and why. That sort of history—the history of how people made up their minds—proves particularly interesting when we consider the substance of the story. The Jews in the provinces and age at hand adopted the policies put forward by the sages who wrote the sources we consider. The entire subsequent world history of the Jews—their politics, social and religious world, the character of the inner life and struggle of their community-nation—refers back to the decisions made at just this time and recorded in the Talmud.

The talmudic corpus stands in a long continuum of thought and culture, stretching back, through the biblical literature for well over a thousand years. Seeing how a collegium of active intellectuals—for the Talmud bears no mark of individual authorship—mediated between their own age and its problems and the authority and legacy of a vivid past teaches lessons about continuities of culture and society not readily available elsewhere. For their culture had endured, prior to their own day, for a longer span of time than separates us from the Magna Charta, on the one side, and Beowulf, on the other. If these revered documents of our politics and culture enjoyed power to define politics and culture today, we should grasp the sort of problem confronting the Talmud's sages. For, after all, the Talmud imagined as normative a society with little in common with that confronting the sages—isolated, independent, free-standing, and not—as sages' Israel was—assimilated in a vast world-empire, autonomous and subordinate, and dependent upon others near and far. Yet these two aspects of the history emergent from the talmudic corpus, while of broad and suggestive interest, scarcely persuade someone primarily interested in historical study, rather than continuities and changes in culture and society, that the document at hands demands sustained attention in particular as a problem for historians. What does is the simple fact that the Talmud provides a striking example, for close analysis, of a problem of acute interest in historical debates even in our own day. I refer to the debates on how we study not the individual but human societies, organized groups, that engage historians from the *Annales* of the 1920s through *Social Science History* today.

History Transcended   161

In describing and interpreting the life of peoples, we seek to generalize about attitudes and shared conceptions, using the French word, "mentalité," for example, to explain that about which we speak. Specifically, we want to know how people form a shared conception of themselves, so as to see themselves as a group, and how, further, what they conceive in common relates to how they each, as individuals, confront and experience life. Louise A. Tilly frames matters in terms of shared emotions and, citing Lucien Febvre, founder, with Marc Bloch, of the *Annales*, quotes Febvre as follows:

> [Emotions] imply relations between men, collective relationships. They are doubtless born within the organic depths specific to a given individual ... [B]ut their expression is the result of a series of experiences of common life, or similar and contemporaneous reactions to the shock of identical situations and encounters of the same nature ... [L]ittle by little ... by linking many participants in turn as initiators and followers—[these] end by becoming a system of interindividual motivations that differ according to circumstances and situations ... [and] a true system of emotions is built. They become something like an institution.[2]

Febvre copes with the deep problems of how peoples' emotions so take shape as to fit a common pattern. That is why he speaks of experiences of common life, identical situations, encounters of the same nature. Now if we take up the same issue in terms framed not of feelings but of the ideas and doctrines that give expression to attitudes and feelings, we find ourselves raising exactly the same questions.

The thesis at hand, that collective relationships expressed through mutually comprehensible emotions emerge from not what is specific to the given individual but what is shared and common pertains all the more so. Specifically, in the talmudic corpus we take up the social expression of attitudes. We turn then to matters of doctrines and institutions, and issues of governance of groups based on a compact of common values. These all together constitute politics, for the secular world, and theology, for the religious one. In the setting of Judaism, with its interest in what people do as much as in what they think, the whole reaches the surface of everyday life in what we call *halakhah*, the rules and laws of life. If, then, we can trace the context of consensus and the progress through which consensus is achieved, we find ourselves providing an exceptionally suggestive example for the inquiry into the interplay between the individual and the group, specifically the formation of collective attitudes out of individual experiences.

What sort of history then? Not manifest but latent, not political but interior, not public but the perspective of a single class of persons, spe-

---

[2] "People's History and Social Science History" (*Social Science History* 1983:7,458).

cifically, sages. But the sages who wrote and preserved the books addressed a large world, and, as a matter of fact, exercised a measure of influence and authority in that world. Accordingly, in the talmudic corpus we have the end-result of half a millennium of the process of attaining concurrence, the achievement of what was at first a caste and class consensus but what was at the end a national compact and agreement. Israel, the Jewish people, in late antiquity produced a minority, the sages under discussion, which to begin with coalesced on its own, and then won adherence to its views, through coercion and persuasion alike, among the nation as a whole. So when we ask what sort of history we may expect from the sources at hand, we find a remarkably relevant sort of discourse. We deal with an example of the long-term formation of collective doctrine, social theory shared among people in diverse times and places, subject to transmission, moreover, from the special circumstances in which the theory took shape to distant and wholly other conditions confronted by the Jewish nation later on. The sources at hand come down from late antiquity because people agreed to copy and preserve them. They came to that agreement because what they found in the sources laid claim on truth and authority. The fundamental theses of the sources attained that status of utter self-evidence that made possible debate on everything but the fundamental issues. These were settled in late antiquity. Where, when, how they were settled, what sort of "experiences of common life, of similar and contemporaneous reactions to the shock of identical situations and encounters of the same nature," in Febvre's language, produced these components of a common consensus and endowed them with self-evidence—these are the issues at hand.

In the conditions of contemporary debate on the nature of historical study, the interest in generalization and the analysis of collectivities, the concern for comparison of group to group, the interest in small details and how these typify large trends, the concern for politics and the influence of ideology—in these conditions the talmudic historian finds remarkably relevant what in itself is remote, particular, and rather special. What we have is a collective biography of a well-organized political and religious estate. But the constant reference to individual opinion characteristic of the sources at hand allows for attention to the individual as well. The vigorous debate, the close study of modes of argument as much as of the substance, likewise allow us to address the formation of shared modes of thought. *Self-evidence*, in the documents at hand, is not conferred by politics alone but achieved by argument. Professor Tilly concludes her article with the following words:

> The genius of social science history is twofold. First, its central

method—collective biography of one kind or another—preserves individual variability while identifying dominant social patterns. Second, its focus on social relationships rather than psychological states remains our surest guarantee of reconstructing how ordinary people of the past lived out their days and made the choices that cumulate into history. Social science history, properly conceived, is the ultimate people's history.

So far as we wish to trace collective biography, our documents exemplify precisely the sort of sources that make that work feasible. So far as we take up the issues of social relationships, both within a social group and also between that group and the outsider, the sources of the talmudic canon address precisely the issue at hand. That is why I claim that, by criteria of contemporary historical debate, the kind of history that bears the adjective "talmudic" and that emerges from a rather circumscribed body of sources indeed falls smack in the center of historical learning today.

Proceeding from the explanation of why the species *talmudic* belongs in the genus *history* to the logical next question, we ask ourselves just what sort of history we may expect to uncover. The Talmud and related literature contain two sorts of historical information: first, stories about events within an estate of clerks; second, data on the debates of those who produced the Talmud. How are these to be used for historical purposes? It is important to specify what those purposes are. We must at the outset recognize that there are many kinds of information we simply do not have, and never shall have, on Jews and Judaism in late antiquity. The Talmud contains very little information on such questions, for instance, as the nature of the inner life, the consciousness and personal hopes of Jews of the day. It has no autobiographical materials, no record of what people thought and felt as private individuals. No one person stands behind a simple sentence. All has been refracted through a shared prism. The whole is a public record, publicly redacted and communally, hence politically, transmitted. Few individuals play a manifest part in the redaction of their own thoughts, much less in their transmission. The absence of records of individual life means that we cannot ask questions about the motives of individuals, their feelings and intentions—the essence of historical inquiry. But there is, in compensation, the record of this collectivity, and, as I have argued, that permits a remarkably contemporary kind of historical study. In the terms of Brian Stock, what we have is the inner history of a textual community.[3]

Our information on various kinds or groups of Jews, moreover, is limited. The Talmud is not a historical document and was never intended as such. It is the record of the laws and logic, exegesis and

---

[3] Brian Stock, *Implications of Literacy* (Princeton, 1986: Princeton University Press).

episodic theology, of a relatively small group of Jews. One may estimate that about three hundred names of Babylonian Amoraim are mentioned, yet we may guess that a minimum of two hundred thousand, and probably more like half a million, Jews lived in Babylonia and Mesopotamia in Parthian and Sasanian times. Whatever judgments one may make about the rabbis' being "normative" or "more significant" than others are fundamentally theological, not historical. Moreover, when we take seriously the facts of rabbinical life—that the rabbis lived within a relatively limited institutional framework, somewhat like the contemporary monastic communities of Mesopotamian and Babylonian Christianity—we may wonder how much what we do know represents what we do not know. Whatever archaeological data we have of the same place and period—the Dura synagogue and the magical bowls—bear little obvious relationship to what we learn in the Talmud. So we cannot ask a great many questions about Jews who are other than rabbis, except in relationship to the rabbis themselves.

The third and most important specification is this: We must at the outset isolate and identify the *viewpoint* of the texts we study and attempt to separate ourselves from that viewpoint for the purposes of historical inquiry. We must always wonder, *Cui bono?* Who is served? What interest advanced? If we neglect to do so, we simply repeat, in modern language, the viewpoint of our sources, rather than attempt to understand and evaluate that viewpoint. When, for example, we concentrate attention on the issues set by the texts, when we merely generalize in historical language the specific stories and ideas presented by the text, then we are doing little more than repeating what is before us in the same propagandistic, tendentious, and partisan spirit in which it was originally composed. This will not serve any useful purpose, for if all we hope for from history is to participate in the world-view of the documents that supply us with information, why study history at all? Why not remain in the tradition of the classical and modern exegetes, who may add their episodic philological *hiddushim* but contribute nothing new and comprehend nothing more than they are told by the discrete texts they study?

What purposes then do we have in reading the Talmud and its canon for the writing of history? It will not suffice, alas, to say we want to know just how things were. This is naive, since "things" encompass information about trivialities as well as important matters. We must confess at the outset the values and interests shaping our mind and imagination and isolate what we regard as important issues. We must criticize those values and interests. And then we may proceed to the historical problems. What we must seek to know is not just how things were, but just how those things were which interest us, and which the documents in their present state may reveal. What interests us is, naturally, a reflection of our, and not their, situation. So the *we* is decisive. And we who read the Talmud for historical purposes are modern historians, who want to know things of no interest whatever to classical Jews, or who want to know the same things but in different ways, in ways congruent to our knowledge and understanding of all aspects of reality.

Yet even though certain kinds of history are not available in the talmudic writings, other kinds are. Let me then specify the type of historical writing I think the talmudic canon makes possible, since that tells us the nature of the historical sense of the authorship that speaks through this corpus of texts. What I want to know, and what I think they wanted to tell us, first, is how a community actually functioned: the dynamics of the relationships among various power-groups, and between those groups and the inchoate masses. In many ways my *History of the Jews in Babylonia*[4] is an essay not merely in historical knowledge—though that lies at the foundation of everything historians do—but an essay in power. What earlier interpreters saw as ethics I see as power. True, what they saw as objective and eternal truths I see as statements of a particular viewpoint, serving a particular group and its interest; statements reflecting the values and ideals, the imagination, of the special interest groups represented in the documents available to us. Alongside concern for power is an interest in myth: namely, the stories people told, the beliefs they held, to verify and justify the power-relationships they experienced. Why did people do what they did? We can ask many questions about ideas widely held, characteristics of specific groups; issues investigated by historians of religion: What were the beliefs that people referred to in order to understand and explain reality? What were the fundamental convictions about reality that underlay all their actions? How did they justify themselves to other people—Israel, gentiles—and before God? In line with my earlier emphasis on the record of the collective consensus of individuals, I further want to know what happened to many people so as to present as self-evident the mythic world at hand. How do we account for the formation of the consensus of myth and of power, expressed in a distinctive mode of powerful discourse, achieved in an iron-consensus within the estate of the clerks, but then, among the nation at large.

These two, then, power and myth, represent the theoretical interests of our day, these and still a third—function: how did things work? Granted the existence of power, the ability of some men to coerce others to say and do their will, either by force or, more amiably, by moving them through an internalization of values; and granted the

---

[4] Leiden, 1965-1970: E.J. Brill, I-V.

knowledge of the imagination of those men and their community, knowledge of their mythic life—granted these two, we ask ourselves, how did the system work? What defined adaptive behavior in such a power-structure? What sort of history took place? What institutions embodied the power and the myth, what programs carried them forward, what was their thrust and dynamism, and what were the events that at specific times and places embodied these abstract forces of power and of myth in historical facts?

But does the Talmud serve to answer these questions, and if so, how? What are the principles of historical knowledge by which I can justify historical results? First, it seems to me important to form a view of the whole, rather than to allow oneself to be paralyzed by the exegesis and eisegesis of the discrete texts within the whole that historians supposed were historical, primarily because of their contents and themes. And that brings us to the unhappy issue of the uncritical uses, for historical purposes, made of the talmudic corpus because of a fundamental misunderstanding of the nature of that corpus. That misunderstanding was in two elements. First, the earlier generations of historians reading the Talmud, as well as many in our own time, assume that the rabbinic authorships cared about what really happened on any particular occasion and wrote that down because they cared; they also assumed that a biographical interest sustained the authorships at hand.[5] Earlier historians of the Talmud took for granted that what a man was said to do is what actually was done. What was attributed to him is what he really said. What people claimed happened actually took place. And the record before us is the accurate, detailed, account of what *really* was said and done. The legal scholar or textual exegete is interested in the content of the texts; it would not matter to him or her whether a man *really* said what is attributed to him, for he wants to know the legal principles at issue and to trace the rabbis' discussion of those principles through legal literature. The literary critic—and the classical scholars produced brilliant literary criticism of a kind—takes the text at face value. He so concentrates on the meaning of words and sentences and their relationships to other words and sentences, that he cannot but accept their content as true. The exegesis and explication of texts, whether by Talmudists or by Biblical schol-

---

[5] See in this connection William Scott Green, "What's In a Name? The Problematic of Rabbinic 'Biography,'" *Approaches to Ancient Judaism: Theory and Practice*, ed. William Scott Green (Chico, 1978: Scholars Press for Brown Judaic Studies), pp. 77-98. That essay buried the possibility of writing biographies of talmudic rabbis. It has since entered the canon of learning in this field, unfortunately not along with the name of the author; Peter Schäfer, "Research into Rabbimic Literature," *Journal of Jewish Studies* 37 (1986), 139-152, provides a fine reprise of Green's arguments and ideas, without crediting him with having originally presented them.

ars, in the very nature of things, tend to produce a fundamentalist spirit.[6]

But if it is time to attempt a critical characterization of the whole, and abandon the gullible reprise and paraphrase of suggestive parts, what to characterize? Here we need to locate questions both pertinent to our own imagination and appropriate to the Talmud. These questions obviously could not concern what the Talmud purports to tell: Was Aqiba really ignorant until he was forty? Did Rabbah b. Nahmani really get taken up to heaven because his Torah was needed in the heavenly academy? On the other hand, the Talmud does accurately tell what those responsible for compiling it thought about the world around them. It contains substantial materials given *en passant*, not in a polemical or tendentious spirit. For example, it preserves numerous reports of what rabbinical courts decided in specific cases. These seem to me to be of great historical value, for, while we may never know whether such a decision was actually made on a given day concerning a given litigation, the fact that the tradents certainly believed such decisions *could* be made is of some sociological interest. The shape of such beliefs, after all, cannot have greatly diverged from the configuration of everyday life, if no polemical or theological interest intervenes.

While the beliefs of the rabbis about times past may be of slight consequence of the description of those times, the belief of the rabbis about what they themselves did every day in their courts seems to me very important in analyzing what the courts actually did. So I do not know whether a man named Samuel really decided thus-and-so in court. But I think the conviction of the generation and school responsible for shaping the story that he had done so accurately portrays how they saw things, and therefore provides us with valuable information on how they viewed the state of their courts and the range of their authority and power. And if, further, we find evidence of a consistent picture, extending for several hundred years, we may then conclude that the courts in general could accomplish pretty much what the rabbis claimed in their behalf. If a picture of an effective court-system emerges, we may then proceed to speculate on the basis for the ability of a group of men to force others to do what they wanted. Obviously, we must take into account not only how the rabbis explained things, but also the facts known to us from quite separate sources of information. In the case of Babylonian Jewry, we need to know about the policies of successive Iranian governments toward the minority communities and *their* government, and also about other groups and

---

[6] In my *Reading and Believing: Ancient Judaism and Contemporary Gullibility* (Atlanta, 1986: Scholars Press for Brown Judaic Studies) I give numerous examples of this sort of work.

institutions within the Jewish community likely to be able to exercise authority, which are not described in much detail in rabbinical sources. When it comes to the mythic life of the rabbinical group, we are on still firmer ground, for the Talmud is a rich resource for information on how the rabbinical circles in particular viewed reality. Here again, we may well have the record only of the final period of talmudic literature. Only through specific and careful investigation can we distinguish what is peculiarly characteristic of the last group of talmudic tradents and redactors, and what also characterized earlier groups in sequence. (I suspect, for instance, that the view concerning the use of graphic images and symbols in Jewish circles probably changed during the history of ancient Judaism, and the literary evidences, when treated separately instead of as a single, unitary-*halakhic* portrait, are likely to help make sense of archaeological data.)

So far I have concentrated on the use of the Talmud's historical information about the life and times of the groups responsible for the Talmud. But what of the numerous specific stories concerning what given rabbis and other Jews actually said and did under specific circumstances—on a given day, at a given place, in a given setting—in other words, exactly the way things were? The philological fundamentalists have generally supposed that once we have established a correct text of a rabbinic work and properly interpreted its language, we then know a set of historical facts. The facticity will be proportionately greater the earlier the manuscript and the better its condition. These suppositions are correct. But these facts will concern only what the compiler of the text wished to tell us. Whether or not the original text was veracious is to be settled neither by textual criticism nor by philological inquiry, valuable though both of these ancillary sciences are for the historical inquiry.

The fundamentalists further suppose that any story, whether occurring early or late in the corpus of rabbinic literature, may well contain valuable information, handed on orally from generation to generation, until it was finally written down. I cannot accept the unexamined opinion held in rabbinical circles, both "scholarly" and traditional, that all rabbinical material was somehow sent floating into the air, if not by Moses, then by someone in remote antiquity (the Men of the Great Assembly, the generation of Jamnia); that it then remained universally available until some authority snatched it down from on high, placed his name on it, and so made it a named tradition and introduced it into the perilous processes of transmission. By this thesis nothing is older than anything else: "there is neither earlier nor later in the Torah." Synoptic studies of the traditions of Yohanan b. Zakkai and of the Pharisees before 70 indicate that versions of a story of saying appearing in later documents normally are demonstrably later than, and literarily dependent upon, versions of the same story or saying appearing in earlier documents. This is important, for it shows that what comes late is apt to be late, and what comes in an early compilation is apt to be early. Admittedly, these are no more than probabilities—extrapolations from a small number of demonstrable cases to a large number in which no demonstration is possible. But at least there are grounds for such extrapolation.

Fundamentalists' convictions about the nature of the historical evidence contained in the Talmud are likely to be false. Whether true or false, the primary conviction of fundamentalism is that the story supplies an accurate account of what actually happened. It is difficult to argue with that conviction. A study of rabbinic sources will not provide much, if any, evidence that we have eyewitness accounts or great events or stenographic records of what people actually said. On the contrary, it is anachronistic to suppose the talmudic rabbis cared to supply such information to begin with. Since they did not, and since they asserted that people had said things of which they had no sure knowledge, we are led to wonder about the pseudepigraphic mentality. By the time we hear about a speech or an event, it has already been reshaped for the purpose of transmission in the traditions. It is rarely possible to know just what, if anything, originally was said or happened. Sometimes we have an obvious gloss, which tells us the tradition originated before the time the glossator made his addition. But knowing that a tradition was shaped within half a century of the life of the man to whom it was attributed helps only a little bit. It is very difficult to build a bridge from the tradition to the event, still more difficult to cross that bridge. The fact is that the entire Talmud is a completely accurate record of the history of those who are responsible for it. But the specification of those people, the recognition of the viewpoint of a particular group, place, and time to which the Talmud's various facts pertain—these remain the fundamental task still facing those who wish to ask of the talmudic literature the kinds of questions we address to sources of a professedly historical character, even of the same time and place as that of the rabbinic literature. What we know at this point is only that the canon of Judaism represented by the two Talmuds and related writings takes slight interest in representing in a systematic and chronological, narrative way things that happened and explaining in that same systematic and essentially chronological narrative what they meant and why they happened in one way rather than in some other. So the character of the sources under study suggests that we deal with an essentially ahistorical Judaism. Nothing could be further from the truth, as we shall now see.

II. Talmudic Judaism and History: The First Stage
The Evidence of the Mishnah (CA A.D. 200)

The framers of the Mishnah, a late second century law code, which along with the Hebrew Bible, forms the foundation of Judaism as we know it, present us with a kind of historical thinking quite different from the one they, along with all Israel, had inherited in Scripture. The legacy of prophecy, apocalypse, and mythic-history ("Heilsgeschichte") handed on by the writers of the books of the Old Testament exhibits a single and quite familiar conception of history seen whole. Events bear meaning, God's message and judgment. What happens is singular, therefore, an event to be noted, and points toward lessons to be drawn for where things are heading and why. If things do not happen at random, they also do not form indifferent patterns of merely secular, social facts. What happens is important because of the meaning contained therein. That meaning is to be discovered and revealed through the narrative of what has happened. So for all forms of Judaism until the Mishnah, the writing of history serves as a form of prophecy. Just as prophecy takes up the interpretation of historical events, so historians retell these events in the frame of prophetic theses. And out of the two—historiography as a mode of mythic reflection, prophecy as a means of mythic construction—emerges a picture of future history, that is, what is going to happen. That picture, framed in terms of visions and supernatural symbols, in the end focuses, as much as do prophecy and history-writing, upon the here and now.

The upshot is simple. History consists of a sequence of one-time events, each singular, all meaningful. These events move from a beginning somewhere to an end at a foreordained goal. History moves toward eschatology, the end of history. The teleology of Israel's life finds its definition in eschatological fulfillment. Eschatology therefore constitutes not a choice within teleology, but the definition of teleology. History done in this way then sits enthroned as the queen of theological science. Events do not conform to patterns. They form patterns. What happens matters because events bear meaning, constitute history. Now, as is clear, such a conception of mythic and apocalyptic history comes to realization in the writing of history in the prophetic pattern or in the apocalyptic framework, both of them mythic modes of organizing events. We have every right to expect such a view of matters to lead people to write books of a certain sort, rather than of some other. In the case of Judaism, obviously, we should expect people to write history books that teach lessons or apocalyptic books that through pregnant imagery predict the future and record the direction and end of time. And in antiquity that kind of writing proves commonplace among all kinds of groups and characteristic of all sorts of Judaisms but one.

History Transcended

The Mishnah contains no sustained narrative whatsoever, a very few tales, and no large-scale conception of history. It organizes its system in non-historical and socially unspecific terms, lacking all precedent in prior systems of Judaism or in prior kinds of Judaic literature. Instead of narrative, it gives description of how things are done, that is, descriptive laws. Instead of reflection on the meaning and end of history, it constructs a world in which history plays little part. Instead of narratives full of didactic meaning, it provides lists of events so as to expose the traits that they share and thus the rules to which they conform. The definitive components of a historical-eschatological system of Judaism—description of events as one time happenings, analysis of the meaning and end of events, and interpretation of the end and future of singular events—none of these commonplace constituents of all other systems of Judaism (including nascent Christianity) of ancient times finds a place in the Mishnah's system of Judaism.

So the Mishnah finds no precedent in prior Israelite writings for its mode of dealing with things that happen. The Mishnah's way of identifying happenings as consequential and describing them, its way of analyzing those events it chooses as bearing meaning, its interpretation of the future to which significant events point—all those in context were unique. Yet to say that the Mishnah's system is ahistorical could not be more wrong. The Mishnah presents a different kind of history. More to the point, it revises the inherited conception of history and reshapes that conception to fit into its own system. When we consider the power of the biblical myth, the force of its eschatological and messianic interpretation of history, the effect of apocalypse, we must find astonishing the capacity of the Mishnah's framers to think in a different way about the same things. As teleology constructed outside the eschatological mode of thought in the setting of the biblical world of ancient Israel proves amazing. Let me now show some of the principal texts that contain and convey this other conception of how events become history and how history teaches lessons.

By "history," as the opening discussion makes clear, I mean not merely events, but how events are so organized and narrated as to teach (for them, theological, for us, religions-historical or social) lessons, reveal patterns, tell us what we must do and why, what will happen to us tomorrow. In that context, some events contain richer lessons than others; the destruction of the Temple of Jerusalem teaches more than a crop failure, being kidnapped into slavery more than stubbing one's toe. Furthermore, lessons taught by events—"history" in the didactic sense—follow a progression from trivial and private to consequential and public. The framers of the Mishnah explicitly refer to very few events, treating those they do mention within a focus quite separate from what happened—the unfolding of the events themselves. They rarely create or use narratives. More probative still, historical events do not supply organizing categories or taxonomic classifications. We find no tractate devoted to the destruction of the Temple, no complete chapter detailing the events of Bar Kokhba, nor even a sustained celebration of the events of the sages' own historical life. When things that have happened are mentioned, it is neither in order to narrate, nor to interpret and draw lessons from, the event. It is either to illustrate a point of law or to pose a problem of the law—always *en passent*, never in a pointed way. So when sages refer to what has happened, this is casual and tangential to the main thrust of discourse.[7] Famous events, of enduring meaning, such as the return to Zion from Babylonia in the time of Ezra and Nehemiah, gain entry into the Mishnah's discourse only because of the genealogical divisions of Israelite society into castes among the immigrants (M. Qiddushin 4:1). Where the Mishnah provides little tales or narratives, moreover, they more often treat how things in the cult are done in general than what, in particular, happened on some one day.[8] It is sufficient to refer casually to well-known incidents. Narrative, in the Mishnah's limited rhetorical repertoire, is reserved for the narrow framework of what priests and others do on recurrent occasions and around the Temple. In all, that staple of history, stories about dramatic events and important deeds, in the minds of the Mishnah's jurisprudents provide little nourishment. Events, if they appear at all, are treated as trivial. They may be well-known, but are consequential in some way other than is revealed in the detailed account of what actually happened.

Sages' treatment of events determines what in the Mishnah is important about what happens. Since the greatest event in the century and a half, from ca. A.D. 50 to ca. 200, in which the Mishnah's materials came into being, was the destruction of the Temple in A.D. 70, we must expect the Mishnah's treatment of that incident to illustrate the document's larger theory of history: what is important and unimportant about what happens. The treatment of the destruction occurs in two ways. First, the destruction of the Temple constitutes a noteworthy fact in the history of the law. Why? Because various laws about

---

[7] For example, the "men slain at Tel Arza" (by the Romans?) come under discussion only because we have to decide whether they are to be declared legally dead so their wives may remarry (M. Yebamot 16:7). The advent of gentiles to Jerusalem (in 70?) raises the question of whether we assume a priest's wife has been raped (M. Ketubot 2:9). A war comes into sight—not named, not important—only because of a queen's vow, taken when her son goes off "to war" (M. Nazir 4:1).

[8] For instance, there is the tale of the burning of the red cow (M. Parah Chapter three) or of the purification of the *mesora* of Lev. 13:2ff. (M. Negaim Chapter Fourteen). The names of Temple officers are catalogued (M. Sheqalim 51:1). But we learn no more about them than the jobs to which they were assigned. Allusions to famous events even within sages' own circles do not demand detailed narration (as at M. Kelim 5:10).

rite and cult had to undergo revision on account of the destruction. The following provides a stunningly apt example of how the Mishnah's philosophers regard what actually happened as being simply changes in the law:

M. Rosh Hashanah 4:1-4

4:1   A.   On the festival day of the New Year which coincided with the Sabbath—
B.   in the Temple they would sound the shofar.
C.   But not in the provinces.
D.   When the Temple was destroyed, Rabban Yohanan ben Zakkai made the rule that they should sound the shofar in every locale in which there was a court.
E.   Said R. Eleazar, "Rabban Yohanan b. Zakkai made that rule in the case of Jamnia alone."
F.   They said to him, "All the same are Jamnia and every locale in which there is a court."

4:2   A.   And in this regard also was Jerusalem ahead of Jamnia:
B.   in every town which is within sight and sound [of Jerusalem], and nearby and able to come to Jerusalem, they sound the shofar.
C.   But as to Jamnia, they sound the shofar only in the court alone.

4:3   A.   In olden times the lulab was taken up in the Temple for seven days, and in the provinces for one day.
B.   When the Temple was destroyed, Rabban Yohanan ben Zakkai made the rule that in the provinces the lulab should be taken up for seven days, as a memorial to the Temple;
C.   and that the day [the sixteenth of Nisan] on which the omer is waved should be wholly prohibited [in regard to the eating of new produce] (M. Suk. 3:12).

4:4   A.   At first they would receive testimony about the new moon all day long.
B.   One time the witnesses came late, and the Levites consequently were mixed up as to [what] song [they should sing].
C.   They made the rule that they should receive testimony [about the new moon] only up to the afternoon offering.
D.   Then, if witnesses came after the afternoon-offering, they would treat that entire day as holy, and the next day as holy too.
E.   When the Temple was destroyed, Rabban Yohanan b. Zakkai made the rule that they should [once more] receive testimony about the new moon all day long.
F.   Said R. Joshua b. Qorha, "This rule too did Rabban Yohanan B. Zakkai make:
G.   "Even if the head of the court is located somewhere else, the witnesses should come only to the location of the council [to give testimony, and not to the location of the head of the court]."

The passages before us leave no doubt about what sages selected as important about the destruction: it produced changes in synagogue rites.

Second, although the sages surely mourned for the destruction and the loss of Israel's principal mode of worship, and certainly recorded the event of the ninth of Ab in the year A.D.70, they did so in their characteristic way: they listed the event as an item in a catalogue of things that are like one another and so demand the same response. But then the destruction no longer appears as a unique event. It is absorbed into a pattern of like disasters, all exhibiting similar taxonomic traits, events to which the people, now well-schooled in tragedy, knows full well the appropriate response. So it is in demonstrating regularity that sages reveal their way of coping. Then the uniqueness of the event fades away, its mundane character is emphasized. The power of taxonomy in imposing order upon chaos once more does its healing work. The consequence was reassurance that historical events obeyed discoverable laws. Israel's ongoing life would override disruptive, one-time happenings. So catalogues of events, as much as lists of species of melons, served as brilliant apologetic by providing reassurance that nothing lies beyond the range and power of ordering system and stabilizing pattern.

M. Taanit 4:6-7

4:6 A. Five events took place for our fathers on the seventeenth of Tammuz, and five on the ninth of Ab.
B. On the seventeenth of Tammuz (1) the tablets [of the Torah] were broken, (2) the daily whole offering was cancelled, (3) the city wall was breached, (4) Apostemos burned the Torah, and (5) he set up an idol in the Temple.
C. On the ninth of Ab (1) the decree was made against our forefathers that they should not enter the land, (2) the first Temple and (3) the second [Temple] were destroyed, (4) Betar was taken, and (5) the city was ploughed up [after the war of Hadrian].
D. When Ab comes, rejoicing diminishes.

4:7 A. In the week in which the ninth of Ab occurs it is prohibited to get a haircut and to wash one's clothes.
B. But on Thursday of that week these are permitted,
C. because of the honor due to the Sabbath.
D. On the eve of the ninth of Ab a person should not eat two prepared dishes, nor should one eat meat or drink wine.
E. Rabban Simeon b. Gamaliel says, "He should make some change from ordinary procedures."
F. R. Judah declares people obligated to turn over beds.
G. But sages did not concur with him.

I include M. Taanit 4:7 to show the context in which the list of M. 4:6 stands. The stunning calamities catalogued at M. 4:6 form groups, reveal common traits, so are subject to classification. Then the laws of M. 4:7 provide regular rules for responding to, coping with, these untimely catastrophes, all (fortuitously) in a single classification. So the raw materials of history are absorbed into the ahistorical, supernatural system of the Mishnah. The process of absorption and regularization of the unique and one-time moment is illustrated in the passage at hand.

Along these same lines, the entire history of the cult, so critical in the larger system created by the Mishnah's lawyers, produced a patterned, therefore sensible and intelligible, picture. As is clear, everything that happened turned out to be susceptible of classification, once the taxonomic traits were specified. A monothetic exercise, sorting out periods and their characteristics, took the place of narrative, to explain things in its own way: first this, and then that, and, in consequence, the other. So in the neutral turf of holy ground, as much as in the trembling earth of the Temple mount, everything was absorbed into one thing, all classified in its proper place and by its appropriate rule. Indeed, so far as the lawyers proposed to write history at all, they wrote it into their picture of the long tale of the way in which Israel served God: the places in which the sacrificial labor was carried on, the people who did it, the places in which the priests ate the meat left over for their portion after God's portion was set aside and burned up. This "historical" account forthwith generated precisely that problem of locating the regular and orderly, which the philosophers loved to investigate: the intersection of conflicting but equally correct taxonomic rules, as we see at M. Zebahim 14:9, below. The passage that follows therefore is history, so far as the Mishnah's creators proposed to write history: the reduction of events to rules forming compositions of regularity, therefore meaning:

M. Zebahim 14:4-8+9

14.4 I. A. Before the tabernacle was set up, (1) the high places were permitted, and (2) [the sacrificial] service [was done by] the first born [Num. 3:12-13, 8:16-18].

B. When the tabernacle was set up, (1) the high places were prohibited, and (2) the [sacrificial] service [was done by] priests.

C. Most Holy Things were eaten within the veils, Lesser Holy Things [were eaten] throughout the camp of Israel.

14:5 II. A. They came to Gilgal.

B. The High places were permitted.

C. Most Holy Things were eaten within the veils, Lesser Holy Things, anywhere.

14:6 III. A. They came to Shiloh.

B. The high places were prohibited.

C. (1) There was no roof-beam there, but below was a house of stone, and hangings above it, and (2) it was "the resting place" [Deut. 12:10].

D. Most Holy Things were eaten within the veils, Lesser Holy Things and second-tithe [were eaten] in any place within sight [of Shiloh].

14:7 IV. A. They came to Nob and Gibeon.
B. The high places were permitted.
C. Most Holy Things were eaten within the evils, Lesser Holy Things, in all the towns of Israel.

14:8 V. A. They came to Jerusalem.
B. The high places were prohibited.
C. And they never again were permitted.
D. And it was "the inheritance" [Deut. 12:9].
E. Most Holy things were eaten within the veils, Lesser Holy Things and second-tithe within the wall.

14:9 A. All the Holy things which one sanctified at the time of the prohibition of the high places and offered at the time of the prohibition of the high places outside—

B. lo, these are subject to the transgression of a positive commandment and a negative commandment, and they are liable on their account to extirpation [for sacrificing outside the designated place, Lev. 17:8-9, M. Zeb. 13:1A].

C. [If] one sanctified them at the time of the permission of high places and offered them up at the time of the prohibition of high places,

D. lo, these are subject to transgression of a positive commandment and to a negative commandment, but they are not liable on their account to extirpation [since if the offerings had been sacrificed when they were sanctified, there should have been no violation].

E. [If] one sanctified them at the time of the prohibition of high places and offered them up at the time of the permission of high places,

F. lo, these are subject to transgression of a positive commandment, but they are not subject to a negative commandment at all.

The authorship at hand had the option of narrative, but chose the way of philosophy: generalization through classification, comparison and contrast. The inclusion of M. Zeb. 14:9, structurally matching M. Taanit 4:7, shows us the goal of the historical composition. It is to set forth rules that intersect and produce confusion, so that we may sort out confusion and make sense of all the data. The upshot may now be stated briefly.

The Mishnah absorbs into its encompassing system all events, small and large. With what happens the sages accomplish what they do with everything else: a vast labor of taxonomy, an immense construction of the order and rules governing the classification of everything on earth and in Heaven. The disruptive character of history—one-time events of ineluctable significance—scarcely impresses the philosophers. They find no difficulty in showing that what appears unique and beyond classification has in fact happened before and so falls within the range of trustworthy rules and known procedures. Once history's components, one-time events, lose their distinctiveness, then history as a didactic intellectual construct, as a source of lessons and rules, also loses all pertinence. So lessons and rules come from sorting things out and classifying them, that is, from the procedures and modes of thought of the philosopher seeking regularity. To this labor of taxonomy, the historian's way of selecting data and arranging them into patterns of meaning to teach lessons, proves inconsequential. One-time events are not what matters. The world is composed of nature and supernature. The repetitious laws that count are those to be discovered in Heaven and, in Heaven's creation and counterpart, on earth. Keep those laws and things will work out. Break them, and the result is predictable: calamity of whatever sort will supervene in accordance with the rules. But just because it is predictable, a catastrophic happening testifies to what has always been and must always be, in accordance with reliable rules and within categories already discovered and well explained. That is why the lawyer-philosophers of the mid-second century produced the Mishnah—to explain how things are. Within the framework of well-classified rules, there could be messiahs, but no single Messiah (in Christian theological terms: *Geschichte*, but no *Historie*).

Up to now I have contrasted "history" with "eternity," and framed matters in such a way that the Mishnah's system appears to have been ahistorical and anti-historical. Yet in fact the framers of the Mishnah recognized the past-ness of the past and hence, by definition, laid out a conception of the past that constitutes a historical doctrine. But it is a different conception from the familiar one. To express the difference, I point out that, for modern history-writing, what is important is to describe what is unique and individual, not what is on-going and unremarkable. History is the story of change, development, movement, not of what does not change, develop, or move. For the thinkers of the Mishnah, historical patterning emerges as today scientific knowledge does, through taxonomy, the classification of the unique and individual, the organization of change and movement within unchanging categories. That is why the dichotomy between history and eternity, change and permanence, signals an unnuanced exegesis of what was, in fact, a subtle and reflective doctrine of history. That doctrine proves entirely consistent with the large perspectives of scribes, from the ones who made omen-series in ancient Babylonia to the ones who made the Mishnah. That is why the category of salvation does not serve, but the one of sanctification fits admirably.

How, then, in the Mishnah as the foundation-document of Judaism, does history come to full conceptual expression. History as an account of a meaningful pattern of events, making sense of the past and giving guidance about the future, begins with the necessary conviction that events matter, one after another. The Mishnah's framers, however, present us with no elaborate theory of events, a fact fully consonant with their systemic points of insistence and encompassing concern. Events do not matter, one by one. The philosopher-lawyers exhibited no theory of history either. Their conception of Israel's destiny in no way called upon historical categories of either narrative or didactic explanation to describe and account for the future. The small importance attributed to the figure of the Messiah as an historical-eschatological figure, therefore, fully accords with the larger traits of the system as a whole. Let me speak with emphasis: If what is important in Israel's existence is sanctification, an ongoing process, and not salvation, understood as a one-time event at the end, then no one will find reason to narrate history.

But Judaism was to emerge from late antiquity: richly eschatological, obsessed with the Messiah and his coming, engaged by the history of Israel and the nations. Judaism at the end did indeed provide an ample account and explanation of Israel's history and destiny. These merged as the generative problematic of Judaism, just as they framed the social reality confronted by Jews wherever they lived. So, to seek the map that shows the road from the Mishnah, at the beginning, to the fully articulated Judaism of the end of the formative age in late antiquity, we have to look elsewhere. For as to the path from the Mishnah through the Tosefta—this is not the way people took.

The centerpiece of the rehistoricization of Judaism accomplished by the framers of the Talmud of the Land of Israel and related writings of course is the reversion to Scripture. The Scriptures that, after all, also lay to hand offered testimony to the centrality of history as a sequence of meaningful events. To the message and uses of history as a source of teleology for an Israelite system, biblical writings amply testified. Prophecy and apocalyptic had long coped quite well with defeat and dislocation. Yet, in the Mishnah, Israel's deeds found no counterpart in Roman history, while, in the Palestinian Talmud, they did. In the Mishnah, time is differentiated entirely in other than national-historical categories. For, as in Abot, "this world" is when one is alive, "the world to come" is when a person dies. True, we find also "this world" and "the time of the Messiah." But detailed differentiation among the ages of "this world" or "this age" hardly generates problems in mishnaic thought. Indeed, no such differentiation appears. Accordingly, the developments briefly outlined here constitute a significant shift in the course of intellectual events, to which the sources at hand—the Mishnah and Talmud of the Land of Israel—amply testify. In ca. A.D. 200 events posed a problem of classification and generalization. In ca. A.D. 400, events were singular and demanded interpretation because, in all their particularity, they bore messages just as, in prophetic thought, they had. In the reconsideration of the singularity of events and the systematic effort at interpreting them and the lessons to be drawn from them, the sages of the Talmud of the Land of Israel regained for their theological thought the powerful resources of history, the single most powerful arena for, and principal medium of, Judaic theology then as now.

CHAPTER TEN

HISTORY INVENTED:
THE CONCEPTION OF HISTORY IN THE TALMUD OF
THE LAND OF ISRAEL

Jacob Neusner

The Mishnah describes a world and presents rules for it. So we may say, in simple language, that the Mishnah is about "life." The Mishnah describes the life of Israel, viewed from one perspective. But the Talmud of the Land of Israel, for its part, is not so much about "life" in general as it is about the Mishnah in particular. Whatever the framers of the Talmud's units of discourse wish to say, they choose to say generally in relationship to something they find in the Mishnah. The Talmud nonetheless follows a distinctive program of topics. At issue here is that which the Mishnah does not choose to treat, but the Talmud for its part wishes to discuss. I refer to the absence in the Mishnah of a taxon defined by the issue of Israel's history, its form, direction, meaning, and end. These fall wholly outside of the Mishnah's frame of reference. On the protean topic, the Mishnah offers no tractate, no chapter, scarcely a reference. Not only do we find no attention to that classical issue of the Israelite world-view, we do not even know how we might find appropriate, specifically Mishnaic, language or categories for discussion of the issue. Suitable words elude us. Whatever discourse we do find in the Talmud pertinent to this formidable and urgent topic therefore lies wholly outside the symbolic and even linguistic-conceptual framework of the Mishnah. As a result, it is principally when the Talmud ignores the Mishnah that it addresses questions important to the present inquiry.

I. The Uses and Meaning of History in the Talmud of the Land of Israel

Disorderly historical events entered the system of the Mishnah and found their place within the larger framework of the Mishnah's orderly world. So to claim that the Mishnah's framers merely ignored what was happening would be incorrect. They worked out their own way of dealing with historical events, the disruptive power of which they not only conceded but freely recognized. Further, the Mishnah's authors to begin with did not intend to compose a history book or a work of prophecy or apocalypse. Even if they had wanted to narrate the course of events, they could hardly have done so through the medium of the Mishnah. Yet the Mishnah presents its philosophy in full awareness of the issues of historical calamity confronting the Jewish nation. So far as the philosophy of the document confronts the totality of Israel's existence, the Mishnah be definition *also* presents a philosophy of history.

The Mishnah's subordination of historical events contradicts the emphasis of a thousand years of Israelite thought. The biblical histories, the ancient prophets, the apocalyptic visionaries—all had testified that what happened mattered. Events carried the message of the living God. That is, events constituted history, pointed toward, and so explained, Israel's destiny. An essentially ahistorical system of timeless sanctification, worked out through construction of an eternal rhythm centered on the movement of the moon and stars and seasons, represented a choice taken by few outside of the priesthood. Furthermore, the pretense that what *happens* matters less than what *is* testified against palpable and remembered reality. For Israel had suffered enormous loss of life. As we shall see, the Talmud of the Land of Israel takes these events seriously and treats them as unique and remarkable. The memories proved real. The hopes evoked by the Mishnah's promise of sanctification of the world in static perfection did not. For they had to compete with the grief of an entire century of mourning:

Y.Taanit 4:5

X. B. Rabbi would derive by exegesis twenty-four tragic events from the verse: *"The Lord has destroyed without mercy all the habitation of Jacob; in his wrath he has broken down the strongholds of the daughter of Judah; he has brought down to the ground in dishonor the kingdom and its rulers"* (Lam. 2:2).

C. R. Yohanan derived sixty from the same verse.

D. Did R. Yohanan then find more than did Rabbi in the same verse?

E. But because Rabbi lived nearer to the destruction of the Temple, there were in the audience old men who remembered what had happened, and when he gave his exegesis, they would weep and fall silent and get up and leave.

We do not know whether things happened as the story-teller says. But the fact remains that the framers of the Yerushalmi preserved the observation that, in Rabbi's time, memories of world-shaking events continued to shape Israel's mind and imagination. For people like those portrayed here, the Mishnah's taxonomic classification of tragedy to accord with trustworthy rules cannot have solved many problems.

Accordingly, we should not be surprised to observe that the Talmud of the Land of Israel contains evidence pointing toward substantial steps taken in rabbinical circles, away from the position of the Mishnah. We find materials that fall entirely outside the framework of historical doctrine established within the Mishnah. These are, first, an interest in the periodization of history, and second, a willingness to include events of far greater diversity than those in the Mishnah. So the Yerushalmi contains an expanded view of the range of human life encompassed to begin with by the conception of history.

Let us take the second point first. So far as things happen that demand attention and so constitute "events," within the Mishnah these fall into two classifications: (1) biblical history, and (2) events involving the Temple. A glance at the catalogue, cited above from M. Ta. 4:6, tells us what kind of happening constitutes an "event," a historical datum demanding attention and interpretation. In the Talmud at hand, by contrast, in addition to Temple-events, we find also two other sorts of *Geschichten*: Torah-events, that is, important stories about the legal and supernatural doings of rabbis, and also political events.

These events, moreover, involved people not considered in the Mishnah: gentiles as much as Jews, Rome as much as Israel. The Mishnah's history, such as it is, knows only Israel. The Talmud greatly expands the range of historical interest when it develops a theory of Rome's relationship to Israel and, of necessity also, Israel's relationship to Rome.

Only by taking account of the world at large can the Talmud's theory of history yield a philosophy of history worthy of the name, that is, an account of who Israel is, the meaning of what happens to Israel, and the destiny of Israel in this world and at the end of time. Israel by itself—as the priests had claimed—lived in eternity, beyond time. Israel and Rome together struggled in historical time: an age with a beginning, a middle, and an end. That is the importance of the expanded range of historical topics found in the present Talmud. When, in the other Talmud, created in Babylonia, we find a still broader interest, in Iran as much as Rome, in the sequence of world empires past and present, we see how rich and encompassing a theory of historical events begins with a simple step toward a universal perspective. It was a step that I think, unlike the ancient prophets and apocalyptists, the scribes and priests represented by the Mishnah were incapable of taking.

The concept of periodization—the raw material of historical thought-hardly presents surprises, since apocalyptic writers began their work by differentiating one age from another. When the Mishnah includes a statement of the "periods" into which time is divided, however, it speaks only of stages of the cult: Shiloh, Nob, Jerusalem. One age is differentiated from the next not by reference to world-historical changes but only by the location of sacrifice and the eating of the victim. The rules governing each locale impose taxa upon otherwise undifferentiated time. So periodization constitutes a function of the larger system of sanctification through sacrifice. The contrast between "this world" and "the world to come," which is not a narrowly historical conception in the Mishnah, now finds a counterpart in the Talmud's contrast between "this age" and the age in which the Temple stood. And that distinction is very much an act of this-worldly historical differentiation. It not only yields apocalyptic speculation. It also generates sober and worldly reflection on the movement of events and the meaning of history in the prophetic-apocalyptic tradition. Accordingly, the Talmud of the Land of Israel presents both the expected amplification of the established concepts familiar from the Mishnah, and also a separate set of ideas, perhaps rooted in prior times but still autonomous of what the Mishnah in particular had encompassed.

Let us first survey what is new and striking. From the viewpoint of the Mishnah, as I have suggested, the single most unlikely development is interest in the history of a nation other than Israel. For the Mishnah views the world beyond the sacred Land as unclean, tainted in particular with corpse-uncleanness. Outside the holy lies the realm of death. The faces of that world are painted in the monotonous white of the grave. Only within the range of the sacred do things happen. There, events may be classified and arranged, all in relationship to the Temple and its cult. But, standing majestically unchanged by the vicissitudes of time, the cult rises above history. Now the ancient Israelite interest in the history of the great empires of the world— perceived, to be sure, in relationship to the history of Israel— reemerges within the framework of the documents that succeeded the Mishnah. Naturally, in the Land os Israel only one empire mattered. This is Rome, which, in the Yerushalmi, is viewed solely as the counterpart to Israel. The world then consists of two nations: Israel, the weaker, Rome, the stronger. Jews enjoy a sense of vastly enhanced importance when they contemplate such a world, containing as it does only two peoples that matter, of whom one is Israel. But from our perspective, the utility for the morale of the defeated people holds no interest. What strikes us in the evidence of the formation of a second and separate system of historical interpretation, beyond that of the Mishnah.

History and doctrine merge, with history made to yield doctrine. What is stunning is the perception of Rome as an autonomous actor, that is, as an entity with a point of origin, just as Israel has a point of origin, and a tradition of wisdom, just as Israel has such a tradition. These are the two points at which the large-scale conception of historical Israel finds a counterpart in the present literary composition. This sense of poised opposites, Israel and Rome, comes to expression in two ways.

First, as we shall now see, it is Israel's own history that calls into being its counterpoint, the anti-history of Rome. Without Israel, there would be no Rome—a wonderful consolation to the defeated nation. For if Israel's sin created Rome's power, then Israel's repentance will bring Rome's downfall. Here is the way in which the Talmud presents the match (all translations are my own):

Y.Abodah Zarah 1:2
IV. E. *Saturnalia* means "hidden hatred" [*sinah temunah*]: The Lord hates, takes vengeance, and punishes
F. This is in accord with the following verse: *"Now Esau hated Jacob"* (Gen. 27:41).
G. Said R. Isaac b. R. Eleazar, "In Rome they call it Esau's Saturnalia."
H. *Kratesis*: It is the day on which the Romans seized power.
K. Said R. Levi, "It is the day on which Solomon intermarried with the family of Phaorah Neccho, King of Egypt. On that day Michael came down and thrust a reed into the sea, and pulled up muddy alluvium, and this was turned into a huge pot, and this was the great city of Rome. On the day on which Jeroboam set up the two golden calves, Remus and Romulus came and built two huts in the city of Rome. On the day on which Elijah disappeared, a king was appointed in Rome: *"There was no king in Edom, a deputy was king"* (1 Kings 22:47).

The important point is that Solomon's sin provoked Heaven's founding of Rome, thus history, lived by Israel, and provoking anti-history, lived by Rome.

Quite naturally, the conception of history and anti-history will assign to the actors in the anti-history—the Romans—motives explicable in terms of history, that is, the history of Israel. The entire world and what happens in it enter into the framework of meaning established by Israel's Torah. So what the Romans do, their historical actions, can be explained in terms of Israel's conception of the world. A striking example of the tendency to explain Romans' deeds through Israel's logic is the reason given for Trojan's war against the Jews:

Y.Sukkah 5:1
VII. A. In the time of Tronianus, the evil one, a son was born to him on the ninth of Ab, and the Israelites were fasting.
B. His daughter died on Hanukkah, and the Israelites lit candles.

C. His wife sent a message to him, saying, "Instead of going out to conquer the barbarians, come and conquer the Jews, who have rebelled against you."
D. He thought that the trip would take ten days, but he arrived in five.
E. He came and found the Israelites occupied in study of the Light [of Torah], with the following verse: "*The Lord will bring a nation against you from afar, from the end of the earth, as swift as the eagle flies, a nation whose language you do not understand*" (Deut. 28:49).
F. He said to them, "With what are you occupied?"
G. They said to him, "With thus-and-so."
H. He said to them, "That man [I] thought that it would take ten days to make the trip, but arrived in five days." His legions surrounded them and killed them.
I. He said to the women, "Obey my legions, and I shall not kill you."
J. They said to him, "What you did to the ones who have fallen do also to us who are yet standing."
K. He mingled their blood with the blood of their men, until the blood flowed into the ocean as far as Cyprus.
L. At that moment the horn of Israel was cut off, and it is not destined to return to its place until the son of David will come.

What is important here is the source of what we might call "historical explanation," deriving, as it does, from the larger framework of sages' conviction. Trajan had done nothing except with God's help and by God's design. Here is another example:

Y.Gittin 5:7
I. A. In the beginning the Romand decreed oppression against Judah, for they had a tradition in their hands from their forefathers that Judah had slain Esau, for it is written, "*Your hand shall be on the neck of your enemies*" (Gen. 49:8).

This means, again, that things make sense wholly in the categories of Torah. The world retains its logic, and Israel knows (and can manipulate) that logic.

At the foundations is the tension between Israel's God and pagan gods. That is, historical explanation here invokes the familiar polemic of Scripture. Accordingly, the development of an interest in Roman history—of a willingness to take as important, events in the history of some nation other than Israel—flows from an established (and rather wooden) notion of the world in which God and gods ("idols") compete. Israel's history of subjugation testifies, not to the weakness of Israel's God, but to his strength. The present prosperity of idolaters, involving the subjugation of Israel, attests only to God's remarkable patience,

God's love for the world he made. This conception, familiar to be sure in the Mishnah itself, now becomes absorbed into historical categories of "now" and "then." That is to say, the notion of competition between God and no-gods, Israel and Rome, is set within the framework of differentiation between (1) "this age" and (2) "the time to come." Since that notion marks a stop beyond the way in which the same theme had come to expression in Mishnah and Tosefta, we had best review the development of the same passage in its literary—hence canonical—sequences. The citation of (1) the Mishnah is *underlined*, the citation of (2) the subsequent Tosefta, in BROKEN UNDERLINE, followed by (3) the Yerushalmi's contribution in ordinary type.

Y.Abodah Zarah 4:7

A. *They asked the sages in Rome, "If God is not in favor of idolatry why does he not wipe it out?"*

B. *They said to them, "If people worshiped something of which the world had no need, he certainly would wipe it out."*

C. *"But lo, people worship the sun, moon, stars, and planets.*

D. *"Now do you think he is going to wipe out his world because of idiots?"*

E. *They said to them, "If so, let them destroy something of which the world has no need, and leave something that the world needs!"*

F. *They said to them, "Then we should strengthen the hands of those who worship these, which would not be destroyed, for then they would say, 'Now you know full well that they are gods, for lo, they were not wiped out!'"*

I. A. *Philosophers asked the sages in Rome, "If God is not in favor of idolatry, why does he not wipe it out?" They said to them, "If people worshiped something of which the world had no need, he certainly would wipe it out. But lo, people worship the sun, moon, and stars. Now do you think he is going to wipe out his world because of idiots?"* [=M. 4:7A-D].

B. *"But let the world be in accord with its accustomed way, and the idiots who behave ruinously will ultimately come and give a full account of themselves. If one has stolen seeds for planting, are they not ultimately going to sprout? If one has had sexual relations with a married woman, will she not ultimately give birth? But let the world follow its accustomed way, and the idiots who behave ruinously will ultimately come and give a full account of themselves"* [T. A.Z. 6:7].

II. A. Said R. Zeira, "If it were written, 'Those who worship them are like them,' there would be a problem. Are those who worship the sun like the sun, those who worship the moon like the moon?! But this is what is written: 'Those who make them are like them; so are all who trust in them' (Ps. 115:8)."

B. Said R. Mana, "If it were written, 'Those who worship them are like them,' it would pose no problem whatsoever. For it also is written, *'Then the moon will be confounded, and the sun ashamed'* (Is. 24:23)."

C. R. Nahman is the name of R. Mana, "Idolatry is destined in the end to come and spit in the face of those that worship idols, and it will bring them to shame and cause them to be nullified from the world."

D. Now what is the scriptural basis for that statement?

E. "*All the worshipers of images will be put to shame, who make their boast in worthless idols*" (Ps. 97:7).

F. R. Nahman is the name of R. Mana, "Idolatry is destined in time to come to bow down before the Holy One, blessed be He, and then be nullified from the world."

G. What is the scriptural basis for that statement?

H. "*All worshipers of images will be put to shame . . .: all gods bow down before him*" (Ps. 97:7).

The important point comes at II.C-H, at which the Talmud's sages present a temporal differentiation absent in the Mishnah. The problem of the Mishnah is a philosophical one. The Tosefta's anonymous authorities make that point explicit. There is a certain logic, an inevitability, upon which Israel may rely. True, idolatry prospers. But idolaters will be called to account. Now that essentially atemporal notion, which can sustain the interpretation of a last judgment for individuals, moves into a social, hence temporal-historical, framework at the third stage. Not merely the idolator, as an individual, comes to account. The *age* of idolatry itself will come to an end. We differentiate between this age, which is bad, and another age, a period in time, which will be good. The notion of temporal sequences upon which historical thinking rests, in no way serves the framers of the Mishnah passage. By contrast, it is essential to the thought, concerning idolatry, of the authorities cited in the Talmud.

The concept of two histories, balanced opposite one another, comes to particular expression, with the Yerushalmi, in the balance of Israelite sage and Roman emperor. Just as Israel and Rome, God and no-gods, compete, with a fore-ordained conclusion, so do sage and emperor. In this age, it appears that the emperor has the power, as does Rome, as do the pagan gods with their temples in full glory. God's Temple, by contrast lies in ruins. But just as sages overcome the emperor through their inherent supernatural power, so too will Israel and Israel's God in the coming age control the course of events.

Y. Terumot 8:10

[Translated by Alan J. Avery-Peck]

IV. A. As to Diocles the swineherd, the students of R. Yudan, the Patriarch, would make fun of him.

B. He [Diocletian] became emperor and moved to Paneas.

C. He sent letters to the rabbis, [saying]: "You must be here [to see] me immediately after the end of the [coming] Sabbath."

D. He instructed the messenger [who was to deliver these orders], "Do not give them the letters until the eve [of Sabbath], just as the sun is setting." [Diocletian hoped to force the rabbis to miss the appointment, for they would not travel on the Sabbath. Then he could have revenge on them because of their cavalier treatment of him, A.]

E. The messenger came to them on the eve [of Sabbath] as the sun was setting.

F. [After receiving the message] R. Yudan the Patriarch and R. Samuel bar Nahman were sitting in the public baths in Tiberias. Antigris, [a certain spirit, appeared and] came to their side.

G. R. Yudan, the Patriarch, wished to rebuke him [and chase him away].

H. R. Samuel bar Nahman said to him [Yudan], "Leave him be. He appears as a messenger of salvation."

I. [Antigris] said to them, "What is troubling the rabbis?"

J. They told him the story [and] he said to them, "[Finish] bathing [in honor of the Sabbath]. For your creator is going to perform miracles [for you]."

K. At the end of the Sabbath [Antigris] took them and placed them [in Paneas].

L. They told [the emperor], "Lo, the rabbis are outside!"

M. He said, "They shall not see my face until they have bathed."

N. [Diocletian] had the bath heated for seven days and nights, [so that the rabbis could not stand the heat].

O. [To make it possible for them to enter, Antigris] went in before them and overpowered the heat.

P. [Afterwards] they went and stood before [the king].

Q. He said to them, "Is it because your creator performs miracles for you that you despise the [Roman] Empire?"

R. They said to him, "Diocles the swineherd did we despise. But Diocletian the emperor we do not despise."

S. Diocletian said to them, "Even so, you should not rebuke [anyone], neither a young Roman, nor a young associate [of the rabbis, for you never know what greatness that individual will attain]."

The this-worldly and practical wisdom contained at the end should not blind us to the importance of the story within the larger theory of history presented in the Yerushalmi. The Mishnah finds ample place for debates between "philosophers" and rabbis. But in the Mishnah the high priest in the Temple and the king upon his throne do not weigh in the balance, or stand poised against, equal and opposite powers, the pagan priest in his temple, the Roman emperor on his throne. The very conception is inconceivable within the context of the Mishnah. For the Yerushalmi, by contrast, two stunning innovations appear: first, the notion of emperor and sage in mortal struggle; second, the idea of an age of idolatry and an age beyond idolatry. The world had to move into a new orbit indeed for Rome to enter into the historical context formerly defined wholly by what happened to Israel.

To our secular eyes these developments seem perfectly natural. After all, the Jews really had been conquered. Their Temple really had been destroyed. So why should they not have taken an interest in the history of the conqueror and tried to place into relationship with their own history the things that happened to him? We find self-evident, moreover, the comfort to be derived from the explanations consequent upon the inclusion of Roman history, in the Yerushalmi's doctrine of the world. But Israel had been defeated many times before the composition of the Mishnah, and the Temple had lain in ruins for nearly a century and a half when Judah the Patriarch promulgated the Mishnah as Israel's code of law. So the circumstances in which the Talmud's materials were composed hardly differed materially from the condition in which, from Bar Kokhba onward, sages selected from what was available and composed the Mishnah.

The Scriptures that, after all, also lay to hand offered testimony to the centrality of history as a sequence of meaningful events. To the message and uses of history as a source of teleology for an Israelite system, biblical writings amply testified. Prophecy and apocalyptic had long coped quite well with defeat and dislocation. Yet, in the Mishnah, Israel's deeds found no counterpart in Roman history, while, in the Palestinian Talmud, they did. In the Mishnah, time is differentiated entirely in other than national-historical categories. For, as in Abot, "this world" is when one is alive, "the world to come" is when a person dies. True, we find also "this world" and "the time of the Messiah." But detailed differentiation among the ages of "this world" or "this age" hardly generates problems in mishnaic thought. Indeed, no such differentiation appears. Accordingly, the developments briefly outlined up to this point constitute a significant shift in the course of intellectual events, to which the sources at hand—the Mishnah, Tosefta, and Talmud of the Land of Israel-amply testify.

Differentiation between the time in which the Temple stood and the present age, of course, hardly will have surprised the authors of the Mishnah. It was a natural outcome of the Mishnah's own division of ages. We recall how time was divided by the location of the altar, and how the divisions were explained by reference to what was done in that regard. Now we find a specification of the exact years involved. Not surprisingly, however, since the Mishnah does not speculate on when the Temple will be rebuilt, as in Tosefta, so here, the framers of the passage in Yerushalmi do not specify the year in which they think the Temple will be rebuilt. The Messiah's coming plays no role at all.

Y.Megillah 1:12
XI. O. So with the tent of meeting: it spent forty years less one in Gilgal. In Gilgal it spent fourteen years, seven when they were conquering the land and seven when they were dividing it.

P. In Shilo it spent three hundred and sixty-nine years.

Q. In Nob and Gibeon it spent fifty-seven years, thirteen in Nob and forty-four in Gibeon.

R. In Jerusalem in the time of the first building it was there for four hundred and ten years.

S. In the time of the second building it was four hundred ten years. This was meant to fulfill the statement of Scripture: *"The latter splendor of this house shall be greater than the former, says the Lord of hosts; and in this place I will give prosperity, says the Lord of hosts"* (Haggai 2:9).

Strikingly absent is any prediction as to *when* the third temple would be rebuilt. In due course many would take up the work of speculation and calculation. But, in his exegesis of the Mishnah, the author of this passage does not do so.

The principal point of differentiation between one age and another, now remained the destruction of the Temple, which, in the spirit of M. Sot. 9:15, marked the turn of the age. Rules held applicable to Temple times were reexamined to see whether they continued to apply. For example, "What is the law as to tearing one's garments *at this time* upon hearing God cursed in euphemisms?" (Y. San.7:8 VII.C). But the important point is the least blatant. Not everything bad in the current age was to be blamed on the destruction. The explanation of contention in discussions of the law, for instance, involved *not* the differentiation between historical periods, but the (timeless) failure of the disciples. "In the beginning there was no contention; but ill-prepared disciples caused it" (Y. Hag. 2:IC). But the end of the matter still turns upon history: "The Torah is not going to be restored to its wholeness until the son of David comes (*ibid.*, E). In context, the meaning is, "a long time from now." The step seems a small one. "This age" and "the other age" shifted at 70. Now, as soon as some other point of differentiation enters, not based upon the destruction of the Temple, a new possibility emerged. Specifically, the potentiality for a theory of Israel's life not spun out of the cult and its history begins to move toward realization. That much we can deduce from the slight evidence at hand.

A further mark of the development of interest in differentiating among historical periods is found in the commemoration of important events. Once one day is differentiated from another because of what happened on that same date a long time ago, we move away from the Mishnah's principal criterion for distinguishing the passage of time.

How so? The framers of the Mishnah, following the priestly tradition, knew that one day differs from another because of the passage of the moon through fixed stars in heaven (e.g. Passover falls at the first full moon after the vernal equinox) and the consequent revision of the cultic offerings on earth (as at Numbers 28-29). True, as we noticed, sages also absorbed into their system one-time historical events, such as the seventeenth of Tammuz and the ninth of Ab. But those events proved incidental to the construction of a larger system, with Mishnah's tractates named for festivals of the natural year and focused upon Temple rites for those days. When, therefore, we discover units of discourse devoted to specific historical events and their meaning, we find ourselves in a new situation. Why? Because events we regard as historical, as distinct from those we see as natural or supernatural, also have now come to be taken seriously. One day differs from another not by virtue of the criterion of creation, but on account of a political or other historical event. As we recognize, the only such historical, non-natural, event absorbed into the Mishnah's system involved the Temple. Accordingly, in what follows, we deal with a different approach to time from the one characteristic of the Mishnah's system.

Let me explain. Having evidently inherited from former times a calendar of celebrations of important events in Israel's history, marked by the prohibition against fasting, the Yerushalmi's sages pursued the issue. In the following unit of discourse we find attention to the traits of commemorative days, consonant with the interest in historical periodization noted earlier:

Y. Megillah 1:4

IX. B. On the twelfth of that month [of Adar] is Tirion's day. [That day on which the decrees of Trajan were annulled is a holiday and it is forbidden to fast on that day, contrary to Meir's view of acceptable behavior on the twelfth of Adar, in line with M. Meg. 1:4G.]

C. And R. Jacob bar Aha said, "Tirion's day has been annulled, for it is the day on which Lulianos and Pappos were killed."

D. The thirteenth of that month of Adar is Nicanor's Day.

E. What is Nicanor's Day? The ruler of the Kingdom of Greece was passing by the Land of Israel on route to Alexandria. He saw Jerusalem and broke out into cursing and execration, saying, "When I come back in peace, I shall break down that tower." The members of the Hasmonaean household went forth and did battle with his troops and killed them until they came to see those nearest the king. When they reached the troops nearest the king, they cut off the hand of the king and chopped off his head and stuck them on a pole, and wrote underneath them, "Here is the mouth that spoke shamefully and the hand that stretched out arrogantly." These he set up on a pike in sight of Jerusalem.

The importance of this passage is that attention focuses upon the meaning of days distinguished because of specific, one-time events that took place on them. There is no further taxonomic interest. The events are of a clearly historical character—that is, in no way related to the cult or the natural course of the moon in the heavens—and bear no claim that what happens matters only if the Temple is directly affected. True, in the background the Temple always is an issue. Further, the days under discussion appear on the so-called Fasting Scroll, on which it is forbidden to mourn; hence all the events fell into a single taxon. Yet the Mishnah's treatment of that matter neglects the very thing the Yerushalmi's authorities take up: the specifics of that happened, the exegesis, in its own terms, of the Scroll and the events to which it refers. And that is the main point. The framers of the passage at hand move out beyond the limits of the Mishnah's system when they narrate events essentially autonomous of happenings in the cult. Such events moreover are distinguished from one another and in no way forced into a uniform taxon. In this step, as in others we have reviewed, we see how the authors represented in the Yerushalmi move into a framework of thought in which Israel's being is described and interpreted in historical-eschatological terms, not in natural-supernatural ones.

Still, the Temple's destruction would always mark the caesura of time. Important political events were to be dated in relationship to that date. Israel lost the right to judge capital cases "forty years before the Temple was destroyed" (Y. San. 7:2III.A). So, too, forty years before the destruction, ominous signs of the coming end began to appear:

Y. Sotah 6:3
IV. A. Forty years before the destruction of the Temple the western light went out, the crimson thread remained crimson, and the lot for the Lord always came up in the left hand.
B. They would close the gates of the Temple by night and get up in the morning and find them wide open.
C. Said Rabban Yohanan ben Zakkai to the Temple, "O Temple, why do you frighten us? We know that you will end up destroyed.
D. "For it has been said, '*Open your doors, O Lebanon, that the fire may devour your cedars!*" (Zech. 11:1).

Reference to the destruction of the Temple as a principal landmark in the division of history, is hardly surprising. The framers of the Mishnah surely will not have been surprised, since, for them, as M. Sot 9:15 shows, with the destruction, the old age had turned into the new and darkening one. What was important to them was to find the counterpart in the life of the sages, since the holy life of the Temple and the holy life of the Torah-circles matched one another. So, in all, the Temple continued to provide the principal, and generative, paradigm—whether historical or cultic.

But as I have emphasized, the definition of significant, hence historical, events now expanded to encompass things that happened beyond the Temple walls, yet still in connection with the Temple's destruction. The main point is that, in the Talmud at hand, the established symmetry was shattered. The Temple's destruction had been made the counterpoise to the decline in the generations of sages. But now the Temple's destruction stood for much more, testified, so to speak, in a wider variety of cases, then solely to the decline of the supernatural world., whether priestly or scribal (to use our terms, not theirs). The message of M. Sot. 9:15 was one thing, the message of the tales at hand, a larger and more encompassing *other* story. That then is the turning point, the transformation of the Temple's destruction into an event bearing consequences in many other ways.

The most important change is the shift in historical thinking adumbrated in the pages of the Yerushalmi, a shift from focus upon the Temple and its supernatural history to close attention to the people, Israel, and its natural, this-worldly history. Once Israel, holy Israel, had come to form the counterpart to the Temple and its supernatural life, that other history—Israel's—would stand at the center of things. Accordingly, a new sort of memorable event came to the fore in the Talmud of the Land of Israel. Let me give this new history appropriate emphasis: *It was the story of the suffering of Israel, the remembrance of that suffering, on the one side, and the effort to explain events of that tragic kind, on the other.* So a composite "history" constructed out of the Yerushalmi's units of discourse pertinent to consequential events would contain long chapters on what happened to Israel, the Jewish people, and not only, or mainly, what had earlier occurred in the Temple.

This expansion in the range of historical interest and theme forms the counterpart to the emphasis, throughout the law, upon the enduring sanctity of Israel, the people, which paralleled the sanctity of the Temple in its time. What is striking in the Yerushalmi's materials on Israel's suffering is the sages' interest in finding a motive for what the Romans had done. That motive derived specifically from the repertoire of explanations already available in Israelite thought. In adducing scriptural reasons for the Soman policy, as we saw, sages extended to the world at large that same principle of intelligibility, in terms of Israel's own Scripture and logic that, in the law itself, made everything sensible and reliable. So the labor of history-writing (or at least, telling stories about historical events) went together with the work of law-making. The whole formed a single exercise in explanation of things that had happened—that is, historical explanation. True, one enterprise involved historical events, the other legal constructions. But the outcome was one and the same.

The components of the historical theory of Israel's sufferings were manifold. First and foremost, history taught moral lessons. Historical events entered into the construction of a teleology for the Yerushalmi's system of Judaism as a whole. What the law demanded reflected the consequences of wrongful action on the part of Israel. So, again, Israel's own deeds defined the events of history. Rome's role, like Assyria's and Babylonia's, depended upon Israel's provoking divine wrath, executed by the great empire. This mode of thought comes to simple expression in what follows.

Y. Erubin 3:9
IV. B. R. Ba, R. Hiyya in the name of R. Yohanan: "*Do not gaze at me because I am swarthy, because the sun has scorched me. My mother's sons were angry with me, they made me keeper of the vineyards; but, my own vineyard, I have not kept!*" (Song 1:6). What made me guard the vineyards? It is because of not keeping my own vineyard.
C. "What made me keep two festival days in Syria? It is because I did not keep the proper festival day in the Holy Land.
D. "I imagined that I would receive a reward for the two days, but I receive a reward only for one of them.
E. "Who made it necessary that I should have to separate two pieces of dough-offering from grain grown in Syria? It is because I did not separate a single piece of dough-offering in the Land of Israel."

Israel had best learn the lesson of its history. When it did so, it also would take command of its own destiny. But this notion of framing one's own destiny should not be misunderstood. The framers of the Talmud of the Land of Israel were not telling the Jews to please God by doing commandments in order that they should thereby gain control of their own destiny.

To the contrary, the paradox of the Yerushalmi's system lies in the fact that Israel frees itself of control by other nations *only* by humbly agreeing to accept God's rule instead. The nations—Rome, in the present instance—rest in one pan of the balance, while God rests, as it were, in the other. Israel must then choose between them. There is no such thing, for Israel, as freedom from both God and the nations, total autonomy and independence. There is only a choice of masters, a ruler on earth or a ruler in Heaven.

With propositions such as these, the framers of the Mishnah will assuredly have concurred. And why not? For the fundamental affirmations of the Mishnah about the centrality of Israel's perfection in stasis—sanctification—readily prove congruent to the attitudes at hand. Once the Messiah's coming had become conditional upon Israel's condition, not upon Israel's actions in historical time, then the Mishnah's system will have imposed *its* fundamental and definitive character upon the Messiah-myth. An eschatological teleology framed through that myth then will prove wholly appropriate to the method of the larger system of the Mishnah.

What, after all, makes a Messiah a false Messiah? In this Talmud, it is not his claim to save Israel, but his claim to save Israel without the help of God. The meaning of the true Messiah is Israel's total submission, through the Messiah's gentle rule, to God's yoke and service. So God is not to be manipulated through Israel's humoring Heaven in rite and cult. The notion of keeping the commandments so as to please Heaven and get God to do what Israel wants—such a nakedly manipulative system is totally incongruent to the text at hand. Keeping the commandments as a mark of submission, loyalty, humility before God—it is this which marks the rabbinic system of salvation. So Israel does not "save itself." Israel never controls its own destiny, either on earth or in Heaven. The only choice is whether to cast one's fate into the hands of cruel, deceitful men, or to trust in the living God of mercy and love. We shall now see how this critical position is spelled out in the setting of discourse about the Messiah in the Talmud of the Land of Israel.

Bar Kokhba, above all, exemplifies arrogance against God. He lost the war because of that arrogance. In particular, he ignored the authority of sages:

Y. *Taanit* 4:5
X. J. Said R. Yohanan, "Upon orders of Caesar Hadrian, in Betar they killed eight hundred thousand."
K. Said R. Yohanan, "There were eighty thousand pairs of trumpeters surrounding Betar. Each one was in charge of a number of troops. Ben Kozeba was there, and he had two hundred thousand troops who, as a sign of loyalty, had but off their little fingers.
L. "Sages sent word to him, 'How long are you going to turn Israel into a maimed people?'
M. "He said to them, 'How otherwise is it possible to test them?'
N. "They replied to him, 'Whoever cannot uproot a cedar of Lebanon while riding on his horse will not be inscribed on your military rolls.'
O. "So there were two hundred thousand who qualified in one way, and another two hundred thousand who qualified in another way."
P. When he would go forth to battle, he would say, "Lord of the world! Do not help and do not hinder us! *'Hast thou not rejected us, O God? Thou dost not go forth, O God, with our armies'* " (Ps. 60:10).

Q. Three and a half years did Hadrian besiege Betar.
R. R. Eleazar of Modiin would sit on sackcloth and ashes and pray every day, saying "Lord of the ages! Do not judge in accord with strict judgment this day!"
S. Hadrian wanted to go to him. A Samaritan said to him, "Do not go to him, until I see what he is doing, and so hand over the city [of Betar] to you. ['Make peace . . . for you.']"
T. He got into the city through a drain pipe. He went and found R. Eleazar of Modiin standing and praying. He pretended to whisper something into his ear.
U. The townspeople saw [the Samaritan] do this and brought him to Ben Kozeba. They told him, "We saw this man having dealings with your friend."
V. [Bar Kokhba] said to him, "What did you say to him, and what did he say to you?"
W. He said to [the Samaritan], "If I tell you, then the king will kill me, and if I do not tell you, then you will kill me. It is better that the king kill me, and not you.
X. "[Eleazar] said to me, 'I should hand over my city.' ['I shall make peace . . .']."
Y. He turned to R. Eleazar of Modiin. He said to him, "What did this Samaritan say to you?"
Z. He replied, "Nothing."
AA. He said to him, "What did you say to him?"
BB. He said to him, "Nothing."
CC. [Ben Kozeba] gave [Eleazar] one good kick and killed him.
DD. Forthwith an echo came forth and proclaimed the following verse:
EE. *"Woe to my worthless shepherd, who deserts the flock! May the sword smite his arm and his right eye! Let his arm be wholly withered, his right eye utterly blinded!* (Zech. 11:17)
FF. "You have murdered R. Eleazar of Modiin, the right arm of all Israel, and their right eye. Therefore may the right arm of that man wither, may his right eye be utterly blinded!"
GG. Forthwith Betar was taken, and Ben Kozeba was killed.

We notice two complementary themes. First, Bar Kokhba treats Heaven with arrogance, asking God merely to keep out of the way. Second, he treats an especially revered sage with a parallel arrogance. The sage had the power to preserve Israel. Bar Kokhba destroyed Israel's one protection. The result was inevitable.

Now in noticing the remarkable polemic in the story, in favor of sages' rule over that of Israelite among men, we should not lose sight of the importance of the tale for our present argument about the Messiah and history.

First, the passage quite simply demonstrates an interest in narrating events other than those involving the Temple, on the one side, or the sages in court, on the other. The story at hand and numerous others, not quoted here, testify to the emergence of a new category of history (or reemergence of an old one), namely, the history not of the supernatural cult, but of Israel the people. It indicates that, for the framers of those units of Yerushalmi which are not concerned with Mishnah-exegesis, and for the editors who selected materials for the final document, the history of Israel the people had now attained importance and demanded its rightful place. Once Israel's history thus reached center-stage, a rich heritage of historical thought would be invoked.

At that point, second, the Messiah, centerpiece of the history of salvation and hero of the tale, would emerge as a critical figure. The historical theory of the framers of the Yerushalmi passage at hand is stated very simply. In their view Israel had to choose between wars, either the war fought by Bar Kokhba or the "war for Torah." "Why had they been punished? It was because of the weight of the war, for they had not wanted to engage in the struggles over the meaning of the Torah" (Y. Ta. 3:9XVI.I). Those struggles, ritual arguments about ritual matter,s promised the one victory worth winning. Israel's history then would be written in terms of wars over the meaning of the Torah and the decision of the law.

True, the skins are new. But the wine is very old. For while we speak of sages and learning, the message is the familiar one. It is Israel's history that works out and expresses Israel's relationship with God. The critical dimension of Israel's life, therefore, is salvation, the definitive trait, movement in time from now to then. It follows that the paramount and organizing category is history and its lessons. As I suggested at the outset, in the Yerushalmi we witness, among the Mishnah's heirs, a striking reversion to biblical convictions about the centrality of history in the definition of Israel's reality. The heavy weight of prophecy, apocalyptic, and biblical historiography, with their emphasis upon salvation and on history as the indicator of Israel's salvation, stood against the Mishnah's quite separate thesis of what truly mattered. What, from their viewpoint, demanded description and analysis and required interpretation? It was the category of sanctification, for eternity. The true issue framed by history and apocalypse was how to move toward the foreordained end of salvation, how so to act in time as to reach salvation at the end of time. The Mishnah's teleology beyond time, its capacity to posit an eschatology lacking all place for a historical Messiah—these take a position beyond the imagination of the entire antecedent sacred literature of Israel. Only one strand or stream, the priestly one, had ever taken so extreme a position on the centrality of sanctification, the peripherality of salvation. Wisdom had stood in between, with its own concerns, drawing attention both to what happened and to what endured. But to wisdom what finally mattered was not nature or supernature, but rather abiding relationships in historical time.

This reversion by the authors of the Talmud to Scripture's paramount motifs, with Israel's history and destiny foremost among them, forms a complement to the Yerushalmi's principal judgment upon the Mishnah itself. For an important exegetical initiative of the Yerushalmi was to provide, for statements of the Mishnah, proof texts deriving from Scripture. Whereas the framers of the Mishnah did not think their statements required evidentiary support, the authors of the Talmud's Mishnah-exegetical units of discourse took proof-texts drawn from Scripture to be the prime necessity. Accordingly, at hand is yet another testimony to the effort, among third and fourth-century heirs of the Mishnah, to draw that document back within the orbit of Scripture, to "biblicize" what the Mishnah's authors had sent forth as a freestanding and "non-biblical" Torah.

The single most interesting indicator of the Talmud's framers' reversion to Scripture lies in the effort to go beyond systematizing biblical events and showing their taxonomic status. Now they proposed to draw lessons from biblical history. True, the framers of the Mishnah would not have been surprised at their heirs' effort to find in ancient Israel's writings lessons for the new day. They had done the same within the pages of the Mishnah itself. A glance, for example, at the homiletical materials at M. Ta. 2:1-4 shows how routinely they invoked biblical events, parallels, analogies. But the Mishnah contains no counterpart to vast stretches of the Yerushalmi's treatment of Scripture, specifically, its amplification of biblical stories with a view to rewriting the repertoire of history of ancient Israel. Evidence of that tendency will be found, for one example, in the rabbinization of the Messiah. So now a single if lengthy, example may suffice to make the point. Before us is a striking instance of the amplification of the narrative of a major event in ancient Israelite history.

Y. Abodah Zarah 1:1
I. V. Said R. Yudan, father of R. Mattenaiah, "The intention of a verse of Scripture [such as is cited below] was only to make mention of the evil traits of Israel.
W. *"On the day of our king when Jeroboam was made king the princes became sick with the heat of wine; he stretched out his hand with mockers'* (Hosea 7:5).
X. "On the day on which Jeroboam began to reign over Israel, all Israel came to him at dusk, saying to him, 'Rise up and make an idol.'
Y. "He said to them, 'It is already dusk. I am partly drunk and partly sober, and the whole people is drunk. But if you want, go and come back in the morning.'

Z. "This is the meaning of the following Scripture, '*For like an oven, their hearts burn with intrigue; all night their anger smolders; in the morning it blazes like a flaming fire*' (Hosea 7:6)."
AA. "'*All night their anger smolders.*'
BB. "'*In the morning it blazes like a flaming fire.*'
CC. "In the morning they came to him. Thus did he say to them, 'I know what you want. But I am afraid of your sanhedrin, lest it come and kill me.'"
DD. "They said to him, 'We shall kill them.'
EE. "That is the meaning of the following verse: '*All of them are hot as an oven. And they devour their rulers*' (Hos. 7:7) . . ."
KK. When he would see an honorable man, he would set up against him two mockers, who would say to him, "Now what generation do you think is the most cherished of all generations?"
LL. He would answer them, "It was the generation of the wilderness which received the Torah."
MM. They would say to him, "Now did they themselves not worship an idol?"
NN. And he would answer them, "Now do you think that, because they were cherished, they were not punished for their deed?"
OO. And they would say to him, "Shut up! The king wants to do exactly the same thing. Not only so, but [the generation of the wilderness] only made one [calf], while [the king] wants to make two."
PP. [*So the king took counsel and made two calves of gold] and he set up one in Bethel, and the other he put in Dan* (1 Kings 12:29).
QQ. The arrogance of Jeroboam is what condemned him decisively.
RR. Said R. Yose bar Jacob, "It was at the conclusion of a sabbatical year that Jeroboam began to rule over Israel. That is the meaning of the following verse: '[*And Moses commanded them]. At the end of every seven years, at the set time of the year of release, at the feast of booths, when all Israel comes to appear before the Lord your God at the place which he will choose, you shall read this law before all Israel in their hearing*' (Deut. 31:10-11).
SS. "[Jeroboam] said, 'I shall be called upon to read [the Torah, as Scripture requires]. If I get up and read first, they will say to me, "The king of the place [in which the gathering takes place, namely, Jerusalem] comes first." And if I read second, it is disrespectful to me. And if I do not read at all, it is a humiliation for me. And, finally, if I let the people go up, they will abandon me and go over to the side of Rehoboam the son of Solomon.'
TT. "That is the meaning of the following verse of Scripture: '[*And Jeroboam said in his heart, Now the kingdom will turn back to the house of David;] if this people go up to offer sacrifices in the house of the Lord at Jerusalem, then the heart of this people will turn again to their Lord, to Rehoboam, king of Judah, and they will kill me and return to rehoboam, king of Judah*' (1 Kings 12:27-28).
UU. "What then did he do? '*He made two calves of gold*' (1 Kings

12:28), and he inscribed on their heart, '. . . lest they kill you' [as counsel to his successors].

VV. "He said, 'Let every king who succeeds me look upon them.'"

Familiar motifs, such as the danger of arrogance, occur here, just as in passages in which sages explain events of their own day. The main point, however, is not to be missed. The extensive recounting of biblical tales, the interest in making points through the narrative of historical events—these do mark a break from the Mishnah's approach. For the framers of the Mishnah rarely found a use for the historical materials of Scripture. It is highly unusual to find in the Mishnah passages like this. Interest in expanding biblical history, apart from the salvific focus imposed by that history, testifies to the process at hand: the renewal, in the pages of the Yerushalmi, of the age-old practice of homiletical retelling of biblical tales. The earlier document contains slight signs of such interest; its successor is rich in such evidence.

The reversion to the prophetic notion of learning the lessons of history carried in its wake reengagement with the Messiah-myth. The climax of the matter comes in an explicit statement that the practice of conduct required by the Torah will bring about the coming of the Messiah. That explanation of the purpose of the holy way of life, focused now upon the end of time and the advent of the Messiah, must strike us as surprising in light of the facts surveyed in an earlier chapter.

For the framers of the Mishnah had found it possible to construct a complete and encompassing teleology for their system with scarcely a single word about the Messiah's coming when the system would be perfectly achieved. So with their interest in explaining events and accounting for history, third- and fourth-century sages represented in the units of discourse at hand invoked what their predecessors had at best found of peripheral consequence to their system. The following contains the most striking expression of the viewpoint at hand.

Y. Taanit 1:1

X. J. *"The oracle concerning Dumah. One is calling to me from Seir, "Watchman, what of the night? Watchman, what of the night?"* (Is. 21:11).

K. The Israelites said to Isaiah, "O our Rabbi, Isaiah, What will come for us out of this night?"

L. He said to them, "Wait for me, until I can present the question."

M. Once he had asked the question, he came back to them.

N. They said to him, "Watchman, what of the night? What did the Guardian of the ages tell you?"

O. He said to them, "The watchman says" *'Morning comes; and also the night. If you will inquire, inquire; come back again'* (Is. 21:12).

P. They said to him, "Also the night?"

Q. He said to the, "It is not what you are thinking. But there will be morning for the righteous, and night for the wicked, morning for Israel, and night for idolaters."
R. They said to him, "When?"
S. He said to them, "Whenever you want, He too wants [it to be]—if you want it. he wants it."
T. They said to him, "What is standing in the way?"
U. He said to them, "Repentance: *'Come back again'* (Is. 21:12.)"
V. R. Aha in the name of R. Tanhum b. R. Hiyya, "If Israel repents for one day, forthwith the son of David will come.
W. "What is the Scriptural basis? *'O that today you would hearken to his voice!'* (Ps. 95:7)."
X. Said R. Levi, "If Israel would keep a single Sabbath in the proper way, forthwith the son of David will come.
Y. "What is the Scriptural basis for this view? *'Moses said, Eat it today, for today is a sabbath to the Lord; today you will not find it in the field'* (Ex. 16:25).
Z. "And it says, *'For thus said the Lord God, the Holy One of Israel, 'In returning and rest you shall be saved; in quietness and in trust shall be your strength.' And you would not'* (Is. 30:15)."

The discussion of the power of repentance would hardly have surprised a Mishnah-sage. What is new is at V-Z, the explicit linkage of keeping the law with achieving the end of time and the coming of the Messiah. That motif stands separate from the notions of righteousness and repentance, which surely do not require it. So the condition of "all Israel," a social category in historical time comes under consideration, and not only the status of individual Israelites in life and in death. The latter had formed the arena for Abot's account of the Mishnah's system's meaning. Now history as an operative category, drawing in its wake Israel as a social entity, comes once more on the scene. But, except for the Mishnah's sages, it had never left the stage.

We must not lose sight of the importance of this passage, with its emphasis on repentance, on the one side, and the power of Israel to reform itself, on the other. The Messiah will come any day that Israel makes it possible. If all Israel will keep a single Sabbath in the proper (rabbinic) way, the Messiah will come. If all Israel will repent for one day, the Messiah will come. "Whenever you want . . .," the Messiah will come. Now, two things are happening here. First, the system of religious observance, including study of Torah, is explicitly invoked as having salvific power. Second, the persistent hope of the people for the coming of the Messiah is linked to the system of rabbinic observance and belief. In this way, the austere program of the Mishnah, with no trace of a promise that the Messiah will come if and when the system is fully realized, finds a new development. A teleology lacking all eschatological dimension here gives way to an explicitly messianic statement that the purpose of the law is to attain Israel's salvation: "If you want it, God wants it too." The one thing Israel commands is its own heart; the power it yet exercises is the power to repent. These suffice. The entire history of humanity will respond to Israel's will, to what happens in Israel's heart and soul. And, with Temple in ruins, repentance can take place only within the heart and mind.

II. *From Sanctification to Salvation*

The framers of the Yerushalmi took over a document portraying a system centered upon sanctifying Israel through the creation of a world in stasis, wholly perfect within itself. They left behind them a document in which that original goal of sanctification in stasis competed with another. For within the pages of the Talmud of the Land of Israel we find a second theory of what matters in Israel's life. A system centered on the salvation of Israel in a world moving toward a goal, a world to be perfected only at the conclusion of the journey through time, now came to full expression. So the bridge formed by the Talmud of the Land of Israel leads from a world in which nothing happens but sanctification *is*, to one in which everything happens *en route* to salvation at the end.

To understand the choices at hand, let us revert to the points of contrast and tension, the specification of opposites, in the materials now reviewed. These indicate the range of permissible choices, hence the boundaries of the reality posited by a given universe of discourse. If we were to administer a psychological test to the storytellers, asking them to state the opposite of a given word, the results cannot be in doubt. If we say, "This world," the storytellers who speak of kings and wars would answer, "the world to come," or "this age," and "the age to come." If, by contrast, we presented to storytellers who relate tales of sages, a given symbol of the natural world, they would reply with a counterpart—a symbol of the supernatural world. As we shall see in a moment, when (supernatural) rabbis die, for example, the (natural) world responds with miracles. In this sense, therefore, we confront two separate constructions of the world—polar possibilities. The one involves historical-messianic explanation of historical events, the other, supernatural explanation of natural ones. True, prayer may speak of either kind of occurrence. But as the climactic moment on the Day of Atonement, the prayer of the high priest turned to the natural world:

> Y. Yoma 5:2
> II. B. This was the prayer of the high priest on the Day of Atonement, when he left the Holy Place whole and in one piece: "May it be pleasing before you, Lord, our God of our fathers, that [a decree of] exile not be issued against us, not this day or this year, but if a decree

of exile should be issued against us, then let it be exile to a place of Torah.

C. "May it be pleasing before you, Lord, our God and God of our fathers, that a decree of want not be issued against us, not this day of this year, but if a decree of want should be issued against us, then let it be a want of [the performance of] religious duties.

D. "May it be pleasing before you, Lord, our God and God of our fathers, that this year be a year of cheap food, full bellies, good business; a year in which the earth forms clods, then is parched so as to form scabs, and then moistened with dew,

E. "so that your people, Israel, will not be in need of the help of one another."

F. "And do not heed the prayer of travelers [that it not rain]."

The high priest's prayer by itself obviously does not prove that, in all circumstances or contexts of sanctification, at issue are nature and supernature alone. But it does at least illustrate the self-evident association proposed at the outset. And the principal point must not be missed. One could speak of the ultimate resolution of Israel's present circumstance without invoking the name of the Messiah or the concept of events leading to a foreordained climax and conclusion with his coming at the end of time. Just as M. Sot. 9:15's author could refer to the resurrection of the dead with in the same breath speaking of the coming of the Messiah, so too it remained possible to do this in the pages of the Yerushalmi.

The main point is that for the framers of the Mishnah, one could speculate about the meaning and end of the holy way of life of the holy people without any reference to the coming of the Messiah. For them and their heirs in the Talmud of the Land of Israel the conception of redemption did not invariably invoke the salvific myth of the Messiah. Other units of discourse in the Yerushalmi carry forward this same treatment of the matter, as in the following.

Y. Yoma 3:2

III. A. One time R. Hiyya the Elder and R. Simeon b. Halapta were talking in the valley of Arabel at daybreak. They saw that the light of the morning star was breaking forth. Said R. Hiyya the Elder to R. Simeon b. Halapta, "Son of my master, this is what the redemption of Israel is like—at first, little by little, but in the end it will go along and burst into light.

B. "What is the Scriptural basis for this view? 'Rejoice not over me, O my enemy; when I fall, I shall rise; when I sit in darkness, the Lord will be a light to me' (Mich. 7:8)."

How then does the Judaism of sanctification, as represented in the Yerushalmi, take up events we should regard as historical? That is, how is Israel to dispose of the events of the day, if not through fervent prayer for the intervention of the Messiah? Bar Kokhba's way, sages maintained, was arrogant. What alternative did they offer? The answer is that, within the framework of sanctification, as in the Mishnah, so in the Yerushalmi, world-shaking events were treated as trivial, with history converted into a symptom of the condition of private life, and great events turned into epiphenomena within the framework of everyday reality. Accordingly, within this system, as the Yerushalmi expresses it, historical events play a decidedly subordinated role. Among the deeds that do make history, mainly personal and private actions come to the fore, not those that bear (to us) self-evident political and social consequence. Accordingly, historical events need not take a leading role in the salvation of Israel—even when salvation is at issue. The "harsh decree" may be averted through piety, charity, right attitude—surely not very consequential deeds in the larger historical scheme of things.

Y. Taanit 2:1
IX. A. Said R. Eleazar, "Three acts nullify the harsh decree, and these are they: prayer, charity, and repentance."
B. And all three of them are to be derived from a single verse of Scripture:
C. *"If my people who are called by my name humble themselves, and pray and seek my face, and turn from their wicked ways, then I will hear from heaven, and will forgive their sin and heal their land"* (2 Chron. 7:14).
D. *"Pray"*—this refers to prayer.
E. *"And seek my face"*—this refers to charity,
F. as you say, *"As for me, I shall behold thy face in righteousness; when I awake, I shall be satisfied with beholding thy form"* (Ps. 17:15).
G. *"And turn from their wicked ways"*—this refers to repentance.
H. Now if they do these things, what is written concerning them?
I. *"Then I will hear from heaven and will forgive their sin and heal their land."*

The forgiveness of sin draws in its wake prosperity, represented by the "healing of the land." These references therefore cannot apply solely to what happens to the individual. They deal with the fate of the whole of society. True, the harsh decree may come from the state; but the outcome is the same. Through repentance and its associated actions Israel can make its own history. In a statement like this, the issue of the coming of the Messiah simply plays no role. The historical-salvific-messianic does not merge with the timeless-sanctifactory-sagacious in materials of this kind; so far as I can see, within the pages of the Yerushalmi, no such union appears.

In Israel there were holy men who bore within themselves the power to save Israel. In this framework, the notion of the Messiah loses all pertinence. How so? Every sage, if sufficiently holy, could effect miracles for Israel. Whether salvation is at issue remains in doubt. For, in context, we deal with supernatural, not this-worldly, events: a miracle in nature, effected by a holy man, rather than a one-for-all historical resolution of Israel's situation, that is, "salvation" in the ordinary sense. The power of the holy or righteous man to save Israel is made explicit in the following:

Y. Yoma 1:1
V. D. Said R. Hiyya bar Ba, "The sons of Aaron died on the first day of Nisan. And why is their death called to mind in connection with the Day of Atonement?
E. "It is to indicate to you that just as the Day of Atonement effects expiation for Israel, so the death of the righteous effects atonement for Israel."
F. Said R. Ba bar Binah, "Why did the Scripture place the story of the death of Miriam side by side with the story of the burning of the red cow?
G. "It is to teach you that, just as the dirt of the red cow [mixed with water] effects atonement for Israel, so the death of the righteous effects atonement for Israel."

The supernatural power associated with the death of the righteous person—in this context, the sage—appears in miracles marking the event.

Y. Abodah Zarah 3:1
II. A. When R. Aha died, a star appeared at noon.
B. When R. Hanan died, the statutes bowed low.
C. When R. Yohanan died, the icons bowed down.
D. They said that [this was to indicate] there were no icons like him [so beautiful as Yohanan himself].
E. When R. Hanina of Bet Hauran died, the Sea of Tiberias split open.
F. They said that [this was to commemorate the miracle that took place] when he went up to intercalate the year, and the sea split open before him.
G. When R. Hoshaiah died, the palm of Tiberias fell down.
H. When R. Isaac b. Eliasheb died, seventy [infirm] thresholds of houses in Galilee were shaken down.
I. They said that [this was to commemorate the fact that] they [were shaky and] had depended on his merit [for the miracle that permitted them to continue to stand].
J. When R. Samuel bar R. Isaac died, cedars of the land of Israel were uprooted.

K. They said that [this was to take note of the fact that] he would take a branch [of a cedar] and [dance, so] praising a bride [at her wedding, and thereby giving happiness to the bride].
L. The rabbis would ridicule them [for lowering himself by doing so]. Said to them R. Zeira, "Leave him be. Does the old man not know what he is doing?"
M. When he died, a flame came forth from heaven and intervened between his bier and the congregation. For three hours there were voices and thunderings in the world: "Come and see what a spring of cedar has done for this old man!"
N. [Further] an echo came forth and said, "Woe that Samuel b. R. Isaac has died, the doer of merciful deeds."
O. When R. Yosa bar Halputa died, the gutters ran with blood in Laodicea.
P. They said [that the reason was] that he had given his life for the rite of circumcision.

The (natural) death of the sage invokes (supernatural) miracles, and so the sage enters into his eternal life. Not *the* Messiah alone, but *any* sufficiently holy and meritorious sage will mask in such a way the shift from one world to the next. But the worlds that are exchanged vary from system to system. For we do not find here the social history of Israel marked by the coming of the Messiah, but rather, the individual life of a sage commemorated in nature through supernature. The type of story at hand therefore calls into question the concept of *one* Messiah only, presiding over a unique event, at the end of a sequence of happenings all pointing toward that one-time eschatological climax. Either Israel is *saved* through the Messiah who resurrects the dead, or Israel is *sanctified* through the presence, in life and in death, of the righteous. We cannot demonstrate that these statements speak of different things to different people. We can only show, as I have here, that, when a unit of discourse deals with the one, it rarely, if ever, mentions the symbols or issues of the other.

But these sets of opposites—time *vs.* eternity, life *vs.* death, nature *vs.* supernature, on the one side, and history *vs.* end of time, this world *vs.* time of the Messiah, death *vs.* resurrection, on the other—need not persist as separate and contradictory. The sage as holy man does his work now and does it mainly through ongoing nature and unchanging supernature. *The* Messiah—as distinct from *a* (any) sage—does his work at the end of time. He does it once. In the resurrection of the dead, he carries out a single, one-time action, by its nature one that need not be repeated. He is a single and therefore unique figure, a kind of holy man to be sure, but one of a kind, who performs a single, unique deed. Once *a* messiah, in the sense of a high priest appointed for a given task to be repeated many times, gives way to *the* Messiah, meaning, a man designed to do a single task, never to be repeated, we leave the framework of the Mishnah altogether.

This does not mean that people faced or even recognized a choice between one teleology and another. It means that the eschatology beyond history, the teleology beyond time, worked out in the Mishnah, stands essentially asymmetrical to the parallel theories spelled out here. They may be harmonized. They may set side by side without colliding. But they may not be represented as one and the same thing. They never meet. And, in the canonical literature of Judaism, the two theories of where things are heading scarcely intersect in a single pericope. The supernatural sage with his power over individual life and the natural world, and the eschatological Messiah with his command over the people of Israel and the whole of history—both within the model of the rabbi, in the image of God—never meet, except when King David is perceived as Rabbi David. And if truth be told, Rabbi David is mostly a rabbi, and only rarely a messiah or the Messiah. If we did not know that David was the prototype of the Messiah, the Yerushalmi would not have made us think so. In all, the eschatological messiah is difficult to locate. "Messiah" defines a category of holy man.

CHAPTER ELEVEN

The Theory of History of Genesis Rabbah

Jacob Neusner

Israel's history constitutes the counterpart of creation, and the laws of Israel's salvation aform the foundation of creation. Therefore a given story out of Genesis, about creation, events from Adam to Noah and Noah to Abraham, the domestic affairs of the patriarchs, or Joseph, will bear a deeper message about what it means to be Israel, on the one side, and what in the end of days will happen to Israel, on the other. So the persistent theological program requires sages' to search in Scripture for meaning for their own circumstance and for the condition of their people. That is the reading of history set forth in Genesis Rabbah. Scripture, the book of Genesis in this case, is turned into future-history, and events of the day—the fourth century—are reshaped into a historical pattern by reading in their light the book of Genesis, and interpreting in the perspective of the book of Genesis those same events—a reciprocal process of mutual illumination. History then formed a sustained and systematic narrative, with the book of Genesis supplying the story line, the condition of Israel, with special reference to the fourth century, providing the plot and narrative tension.

Let us begin with a single example of the way in which Genesis Rabbah, a late fourth or early fifth century discourse organized as a commentary to the book of Genesis, treats a historical event. It derives from the single critical moment, in sages' view, in the narrative of Genesis. The binding of Isaac, critical in sages' reading of lessons taught by Abrahams' deeds for the direction of their descendants, formed the centerpiece of their quest for the laws of history as well. At each point, in each detail, they discovered not only what we going to happen but also why. The single most important paradigm for history therefore emerged from the deed at Moriah. The Roman numeral refers to the chapter in Genesis Rabbah and the subdivision of that chapter, the Arabic numeral, to the paragraph of that subdivision, and the letter, the sentence of that paragraph; we deal with Genesis Rabbah Chapter Fifty-Six, the first and second subdivisions, as indicated.

LVI:I.1.A. "On the third day Abraham lifted up his eyes and saw the place afar off"(Gen. 22:4):

B. "After two days he will revive us, on the third day he will raise us up, that we may live in his presence"(Hos. 16:2).

C. On the third day of the tribes: "And Joseph said to them on the third day, 'This do and live' "(Gen. 42:18).

D. On the third day of the giving of the Torah: "And it came to pass on the third day when it was morning"(Ex. 19:16).

E. On the third day of the spies: "And hide yourselves there for three days"(Josh 2:16).

F. On the third day of Jonah: "And Jonah was in the belly of the fish three days and three nights"(Jonah 2:1).

G. On the third day of the return from the Exile: "And we abode there three days"(Ezra 8:32).

H. On the third day of the resurrection of the dead: "After two days he will revive us, on the third day he will raise us up, that we may live in his presence"(Hos. 16:2).

I. On the third day of Esther: "Now it came to pass on the third day that Esther put on her royal apparel"(Est. 5:1).

J. She put on the monarchy of the house of her fathers.

K. On account of what sort of merit?

L. Rabbis say, "On account of the third day of the giving of the Torah."

M. R. Levi said, "It is on account of the merit of the third day of Abraham: 'On the third day Abraham lifted up his eyes and saw the place afar off'(Gen. 22:4)."

2.A. ". . . lifted up his eyes and saw the place afar off"(Gen. 22:4):

B. What did he see? He saw a cloud attached to the mountain. He said, "It would appear that that is the place concerning which the Holy One, blessed be he, told me to offer up my son."

The third day marks the fulfillment of the promise, at the end of time of the reserection of the dead, and, at appropriate moments, of Israel's redemption. The reference to the third day at Gen. 22:2 then invokes the entire panoply of Israel's history. The relevance of the composition emerges at the end. Prior to the concluding segment, the passage forms a kind of litany and falls into the category of a liturgy. Still, the recurrent hemeneutic which teaches that the stories of the patriarchs prefigure the history of Israel certainly makes its appearance.

We may now generalize on the theory of history in Genesis Rabbah. The sages who produced that book understood that stories about the progenitors, presented in the book of Genesis, define the human condition and proper conduct for their children, Israel in time to come. Accordingly, they systematically asked Scripture to tell them how they were supposed to conduct themselves at the critical turnings of life. The first thing to notice is how a variety of events is made to prove a syllogism. The stories of Genesis therefore join stories of other times and persons in Israel's history. All of them equally, and timelessly, point to prevailing rules. Syllogistic argument, resting on lists of facts of the same classification, wrests the narrative out of its one-time and time-bound esetting and turns it into a statement of rules that prevail everywhere and all the time for Israel. Here is a good example of the mode of argument of the document:

> XCVI:III.1.A. "And when the time drew near that Israel must die, [he called his son Joseph and said to him, 'If now I have found favor in your sight, put your hand under my thigh and promise to deal loyally and truly with me. Do not bury me in Egypt, but let me lie with my fathers; carry me out of Egypt and bury me in their burying place.' He answered, I will do as you have said.' And he said, 'Swear to me.' And he swore to him. Then Israel bowed himself upon the head of his bed]"(Gen. 47:29-31):
>
> B. "There is no man that has power of the spirit . . . neither is there dominion in the day of death"(Qoh. 8:8).
>
> C. Said R. Joshua of Sikhnin in the name of R. Levi, "As to the trumpets that Moses made in the wilderness, when Moses lay on the point of death, the Holy One, blessed be he, hid them away, so that he would not blow on them and summon the people to him.
>
> D. "This was meant to fulfill this verse: '. . . neither is there dominion in the day of death'(Qoh. 8:8).
>
> E. "When Zimri did his deed, what is written? 'And Phineas went after the man of Israel into the chamber' (Num. 25:8). So where was Moses, that Phineas should speak before he did?
>
> F. "'. . . neither is there dominion in the day of death'(Qoh.8:8).
>
> G. "But the formulation expresses humiliation. Salvation was handed over to Phineas, [and Moses] abased himself.
>
> H. "So too with David: 'How king David was old' (1 Kgs. 1:1). What is stated about him when he lay dying? 'Now the days of David drew near, that he should die' (1 Kgs. 21:1).
>
> I. "What is said is not 'king David,' but merely 'David.'
>
> J. "The same applies to Jacob, when he was on the point of death, he humbled himself to Joseph, saying to him, 'If now I have found favor in your sight.' [So he abased himself, since there is no dominion on the day of death.]
>
> K. "When did this take place? As he drew near the end: 'And when the time drew near that Israel must die.'"

What strikes the exegete is the unprepossessing language used by Jacob in speaking to Joseph. The intersecting verse makes clear that, on the day of one's death, one no longer rules. Several examples of that fact are given, Moses, David, finally Jacob. So the syllogism about the loss of power on the occasion of death derives proof from a number of sources, and the passage has not been worked out to provide the exegesis of our base verse in particular. The exposition is all the more moving because the exegete focuses upon his proposition, rather than on the great personalities at hand. His message obviously is that even the greatest lose all dominion when they are going to die. In this way the deeds of the founders define the rule for the descendants.

As a corollary to the view that the biography of the fathers prefigures the history of the descendants, sages maintained that the deeds of the children—the holy way of life of Israel—follow the model established by the founders long ago. So they looked in Genesis for the basis for the things they held to be God's will for Israel. And they found ample proof. Sages invariably searched the stories of Genesis for evidence of the origins not only of creation and of Israel, but also of Israel's cosmic way of life, its understanding of how, in the passage of nature and the seasons, humanity worked out its relationship with God. The holy way of life that Israel lived through the seasons of nature therefore would make its mark upon the stories of the creation of the world and the beginning of Israel.

Part of the reason sages pursued the interest at hand derived from polemic. From the first Christian century theologians of Christianity maintained that salvation did not depend upon keeping the laws of the Torah. Abraham, after all, had been justified and he did not keep the Torah, which, in his day, had not yet been given. So sages time and again would maintain that Abraham indeed kept the entire Torah even before it had been revealed. They further attributed to Abraham, Isaac, and Jacob rules of the Torah enunciated only later on, for example, the institution of prayer three times a day. But the passage before us bears a different charge. It is to Israel to see how deeply embedded in the rules of reality were the patterns governing God's relationship to Israel. That relationship, one of human sin and atonement, divine punishment and forgiveness, expresses the most fundamental laws of human existence. Here is yet another rule that tells sages what to find in Scripture.

> XCVIII:I.1.A. "Then Jacob called his sons [and said, 'Gather yourselves together, that I may tell you what shall befall you in days to come. Assemble and hear, O sons of Jacob, and hearken to Israel, your father. Reuben, you are my first-born, my might and the first fruits of my strength, pre-eminent in pride and pre-eminent in power. Unstable as water, you shall not have pre-eminence, because you went up to your father's bed, then you defiled it, you went up to my couch!]"(Gen. 49:1-4):
>
> B. "I will cry to God Most High, [unto God who completes it for me]"(Ps. 57:3):
>
> C. "I will cry to God Most High:" on the New Year.
>
> D. ". . . unto God who completes it for me:" on the Day of Atonement.

E. To find out which [goat] is for the Lord and which one is for an evil decree.

2.A. Another matter: "I will cry to God Most High, [unto God who completes it for me]"(Ps. 57:3):

B. "I will cry to God Most High:" refers to our father, Jacob.

C. "... unto God who completes it for me:" for the Holy One, blessed be he, concurred with him to give each of the sons a blessing in accord with his character.

D. "Then Jacob called his sons [and said, 'Gather yourselves together, that I may tell you what shall befall you in days to come]."

The intersecting verse invites the comparison of the judgment of the Days of Awe to the blessing of Jacob, and that presents a dimension of meaning that the narrative would not otherwise reveal. Just as God decides which goat serves what purpose, so God concurs in Jacob's judgment of which son/tribe deserves what sort of blessing. So Jacob stands in the stead of God in this stunning comparison of Jacob's blessing to the day of judgment. The link between Jacob's biography and the holy life of Israel is fresh.

What, then, tells sages how to identify the important and avoid the trivial? The answer derives from the fundamental theological conviction that gives life to their search of Scripture. It is that the task of Israel is to hope, and the message of Genesis—there for the sages to uncover and make explicit—is always to hope. For a Jew it is a sin to despair. This I think defines the iron law of meaning, telling sages what matters and what does not, guiding their hands to take up those verses that permit expression of hope—that above all. Given the definitive event of their day—the conversion of the great empire of Rome to Christianity—the task of hope proved not an easy assignment.

XCVIII:XIV.4.A. "I hope for your salvation, O Lord" (Gen. 49:18):

B. Said R. Isaac, "All things depend on hope, suffering depends on hope, the sanctification of God's name depends on hope, the merit attained by the fathers depends on hope, the lust for the age to come depends on hope.

C. "That is in line with this verse: 'Yes, in the way of your judgments, O Lord, we have hoped for you, to your name, and to your memorial, is the desire of our soul'(Is. 26:8). 'The way of your judgments refers to suffering.

D. "'... to your name:' this refers to the sanctification of the divine name.

E. "'... and to your memorial:' this refers to the merit of the fathers.

F. "'... is the desire of our soul:' this refers to the lust for the age to come.

G. "Grace depends on hope: 'O Lord, be gracious to us, we have hoped for you'(Is. 33:2).

H. "Forgiveness depends on hope: 'For with you is forgiveness' (Ps. 133:4), then: 'I hope for the Lord'(Ps. 130:5)."

The interesting unit is No. 4, which is explicit on the critical importance of hope in the salvific process, and which further links the exclamation to the setting in which it occurs. This seems to me to typify the strength of the exegesis at hand, with its twin-powers to link all details to a tight narrative and to link the narrative to the history of Israel.

Sages read the narrative of creation and the fall of Adam to testify to the redemption and the salvation of Israel. Let me begin with a single example of the syllogism at hand and then offer a more general statement of it. The following passage provides a stunning example of the basic theory of sages on how the stories of creation are to be read:

XXIX:III.1.A. "And Noah found grace"(Gen. 6:8):
B. Said R. Simon, "There were three acts of finding on the part of the Holy One, blessed be he:
C. "'And you found [Abraham's] heart faithful before you'(Neh. 9:8).
D. "'I have found David my servant'(Ps. 89:21).
E. "'I found Israel like grapes in the wilderness'(Hos. 9:10)."
F. His fellows said to R. Simon, "And is it not written, 'Noah found grace in the eyes of the Lord'(Gen. 6:8)?"
G. He said them, "He found it, but the Holy One, blessed be he, did not find it."
H. Said R. Simon, "'He found grace in the wilderness'(Jer. 31:1) on account of the merit of the generation of the Wilderness."

The proposition draws on the verse at hand, but makes its own point. It is that the grace shown to Noah derived from Israel. Noah on his own—that is, humanity—enjoyed salvation only because of Israel's merit. The proposition is striking and daring. God "found," that is, made an accidental discovery, of a treasure, consisting only of three: Abraham, David, and Israel. These stand for the beginning, the end, and the holy people that started with Abraham and found redemption through David. As if to underline this point, we refer, H, to the generation of the Wilderness and its faith, which merited gaining the Land.

A cogent and uniform world-view accompanied the sages at hand when they approached the text of Genesis. This world-view they systematically joined to that text, fusing the tale at hand with that larger context of imagination in which the tale was received and read. Accordingly, when we follow the sages' mode of interpreting the text, we find our way deep into their imaginative life. Scripture becomes the set of facts that demonstrate the truth of the syllogisms that encompassed and described the world, as sages saw it. The next stage in my demonstration of the systematic and deeply polemical reading at hand will take the simple form of successive illustration of the basic thesis.

That thesis is that Israel's salvific history informs and infuses the creation of the world. That story takes on its true meaning from what happened to Israel, and it follows that Israel's future history accounts for the creation of the world.

> XX:I.1.A. "Then the Lord God said to the serpent, 'Because you have done this, cursed are you above all cattle and above all wild animals' "(Gen. 3:14):
> B. "A slanderer shall not be established in the earth; the violent and wicked man shall be hunted with thrust upon thrust"(Ps. 140:12).
> C. Said R. Levi, "In the world to come the Holy One, blessed be he, will take the nations of the world and bring them down to Gehenna. He will say to them, 'Why did you impose fines upon my children.' They will say to him, 'Some of them slandered others among them.' The Holy One, blessed be he, will then take these [Israelite slanderers] and those and bring them down to Gehenna."
> 2.A. Another interpretation: "A slanderer" refers to the snake, who slandered his creator.
> B. "Will not be established [standing upright] on earth:" "Upon your belly you shall go"(Gen.3:14).
> C. "The violent and wicked man shall be hunted:" What is written is not "with a thrust" but "with thrust after thrust," [since not only the serpent was cursed]. What is written is "thrust after thrust," for man was cursed, woman was cursed, and the snake was cursed.
> D. "And the Lord God said to the serpent. . . ."

We have an exegesis of a base verse and intersecting verse, that is in that "classic" form in which the intersecting verse is fully worked out and only then drawn to meet the base verse. No. 1 treats the intersecting verse as a statement on its own, and then No. 2 reads the verse in line with Gen. 3:14. But the intersecting verse is hardly chosen at random, since it speaks of slander in general, and then at No. 2 the act of slander of the snake is explicitly read into the intersecting verse. So the intersection is not only thematic, not by any means. The upshot of the exercise links Israel's history to the history of humanity in the garden of Eden. No. 1 focuses upon the sacred history of Israel, making the point that slanderers in Israel cause the nation's downfall, just as the snake caused the downfall of humanity, the point

> XIX:VII.1.A. "And they heard the sound of the Lord God walking in the garden in the cool of the day"(Gen. 3:8):
> 2.A. Said R. Abba bar Kahana, "The word is not written, 'move,' but rather, 'walk,' bearing the sense that [the Presence of God] lept about and jumped upward.
> B. "[The point is that God's presence lept upward from the earth on account of the events in the garden, as will now be explained:] The principal location of the Presence of God was [meant to be] among the creatures

down here. When the first man sinned, the Presence of God moved up to the first firmament. When Cain sinned, it went up to the second firmament. When the generation of Enosh sinned, it went up to the third firmament. When the generation of the Flood sinned, it went up to the fourth firmament. When the generation of the dispersion [at the tower of Babel] sinned, it went up to the fifth. On account of the Sodomites it went up to the sixth, and on account of the Egyptians in the time of Abraham it went up to the seventh.

C. "But, as a counterpart, there were seven righteous men who rose up: Abraham, Isaac, Jacob, Levi, Kahath, Amram, and Moses. They brought the Presence of God [by stages] down to earth.

D. "Abraham brought it from the seventh to the sixth, Isaac brought it from the sixth to the fifth, Jacob brought it from the fifth to the fourth, Levi brought it down from the fourth to the third, Kahath brought it down from the third to the second, Amram brought it down from the second to the first. Moses brought it down to earth."

E. Said R. Isaac, "It is written, 'The righteous will inherit the land and dwell therein forever'(Ps.37:29). Now what will the wicked do? Are they going to fly in the air? But that the wicked did not make it possible for the Presence of God to take up residence on earth [is what the verse wishes to say]."

What is striking is the claim that while the wicked (gentiles) drove God out of the world, the righteous (Israelites) brought God back into the world. This theme, linking the story of the fall of man to the history of Israel, with Israel serving as the counterpart and fulfilment of the fall at creation. The next composition still more strikingly shows that the creation and fall of man finds its counterpart in the formation and sanctification of Israel. So Israel serves, as did the first man, as the embodiment of humanity. But while Adam sinned and was driven from paradise, Israel through atonement will bring humanity salvation. In this way the book of Genesis serves a purpose quite pertinent to the theological program of the compilers of Genesis Rabbah.

XIX:IX.1.A. "And the Lord God called to the man and said to him, 'Where are you?' "(Gen. 3:9):

B. [The word for "where are you" yields consonants that bear the meaning,] "How has this happened to you?"

C. [God speaks:] "Yesterday it was in accord with my plan, and now it is in accord with the plan of the snake. Yesterday it was from one end of the world to the other [that you filled the earth], and now: 'Among the trees of the garden'(Gen. 3:8)[you hide out]."

2.A. R. Abbahu in the name of R. Yose bar Haninah: "It is written, 'But they are like a man [Adam], they have transgressed the covenant'(Hos. 6:7).

B. "'They are like a man,' specifically, like the first man. [We shall now compare the story of the first man in Eden with the story of Israel in its land.]

C. " 'In the case of the first man, I brought him into the garden of Eden, I commanded him, he violated my commandment, I judged him to be sent away and driven out, but I mourned for him, saying "How. . ." ' " [which begins the book of Lamentations, hence stands for a lament, but which, as we just saw, also is written with the consonants that also yield, 'Where are you'].

D. " 'I brought him into the garden of Eden,' as it is written, 'And the Lord God took the man and put him into the garden of Eden'(Gen. 2:15).

E. " 'I commanded him,' as it is written, 'And the Lord God commanded. . .'(Gen. 2:16).

F. " 'And he violated my commandment,' as it is written, 'Did you eat from the tree concerning which I commanded you'(Gen. 3:11).

G. " 'I judged him to be sent away,' as it is written, "And the Lord God sent him from the garden of Eden'(Gen. 3:23).

H. " 'And I judged him to be driven out.' 'And he drove out the man'(Gen. 3:24).

I. " 'But I mourned for him, saying, 'How. . .".' 'And he said to him, "Where are you' "(Gen. 3:9), and the word for 'where are you' is written, 'How. . . .'

J. " 'So too in the case of his descendants, [God continues to speak,] I brought them into the Land of Israel, I commanded them, they violated my commandment, I judged them to be sent out and driven away but I mourned for them, saying, "How. . . ." ' "

K. " 'I brought them into the Land of Israel.' 'And I brought you into the land of Carmel' (Jer. 2:7).

L. " 'I commanded them.' 'And you, command the children of Israel' (Ex. 27:20). 'Command the children of Israel' (Lev. 24:2).

M. " 'They violated my commandment.' 'And all Israel have violated your Torah' (Dan. 9:11).

N. " 'I judged them to be sent out.' 'Send them away, out of my sight and let them go forth' (Jer 15:1).

O. " '. . . .and driven away.' 'From my house I shall drive them' (Hos. 9:15).

P. " 'But I mourned for them, saying, "How. . . ." ' 'How has the city sat solitary, that was full of people' (Lam. 1:1)."

No. 1 simply contrasts one day with the next, a stunning and stark statement, lacking all decoration. No. 1 certainly sets the stage for No. 2 and the whole must be regarded as a cogent, thoughtful composition. The other, No. 2, equally simply compares the story of man in the Garden of Eden with the tale of Israel in its Land. Every detail is in place, the articulation is perfect, and the result, completely convincing as an essay in interpretation. All of this rests on the simple fact that the word for "where are you" may be expressed as "How. . .," which, as is clear, invokes the opening words of the book of Lamentations. So

Israel's history serves as a paradigm for human history, and vice versa. What then is the point? It is obedience, as the following indicates:

> XIX:XI.1.A. "The man said, 'The woman whom you gave to be with me gave me fruit of the tree, and I ate' "(Gen. 3:12):
> B. There are four on whose pots the Holy One, blessed be he, knocked, only to find them filled with piss, and these are they: Adam, Cain, the wicked Balaam, and Hezekiah.
> C. Adam: "The man said, 'The woman whom you gave to be with me gave me fruit of the tree and I ate"(Gen. 3:12).
> D. Cain: "And the Lord said to Cain, 'Where is Abel, your brother'?"(Gen. 4:9).
> E. The wicked Balaam: "And God came to Balaam and said, 'What men are these with you?' "(Num. 22:9)
> F. Hezekiah: "Then came Isaiah the prophet to king Hezekiah and said to him, 'What did these men say?' "(2 Kgs. 20:14).
> G. But Ezekiel turned out to be far more adept than any of these: " 'Son of man, can these bones live?' And I said, 'O Lord God, you know' "(Ez. 37:3).
> H. Said R., Hinena bar Pappa, "The matter may be compared to the case of a bird that was caught by a hunter. The hunter met someone who asked him, 'Is this bird alive or dead?'
> I "He said to him, 'If you want, it is alive, but if you prefer, it is dead.' So: " 'will these bones live?" And he said, "Lord God, you know.' "

The colloquy once more serves to find in Israel's history a counterpart to the incident at hand. Only Ezekiel knew how to deal with a question that bore with it the answer: God will do as God likes, God knows the answer. That is, the sole appropriate response is one of humility and acceptance God's will. With what result? With the result of the salvation of humanity through Israel. History through Israel becomes the story of the salvation of humanity:

> XXI:I.1.A. "Then the Lord God said, 'Behold, the man has become like one of us, [knowing good and evil, and now, lest he put forth his hand and take also of the tree of life and eat and live forever]' "(Gen. 3:22):
> B. "It is written, 'Then I heard a holy one speaking, and another holy one said to that certain one who spoke' "(Dan. 8:13).
> C. "The one" refers to the Holy One, blessed be he: "The Lord, our God, the Lord is One"(Deut. 6:4).
> D. "Holy," for everyone says before him, "Holy. . . ."
> E. "Speaking" means "issuing harsh decrees against his creatures."
> F. [For example,] "Thorns and thistles it shall bring forth to you"(Gen. 3:18).
> G. "And another holy one said to that certain one who spoke:"
> H. R. Huna said, "It was to Mr. So-and-so."
> I. Aqilas translated the passage, "It was to one who was within that he

spoke, meaning the first man, whose presence lay within [and closer to God than] that of the serving angels [since he stood closer to God than they did]." [The remainder of the exegesis flows from Aqilas's view of the locus of discourse.]

J. "How long shall be the vision concerning the continual burnt offering?"(Dan. 8:13);

K. "Will the decree that has been issued against the first man go on forever?"

L. "And the transgression that causes desolation"(Deut. 8:13):

M. "So too will his transgression desolate him even in the grave?"

N. "To give both the sanctuary and the host to be trampled underfoot"(Dan. 8:13):

O. "Will he and his descendants be made into chaff before the angel of death?"

P. "And he said to me, 'Until evening, morning two thousand and three hundred, then shall the sanctuary be victorious' "(Dan. 8:14):

Q. R. Azariah, R. Jonathan b. Haggai in the name of R. Isaac: "In any case in which it is evening, it is not morning, and in any case in which it is morning, it surely is not evening. [So what is the sense of this passage?] But when it is morning for the nations of the world, it is evening for Israel, and as to 'morning,' at that time [at which it is morning for Israel],' then 'shall the sanctuary be victorious,' for at that time I shall declare him justified of that decree: 'Behold, let the man become like one of us'(Gen. 3:22)."

The fully exploited intersection of the intersecting and base verses turns the statement of Gen.3:22 into a powerful promise. Man will indeed become like the One, at the time that the gentiles reach their evening, and Israel, morning. So once more the condition of Israel serves as a paradigm for the human situation, but this in a most concrete and specific way. The nations of the world embody the curse of God to man, and Israel, the promised future blessing. The framer of the passage carefully avoids speculation on the meaning of the numbers used in Daniel's passage, so the apocalyptic power of Daniel's vision serves the rather generalized messianic expectations of sages, without provoking dangerous speculation on the here and now.

XXI:VII.2.A. Judah b. Padaiah interpreted, "Who will remove the dust from between your eyes, O first man! For you could not abide in the commandment that applied to you for even a single hour, and lo, your children can wait for three years to observe the prohibition of the use of the fruit of a tree for the first three years after it is planted: 'Three years shall it be as forbidden to you, it shall not be eaten'(Lev. 19:23)."

B. Said R. Huna, "When Bar Qappara heard this, he said, 'Well have you expounded matters, Judah, son of my sister!' "

No. 3 then compares the character of Israel to the character of the first man, calling Israel "descendants of the first man" and pointing out that they can observe a commandment for a long time. The example is apt, since Israel observes the prohibition involving the fruit of a newly planted tree, and does so for three years, while the first man could not keep his hands off a fruit tree for even an hour. This of course restates with enormous power the fact that Israel's history forms the counterpart to the history of humanity. But while the first man could not do what God demanded, Israel can and does do God's will. We come at the end of a simple and clear statement of the main point of it all:

> LXXXIII:V.1.A. Wheat, Straw, and stubble had a fight.
> B. Wheat said, "It was on my account that the field was sown."
> C. Stubble said, "It was on my account that the field was sown."
> D. Wheat said, "The day will come and you will see."
> E. When the harvest time came, the householder began to take the stubble and burn it, and the straw and spread it, but the when he made into heaps.
> F. Everyone began to kiss the wheat. [I assume this is a reference to the messianic passage, "Kiss the son" which is also to be translated, "Kiss the wheat"(Ps. 2:12).]
> G. So too Israel and the nations of the world have a fight.
> H. These say, "It was on our account that the world was created," and those say, "It was on our account that the world was created."
> I. Israel says, "The day will come and you will see."
> J. In the age to come: "You shall fan them and the wind will carry them away"(Is. 41:16).
> K. As to Israel: "And you shall rejoice in the Lord, you shall glory in the Holy One of Israel"(Is. 41:16).

Here at the end sages make explicit their basic view. The world was created for Israel, and not for the nations of the world. At the end of days everyone will see what only Israel now knows. Since sages read Genesis as the history of the world with emphasis on Israel, the lives portrayed, the domestic quarrels and petty conflicts with the neighbors, as much as the story of creation itself, all serve to yield insight into what was to be. We now turn to a detailed examination of how sages spelled out the historical law at hand. The lives of the patriarchs signaled the history of Israel. Every detail of the narrative therefore served to prefigure what was to be, and Israel found itself, time and again, in the revealed facts of the history of the creation of the world, the decline of humanity down to the time of Noah, and, finally, its ascent to Abraham, Isaac, and Israel. In order to illustrate the single approach to diverse stories, whether concerning Creation, Adam, and Noah, or concerning Abraham, Isaac, and Jacob, we focus on two matters, Abraham, on the one side, and Rome, on the other. In the former we see that Abraham serves as well as Adam to prove the point of it all. In the latter we observe how, in reading Genesis, the sages who compiled Genesis Rabbah discovered the meaning of the events of their own day.

Let us begin with an exemplary case of how sages discovered social laws of history in the facts of Scripture. What Abraham did corresponds to what Balaam did, and the same law of social history derives proof from each of the two contrasting figures.

> LV:VIII.1.A. "And Abraham rose early in the morning, [saddled his ass, and took two of his young men with him, and his son Isaac, and he cut the wood for the burnt offering and arose and went to the place which God had told him]"(Gen. 22:3):
>
> B. Said R. Simeon b. Yohai, "Love disrupts the natural order of things, and hatred disrupts the natury order of things.
>
> C. "Love disrupts the natural order of things we learn from the case of Abraham: '. . . he saddled his ass.' But did he not have any number of servants? But that proves love disrupts the natural order of things.
>
> D. "Hatred disrupts the natural order of things we learn from the case of Balaam: 'And Balaam rose up early in the morning and saddled his ass' (Num. 22:21). But did he not have any number of servants? But that proves hatred disrupts the natural order of things.
>
> E. "Love disrupts the natural order of things we learn from the case of Joseph: 'And Joseph made his chariot ready' (Gen. 46:29). But did he not have any number of servants? But that proves love disrupts the natural order of things.
>
> F. "Hatred disrupts the natural order of things we learn from the case of Pharoah: 'And he made his chariot ready' (Ex. 14:6). But did he not have any number of servants? But that proves hatred disrupts the natural order of things."
>
> 2A. Said R. Simeon b. Yohai, "Let one act of saddling an ass come and counteract another act of saddling the ass. May the act of saddling the ass done by our father Abraham, so as to go and carry out the will of him who speak and brought the world into being counteract the act of saddling that was carried out by Balaam when he went to curse Israel.
>
> B. 'Let one act of preparing counteract another act of preparing. Let Joseph's act of preparing his chariot so as to meet his father serve to counteract Pharaoh's act of perparing to go and pursue Israel."
>
> C. R. Ishmael taught on Tannaite authority, "Let the sword held in the hand serve to counteract the sword held in the hand.
>
> D. "Let the sword held in the hand of Abraham, as it is said, 'Then Abraham put forth his hand and took the knife to slay his son' (Gen. 22:10) serve to counteract the sword taken by Pharoah in hand: 'I will draw my sword, my hand shall destroy them' (Ex. 15:9)"

We see that the narrative is carefully culled for probative facts, yielding laws. One fact is that there are laws of history. The other is that laws may be set aside, by either love or hatred. Yet another law of history applies in particular to Israel, as distinct from the foregoing, deriving from the life of both Israel and the nations, Abraham and Balaam. What follows presents the law that Israel never is orphaned of holy and heroic leaders.

LVIII:II.1.A. "The sun rises and the sun goes down"(Qoh. 1:5):

B. Said R. Abba, "Now do we not know that the sun rises and the sun sets? But the sense is this: before the Holy One, blessed be he, makes the sun of one righteous man set, he brings up into the sky the sun of another righteous man.

C. "On the day that R. Aqiba died, Our Rabbi [Judah the Patriarch] was born. In his regard, they recited the following verse: 'The sun rises and the sun goes down'(Qoh. 1:5).

D. "On the day on which Our Rabbi died, R. Adda bar Ahbah was born. In his regard, they recited the following verse: 'The sun rises and the sun goes down'(Qoh. 1:5)

E. "On the day on which R. Ada died, R. Abin was born. In his regard, they recied the following verse: 'The sun rises and the sun goes down'(Qoh. 1:5).

F. "On the day on which R. Abin died, R. Abin his son was born. In his regard they recited the following verse: 'The sun rises and the sun goes down'(Qoh. 1:5).

G. "On the day on which R. Abin died, Abba Hoshaiah of Taraya was born. In his regard they recited the following verse: 'The sun rises and the sun goes down'(Qoh. 1:5).

H. "On the day on which Abba Hoshaiah of Taraya died, R. Hoshaiah was born. In his regard they recited the following verse: 'The sun rises and the sun goes down'(Qoh. 1:5).

I. "Before the Holy One, blessed be he, made the sun of Moses set, he brought up into the sky the sun of Joshua: 'And the Lord said to Moses, Take you Joshua, the son of Nun' (Num. 27:18).

J. "Before the Holy One, blessed be he, made the sun of Joshua set, he brought up into the sky the sun of Othniel, son of Kenaz: 'And Othniel the son of Kenaz took it' (Joshua 15:17).

K. "Before the Holy One, blessed be he, made the sun of Eli set, he brought up into the sky the sun of Samuel: 'And the lamp of God was not yet gone out, and Samuel was laid down to sleep in the Temple of the Lord'(1 Sam. 3:3)."

L. Said R. Yohanan, "He was like an unblemished calf."

M. [Reverting to K:] "Before the Holy One, blessed be he, made the sun of Sarah set, he brought up into the sky the sun of Rebecca: 'Behold Milcah also has borne children' (Gen. 22:20). 'Sarah lived a hundred and twenty-seven years. These were the years of the life of Sarah'(Gen. 23:1)."

One rule of Israel's history is yielded by the facts at hand. Israel is never left without an appropriate hero or heroine. The relevance of the long discourse becomes clear at the end. Each story in Genesis may forecast the stages in Israel's history later on, beginning to end. A matter of deep concern focused sages' attention on the sequence of world-empires to which, among other nations, Israel was subjugated, Babylonia, Media, Greece, and Rome—Rome above all. What will follow? Sages maintained that beyond the rule of Rome lay the salvation of Israel:

> XLII:IV.1.A. "And it came to pass in the days of Amraphel"(Gen. 4:1):
> 4.A. Another matter: "And it came to pass in the days of Amraphael, king of Shinar"(Gen. 14:1) refers to Babyulonia.
> B. "Arioch, king of Ellasar"(Gen. 14:1) refers to Greece.
> C. "Chedorlaomer, king of Elam" (Gen. 14:1) refers to Media.
> D. "And Tidal, king of Goiim [nations]" (Gen. 14:1) refers to the wicked government [Rome], which conscripts troops from all the nations of the world.
> E. Said R. Eleazar bar Abina, "If you see that the nations contend with one another, look for the footsteps of the king-messiah. You may know that that is the case, for lo, in the time of Abraham, because the kings struggled with one another, a position of greatness came to Abraham."

Obviously, No.4 presents the most important reading of Gen.14:1, since it links the events of the life of Abraham to the history of Israel and even ties the whole to the messianic expectation. I suppose that any list of four kings will provoke inquiry into the relationship of the entries of that list to the four kingdoms among which history, in Israel's experience, is divided. The process of history flows in both directions. Just as what Abraham did prefigured the future history of Israel, so what the Israelites later on were to do imposed limitations on Abraham. Time and again events in the lives of the patriarchs prefigure the four monarchies, among which, of course, the fourth, last, and most intolerable was Rome. Here is another such exercise in the recurrent proof of a single proposition.

> XLIV:XVII.4.A. "[And it came to pass, as the sun was going down,] lo, a deep sleep fell on Abram, and lo, a dread and great darkness fell upon him"(Gen. 15:12):
> B. ". . . lo, a dread" refers to Babylonia, as it is written, "Then was Nebuchadnezzar filled with fury"(Gen. 3:19).
> C. " and darkness" refers to Media, which darkened the eyes of Israel by making it necessary for the Israelites to fast and conduct public mourning.
> D. ". . .great. . ." refers to Greece.
> E. R. Simon said, "The kingdom of Greece set up one hundred and twenty commanders, one hundred and twenty hyparchs, and one hundred and twenty generals."

F. Rabbis said, "It was sixty of each, as it is written, 'Serpents, fiery serpents, and scropions' (Gen. 8:15). Just as the scorpion produces sixty eggs at a time, so the kingdom of Greece set up sixty at a time."

G. ". . . fell upon him" refers to Edom, as it is written, "The earth quqakes at the noise of their fall"(Jer. 49:21).

H. Some reverse matters:

I. ". . . fell upon him" refers to Babylonia, since it is written, "Fallen, fallen is Babylonia"(Is. 21:9).

J. ". . .great. . ." refers to Media, in line with this verse: "King Ahasuerus did make great"(Est. 3:1).

K. " and darkness" refers to Greece, which darkened the eyes of Israel by its harsh decrees.

L. ". . .lo, a dread" refers to Edom, as it is written, "After this I saw . . . , a fourth beast, dreadful and terrible"(Dan. 7:7).

No. 4 successfully links the cited passage once more to the history of Israel. Israel's history falls under God's domiinion. Whatever will happen carries out God's plan. The fourth kingdom is part of that plan, which we can discover by carefully studying Abraham's life and God's word to him. What of Rome in particular? Edom, Ishmael, and Esau all stand for Rome, perceived as a special problem, an enemy who also is a brother. In calling now-Christian Rome brother, sages conceded the Christian claim to share in the patrimony of Israel. For example, Ishmael, standing for Christian Rome, claims God's blessing, but Isaac gets it, as Jacob will take it from Esau.

XLVII:V.1.A. "God said, 'No, but Sarah your wife [shall bear you a son, and you shall call his name Isaac. I will establish my covenant with him as an everlasting covenant for his descendants after him.] As for Ishmael, I have heard you. Behold, I will bless him and make him fruitful and multiply him exceedingly. He shall be the father of twelve princes, and I will make him a great nation]' "(Gen. 17:19-20).

B. R. Yohanan in the name of R. Joshua b. Hananiah, "In this case the son of the servant-woman might learn from what was said concerning the son of the mistress of the household:

C. " 'Behold, I will bless him' refers to Isaac.

D. " '. . .and make him fruitful' refers to Isaac.

E. " '. . .and multiply him exceedingly' refers to Isaac.

F. " '. . .As for Ishmael, I have informed you' through the angel. [The point is, Freedman, *Genesis Rabbah* (London, 1948), p.401, n.4, explains, Ishmael could be sure that his blessing too would be fulfilled.]"

G. R. Abba bar Kahana in the name of R. Birai: "Here the son of the mistress of the household might learn from the son of the handmaiden:

H. " 'Behold, I will bless him' refers to Ishmael.

I. " '. . .and make him fruitful' refers to Ishmael.

J. " '. . .and multiply him exceedingly' refers to Ishmael.

K. "and by an argument *a fortiori*: 'But I will establish my covenant with Isaac' (Gen. 17:21)."

2.A. Said R. Isaac, "It is written, 'All these are the twelve tribes of Israel'(Gen. 49:28). These were the descandants of the mistress [Sarah].

B. "But did Ishmael not establish twelve?

C. "The reference to those twelve is to princes, in line with the following verse: 'As princes and wind' (Prov. 25:14). [But the word for *prince* also stands for the word *vapor*, and hence the glory of the sons of Ishmael would be transient (Freedman, p. 402, n.2).]

D. "But as to these [descended from Isaac], they are in line with this verse: 'Sworn are the tribes of the word, selah' (Hab. 3:9). [Freedman, p. 402, n.3: The word for *tribe* and for *staff* or *rod*, in the cited verse, are synonyms, both meaning tribes, both meaning rods, and so these tribes would endure like rods that are planted.]"

Nos. 1 and 2 take up the problem of the rather fulsome blessing assigned to Ishmael. One authority reads the blessing to refer to Isaac, the other maintains that the blessing refers indeed to Ishmael, and Isaac will gain that much more. No. 2 goes over the same issue, now with the insistence that the glory of Ishmael will pass like vapor, while the tribes of Isaac will endure as well planted rods. The polemic against Edom/Rome, with its transient glory, is familiar.

By this point readers must find themselves altogether at home in reading the book of Genesis as if it portrayed the history of Israel and Rome. For that is the single obsession binding sages of the document at hand to common discourse with the text before them. Why Rome in the form it takes in Genesis Rabbah? And how come the obsessive character of sages disposition of the theme of Rome? Were their picture merely of Rome as tyrant and destroyer of the Temple, we should have no reason to link the text to the problems of the age of redaction and closure. But now it is Rome as Israel's brother, counterpart, and nemesis, Rome as the one thing standing in the way of Israel's, and the world's ultimate salvation. So the stakes are different, and much higher. It is not a political Rome but a Christian and messianic Rome that is at issue: Rome as surrogate for Israel, Rome as obstacle to Israel. Why? It is because Rome now confronts Israel with a crisis, and, I argue, the program of Genesis Rabbah constitutes a response to that crisis. Rome in the fourth century became Christian. Sages respond by facing that fact quite squarely and saying, "Indeed, it is as you say, a kind of Israel, an heir of Abraham as your texts explicitly claim. But we remain the sole legitimate Israel, the bearer of the birthright—we and not you. So you are our brother: Esau, Ishmael, Edom." And the rest follows.

By rereading the story of the beginnings, sages discovered the answer and the secret of the end. Rome claimed to be Israel, and, indeed, sages conceded, Rome shared the patrimony of Israel. That claim took the form of the Christians' appropriate of the Torah as "the Old Testament," so sages acknowledged a simple fact in acceding to the notion that, in some way, Rome too formed part of Israel. But it was the rejected part, the Ishmael, the Esau, not the Isaac, not the Jacob. The advent of Christian Rome precipitated the sustained, polemical, and, I think, rigorous and well-argued rereading of beginnings in light of the end. Rome then marked the conclusion of human history as Israel had known it. Beyond? The coming of the true Messiah, the redemption of Israel, the salvation of the world, the end of time. So the issues were not inconsiderable, and when the sages spoke of Esau/Rome, as they did so often, they confronted the life-or-death decision of the day.

Let us begin with a simple example of how ubiquitous is the shadow of Ishmael/Esau/Edom/Rome. Whever sages reflect on future history, their minds turn to their own day. They found the hour difficult, because Rome, now Christian, claimed that very birthright and blessing that they understood to be theirs alone. Christian Rome posed a threat without precedent. Now another dominion, besides Israel's claimed the rights and blessings that sustained Israel. Wherever in Scripture they turned, sages found comfort in the iteration that the birthright, the blessing, the Torah, and the hope—all belonged to them and to none other. As the several antagonists of Israel stand for Rome in particular, so the traits of Rome, as sages perceived them, characterized the biblical heroes. Esau provided a favorite target. From the womb Israel and Rome contended.

> LXII:VI.11.A. "And the children struggled together [within her, and she said, 'If it is thus, why do I live?' So she went to inquire of the Lord. And the Lord said to her, 'Two nations are in your womb, and two peoples, born of you, shall be divided; the one shall be stronger than the other, and the elder shall serve the younger']"(Gen. 25:22-23):
> B. R. Yohanan and R. Simeon b. Laqish:
> C. R. Yohanan said, "[Because the word, 'struggle,' contains the letters for the word, 'run,'] this one was running to kill that one and that one was running to kill this one."
> D. R. Simeon b. Laqish: "This one releases the laws given by that one, and that one releases the laws given by this one."
> 2.A. R. Berekhiah in the name of R. Levi said, "It is so that you should not say that it was only after he left his mother's womb that [Esau] contended against [Jacob].
> B. "But even while he was yet in his mother's womb, his fist was stretched forth against him: 'The wicked stretch out their fists [so Freedman] from the womb' (Ps. 58:4)."
> 3.A. "And the children struggled together within her:"
> B. [Once more referring to the letters of the word "struggled," with

special attention to the ones that mean, "run,"] they wanted to run within her.

C. When she went by houses of idolatry, Esau would kick, trying to get out: "The wicked are estranged from the womb" (Ps. 58:4).

D. When she went by synagogues and study-houses, Jacob would kick, trying to get out: "Before I formed you in the womb, I knew you" (Jer. 1:5)."

Nos. 1-3 take for granted that Esau represents Rome, and Jacob, Israel. Consequently the verse underlines the point that there is natural enmity between Israel and Rome. Esau hated Israel even while he was still in the womb. Jacob, for his part, revealed from the womb those virtues that would characterize him later on, eager to serve God as Esau was eager to worship idols

LXIII:VII.2.A. "Two nations are in your womb, [and two peoples, born of you, shall be divided; the one shall be stronger than the other, and the elder shall serve the younger]" (Gen. 25:23):

B. There are two proud nations in your womb, this one takes pride in his world, and that one takes pride in his world.

C. This one takes pride in his monarchy, and that one takes pride in his monarchy.

D. There are two proud nations in your womb.

E. Hadrian represents the nations, Solomon, Israel.

F. There are two who are hated by the nations in your womb. All the nations hate Esau, and al the nations hate Israel.

G. [Following Freedman's reading:] The one whom your creator hates is in your womb: "And Esau I hated"(Mal. 1:3).

The syllogism invokes the base-verse as part of its repertoire of cases. No. 2 augments the statment at hand, still more closely linking it to the history of Israel. What follows explicitly introduces the issue of the Messiah:

LXIII:VIII.3.A. "The first came forth red:"

B. R. Haggai in the name of R. Isaac: "On account of the merit attained by obeying the commandment, 'You will take for yourself on the first day. . . ,' (Lev. 23:40),

C. "I shall reveal myself to you as the First, avenge you on the first, rebuild the first, and bring you the first.

D. "I shall reveal myself to you the First: 'I am the first and I am the last' (Is. 44:6).

E. "'. . .avenge you on the first: 'Esau, 'the first came forth red.'

F. "'. . .rebuild the first: that is the Temple, of which it is written, 'You throne of glory, on high from the first, you place of our sanctuary' (Jer. 17:12).

G. "'. . .and bring you the first: that is, the messiah-king: 'A first unto Zion will I give, behold them, and to Jerusalem' (Is. 41:27)."

LXII:X.1.A. "[When the boys grew up,] Esau was a skilful hunter, [a man of the field, while Jacob was a quiet man, dwelling in tents]"(Gen. 25:27):

B. He hunted people through snaring them in words [as the Roman prosecutors do:] "Well enough, you did not steal. But who stole with you? You did not kill, but who killed with you?"

2.A. R. Abbahu said, "He was a trapper and a fieldsman, trapping at home and in the field.

B. "He trapped at home: 'How do you tithe salt?' [which does not, in fact, have to be tithed at all!]

C. "He trapped in the field: 'How do people give tithe for straw?' [which does not, in fact, have to be tithed at all!]"

3.A. R. Hiyya bar Abba said, "He treated himself as totally without responsibility for himself, like a field [on which anyone tramples].

B. "Said the Israelites before the Holy One, blessed be he, 'Lord of all ages, is it not enough for us that you have subjugated us to the seventy nations, but even to this one, who is subjected to sexual intercourse just like a woman?'

C. "Said to them the Holy One, blessed be he, 'I too will exact punishment from him with those same words: 'And the heart of the mighty men of Edom at that day shall be as the heart of a woman in her pangs' " (Jer. 49:22).

4.A. "'. . .while Jacob was a quiet man, dwelling in tents" (Gen. 25:27):

B. There is a reference to two tents, that is, the school house of Shem and the school house of Eber.

Nos. 1-3 deal with the description of Esau, explaining why he was warlike and aggressive. Nothing Esau did proved sincere. He was a hypocrite, even when he tried to please his parents.

LXV:I.1.A. "When Esau was forty years old, he took to wife Judith, the daughter of Beeri, the Hittite, and Basemath the daughter of Elon the Hittite; and they made life bitter for Isaac and Rebecca" (Gen. 26:34-35):

B. "The swine out of the wood ravages it, that which moves in the field feeds on it" (Ps. 80:14).

C. R. Phineas and R. Hilqiah in the name of R. Simon: "Among all of the prophets, only two of them spelled out in public [the true character of Rome, represented by the swine], Asaf and Moses.

D. "Asaf: 'The swine out of the wood ravages it.'

E. "Moses: 'And the swine, because he parts the hoof' (Deut. 14:8).

F. "Why does Moses compare Rome to the swine? Just as the swine, when it crouches, puts forth its hoofs as if to say, 'I am clean,' so the wicked kingdom steals and grabs, while pretending to be setting up courts of justice.

G. "So Esau, for all forty years, hunted married women, ravished them, and when he reached the age of forty, he presented himself to his father, saying, 'Just as father got married at the age of forty, so I shall marry a wife at the age of forty.'

H. " 'When Esau was forty years old, he took to wife Judith, the daughter of Beeri, the Hittite, and Basemath the daughter of Elon the Hittite.' "

The exegesis of course once more identifies Esau with Rome. The round-about route linking the fact at hand, Esau's taking a wife, passes through the territory of Roman duplicity. Whatever the government does, it claims to do in the general interest. But it really has no public interest at all. Esau for his part spent forty years pillaging women and then, at the age of forty, pretended, to his father, to be upright. That, at any rate, is the parallel clearly intended by this obviously unitary composition. The issue of the selection of the intersecting verse does not present an obvious solution to me; it seems to me only the identification of Rome with the swine accounts for the choice. The contrast between Israel and Esau produced the following anguished observation. But here the Rome is not yet Christian, so far as the clear reference is concerned. The union of the two principal motifs of exegesis, the paradigmatic character of the lives of the patriarchs and matriarchs, the messianic message derived from those lives, is effected in the following:

LXXXII:I.1.A. "There are the kings who reigned in the land of Edom before any king reigned over the Israelites: Bela the son of Beor reigned in Edom, the name of his city being Dinhabah" (Gen. 36:31-32):

B. R. Isaac commenced discourse by citing this verse: "Of the oaks of Bashan they have made your oars" (Ez. 27:6).

C. Said R. Isaac, "The nations of the world are to be compared to a ship. Just as a ship has its mast made in one place and its anchor somewhere else, so their kings: 'Samlah of Masrekah' (Gen. 36:36), 'Shaul of Rehobot by the river' (Gen. 36:27), and: 'These are the kings who reigned in the land of Edom before any king reigned over the Israelites.' "

2.A. ["An estate may be gotten hastily at the beginning, but the end thereof shall not be blessed" (Prov. 20:21)]: "An estate may be gotten hastily at the beginning:" "These are the kings who reigned in the land of Edom before any king reigned over the Israelites."

B. " '. . .but the end thereof shall not be blessed:" "And saviors shall come up on mount Zion to judge the mount of Esau"(Ob. 1:21).

No. 1 contrasts the diverse origin of Roman rulers with the uniform origin of Israel's king in the house of David. No. 2 makes the same point still more forcefully. How so? Though Esau was the first to have kings, his land will eventually be overthrown (Freedman, p.766, n.3). So the point is that Israel will have kings after Esau no longer does, and the verse at hand is made to point to the end of Rome, a striking revision to express the importance is Israel's history to events in the lives of the patriarchs.

The final passage once more stresses the correspondence between Israel's and Edom's governments, respectively. The reciprocal character of their histories is then stated in a powerful way, with the further implication that, when the one rules, the other waits. So now Israel waits, but it will rule. The same point is made in what follows, but the expectation proves acute and immediate.

> LXXXIII:IV.3.A. "Magdiel and Iram: these are the chiefs of Edom, that is Esau, the father of Edom, according to their dwelling places in the land of their possession" (Gen. 36:42):
> B. On the day on which Litrinus came to the throne, there appeared to R. Ammi in a dream this message: "Today Magdiel has come to the throne."
> C. He said, "One more king is required for Edom [and then Israel's turn will come]."
> 4.A. Said R. Hanina of Sepphoris, "Why was he called Iram? For he is destined to amass [a word using the same letters] riches for the king-messiah."
> B. Said R. Levi, "There was the case of a ruler in Rome who wasted the treasuries of his father. Elijah of blessed memory appeared to him in a dream. He said to him, 'Your fathers collected treasures and you waste them.'
> C. "He did not budge until he filled the treasuries again."

Nos. 3 presents once more the theme that Rome's rule will extend only for a foreordained and limited time, at which point the Messiah will come. No. 4 explains the meaning of the name Iram. The concluding statement also alleges that Israel's saints even now make possible whatever wise decisions Rome's rulers make. That forms an appropriate conclusion to the matter. Like Eusebius, therefore, the authorship of Genesis Rabbah has rewritten the history of the world as classified and defined by Israel, and the issues prove profoundly theological, just as is the case with Eusebius. But the theological focus is entirely different. Eusebius addressed the Church with an inner-directed exposition of problems of free will and fate, the authorship of Genesis Rabbah spoke to Israel, the Jewish people, with an inward exposition of the problems of Israel's salvation. History was (re)invented, in Christianity and Judaism, as a new medium for theological discourse. Why that medium should have proved urgent in the fourth and early fifth centuries and not earlier then is clear. What changed? The advent of Christianity to power, that is, to a political standing in the world, demanded a new mode of thought, and history supplied it. And Judaism, facing in a new way the old question of postponed salvation, followed suit.

PART THREE

CONCLUSION

CHAPTER TWELVE

THE ROLE OF HISTORY IN JUDAISM: THE INITIAL DEFINITION

Jacob Neusner

While the Judaism of the dual Torah makes ample use of the Old Testament in its account of itself, in the end, the the canon of the dual Torah - written and oral, encompassing the two Talmuds and various Midrash-compilations - appealed to events but produced very little history. There is no counterpart, for example, to Eusebius, none to Augustine. We should expect that the canon of heirs to the the Deuteronomic historians would encompass narrative history, but it does not. We should expect to find therein accounts of events of not only times past but also the present explained by the past, but we do not. We should go in search of the description of one-time, unique happenings - events in the conventional sense - but, if we did, we should return disappointed. The result will be quite opposite. When we read matters properly, we shall find out how to read. For the archaeology of texts uncovers abstract structure in the identification and explication of the concrete event.

If we ask ourselves, then, how the Judaic invention of history served the larger systemic interests of the Judaism that reverted to historical thinking, the answer is by no means the one we should anticipate. Specifically, that Judaism utilized events, but produced no history, and the precise character of the Judaic utilization of history requires definition. The answer, not surprisingly, is that history served at the altar of theology - and, as a matter of fact, did not take a principal part in that service. We see that fact with great clarity when we ask ourselves what exactly does Judaism mean by "events"? For, until our own time, "events" formed the raw material of history, the source of probative evidence of propositions, the pattern that, all together and all at once, pointed to that truth that history proved. When, therefore, we can say how the Judaism of the canon of the dual Torah defined and utilized events, we shall have a clear picture of the theological uses to which, in Judaism, history was put.

To find the answer that question succinctly is simple. When we know how Judaism *classifies* events, we shall have the answer to the question of defining events - a perfectly routine procedure in the natural history of ideas. So too, when we know how Judaism *utilizes* events, assessing with accuracy, and on the basis of a vast and characteristic kind of writing, the heuristic value, the probative standing, of events, we once again shall have our answer.

In the canonical literature of the Judaism of the dual Torah, formed between the second and the seventh centuries and authoritative to this day, events find their place, within the science of learning of *Listenwissenschaft* that characterizes this literature, along with sorts of things that, for our part, we should not characterize as events at all. It follows that the Judaism of the canon in no way appeals to history as a sequence of ordered events, yielding a clear truth and meaning, in the way, for instance, that history in the Deuteronomic sequence of Deuteronomy, Joshua, Judges, Samuel, and Kings forms a sequence of events that comprise history. In canonical Judaism, by contrast, events have no autonomous standing; events are not unique, each unto itself; events have no probative value on their own; and events are not to be strung together as explanations for how things are. In this writing, philosophical and scientific, rather than (in the aggregate) historical and theological, events form cases, along with a variety of other cases, making up lists of things that, in common, point to or prove one thing.

Not only so, but events do not make up their own list at all, and this is what I found rather curious when I first noted that fact. That is to say, just as in the canon of Judaism of the dual Torah is not a single piece of writing of sustained narrative, something we might call history as Josephus or the Deuteronomists wrote history, so we have only episodically and then unsustainedly the representation of events as merely exemplary, never probative by reason of connection and sequence and order. Events therefore do not form components of an independent variable, and history constitutes no independent variable. Events will appear on - form components of - the same list as persons, places, things. That means that events not only have no autonomous standing on their own, but also that events constitute no species even within a genus, the historical order. For persons, places, and things in our way of thinking do not belong on the same list as events; they are not of the same order. Within the logic of our own minds, we cannot classify the city, Paris, within the same genus as the event, the declaration of the rights of man, for instance, nor is Sinai of the same order of things as the Torah.

What then are we to make of a list that encompasses within the same taxic composition events and things? One such list made up of events, persons, and places, is as follows: [1] Israel at the sea; [2] the ministering angels; [3] the tent of meeting; [4] the eternal house [=the Temple]; [5].Sinai. That mixtures an event (Israel redeemed at the sea), a category of sensate being (angels), a location (tent of meeting, Temple), and then Sinai, which can stand for a variety of things but in context stands for the Torah. In such a list an event may or may not stand for a value or a proposition, but it does not enjoy autonomous standing; the list is not defined by the eventfulness of events and their meaning, the compilation of matters of a single genus or even a single species (tent of meeting, eternal house, are the same species here). The notion of event as autonomous, even unique, is quite absent in this taxonomy.

Another such list moves from events to other matters altogether, finding the whole subject to the same metaphor, hence homogenized. First come the events that took place at these places or with these persons: Egypt, the sea, Marah, Massah and Meribah, Horeb, the wilderness, the spies in the Land, Shittim, for Achan/Joshua and the conquest of the Land. Now that mixture of places and names clearly intends to focus on particular things that happened, and hence, were the list to which I refer to conclude at this point, we could define an event for Judaism as a happening that bore consequence, taught a lesson or exemplified a truth, in the present case, an event matters because it the mixture of rebellion and obedience. But there would then be no doubt that "event" formed a genus unto itself, and that a proper list could not encompass both events, defined conventionally as we should, and also other matters altogether.

But the literary culture at hand, this textual community proceeds, in the same literary context, to the following items: [1] the Ten Commandments; [2] the show-fringes and phylacteries; [3] the *Shema* and the Prayer; [4] the tabernacle and the cloud of the Presence of God in the world to come. Why we invoke, as our candidates for the metaphor at hand, the Ten Commandments, show-fringes and phylacteries, recitation of the *Shema* and the Prayer, the tabernacle and the cloud of the Presence of God, and the mezuzah, seems to me clear from the very catalogue. These reach their climax in the analogy between the home and the tabernacle, the embrace of God and the Presence of God. So the whole is meant to list those things that draw the Israelite near God and make the Israelite cleave to God. And to this massive catalogue, events are not only exemplary - which historians can concede without difficulty - but also subordinated.

They belong on the same list as actions, things, persons, places, because they form an order of being that is not to be differentiated between events (including things that stand for events) and other cultural artifacts altogether. A happening is no different from an object, in which case "event" serves no better, and no worse, than a hero, a gesture or action, recitation of a given formula, or a particular locale, to establish a truth. It is contingent, subordinate, instrumental. I can think of no more apt illustration of Geertz's interesting judgment cited by Sahlins, that "an event is a unique actualization of a general phenomenon, a contingent realization of the cultural pattern." And why find that fact surprising, since all history comes to us in writing, and it is the culture that dictates how writing is to take place; that is why history can only paraphrase the affirmations of a system, and that is why events recapitulate in acute and concrete ways the system that classifies one thing that happens as event, but another thing is not only not an event but is not classified at all. In the present instance, an event is not at all eventful; it is merely a fact that forms part of the evidence for what is, and what is eventful is not an occasion at all, but a condition, an attitude, a perspective and a viewpoint. Then, it is clear, events are subordinated to the formation of attitudes, perspectives, viewpoints - the formative artifacts of not history in the conventional sense but culture in the framework of Sahlin's generalization, "history is culturally ordered, differently so in different societies, according to meaningful schemes of things."

To make more concrete the evidence on which I have drawn to join the public discussion, let me refer to one important compilation of lists, of the sixth century A.D., contemporary with the Talmud of Babylonia, a compilation of exegesis of Song of Songs called Song of Songs Rabbah.[1] That compilation presents a reading of the Song of Songs as a metaphorization of God's relationship of intense love for Israel, and Israel's relationship of intense love for God. In that document we find sequences, or combinations, of references to Old Testament persons, events, actions, and the like. These bear the rhetorical emblem, "another matter," in long lists of composites of well-framed compositions.[2] Each entry on a given list will be represented as "another matter," meaning, another interpretation of reading of a given verse in the Song of Songs. As a matter of fact, however, that "other matter," one following the other, turns out to be the same matter in other terms. These constructions form lists out of diverse entries.

---

[1] My translation and analysis of the document are in the following: *Song of Songs Rabbah. An Analytical Translation.* Volume One. *Song of Songs Rabbah to Song Chapters One through Three.* Atlanta, 1990: Scholars Press for Brown Judaic Studies; *Song of Songs Rabbah. An Analytical Translation.* Volume Two. *Song of Songs Rabbah to Song Chapters Four through Eight.* Atlanta, 1990: Scholars Press for Brown Judaic Studies; and *The Midrash Compilations of the Sixth and Seventh Centuries: An Introduction to the Rhetorical Logical, and Topical Program. IV. Song of Songs Rabbah.* Atlanta, 1990: Scholars Press for Brown Judaic Studies.

[2] I estimate that approximately 80% of the document in bulk is comprised of "another-matter" compositions. The list in this form defines the paramount rhetorical medium and logical structure of the document.

When in Song of Songs Rabbah we have a sequence of items alleged to form taxon, that is, a set of things that share a common taxic indicator, of course what we have is a list. The list presents diverse matters that all together share, and therefore also set forth, a single fact or rule or phenomenon. That is why we can list them, in all their distinctive character and specificity, on a common catalogue of "other things" that pertain all together to one thing.

Since, on these lists, we find classified within a single taxon events, persons, places, objects and actions, it is important to understand how they coalesce.[3] The rhetoric is the key-indicator, since it is objective and superficial. When we find the rhetorical formula, "another matter," that is, *davar aher*, what follows says the same thing in other words, or at least something complementary and necessary to make some larger point. That is why I insist the constructions form lists. William Scott Green states the matter, in his analysis of a single passage, in these words:

> Although the interpretations in this passage are formally distinguished from one another...by the disjunctive device *davar aher* ('another interpretation'), they operate within a limited conceptual sphere and a narrow thematic range. Thus rather than 'endless multiple meanings,' they in fact ascribe to the words 'doing wonders' multiple variations of a single meaning. By providing multiple warrant for that message, the form effectively restricts the interpretive options...[4]

When we have a sequence of *davar-aher* passages forming a davar-aher construction, the message is cumulative, and the whole as a matter of fact forms a sum greater than that of the parts; it will then be that accumulation that guides us to what is if implicit yet fundamental in the exact sense: at the foundation of matters; there is where we should find that system, order, proportion, cogency that all together we expect a theology to impart to discrete observations about holy matters.

In general, "another matter" signals "another way of saying the same thing;" or the formula bears the sense, "these two distinct things add up to one thing," with the further proviso that both are necessary

---

[3] The archaeological evidence of ancient synagogues yields counterpart "lists," that is to say, recurrent groups of iconic symbols that appear together, but with no other items, from one synagogue to another, e.g., the ram's horn, the palm branch, the candelabrum, are commonly grouped, but no other iconic symbols then appear in groups or what we should call "iconic lists." I have compared the iconic lists with the "another-matter-lists" in *Theology and Symbol in Judaism*. Minneapolis, 1990: Fortress Press.

[4] In Jacob Neusner with William Scott Green, *Writing with Scripture. The Authority and Uses of the Hebrew Bible in the Torah of Formative Judaism* (Minneapolis, 1989: Fortress Press), p. 19.

to make one point that transcends each one. Not only so, but in Song of Songs Rabbah the fixed formula of the *davar-aher*-compilation points toward fixed formulas of theological thought: sets of coherent verbal-symbols that work together. These "other things" encompass time, space, person and object, action and attitude, and join them all together, for instance, David, Solomon, Messiah at the end of time; this age, the age to come; the Exodus from Egypt, Sinai, the age to come all may appear together within a single list. Let me give a single example of the list that makes it possible to redefine "event" into a category of quite a-historical valence.

Chapter Five. Song of Songs Rabbah to Song 1:5

V:i.1   A.   "I am very dark, but comely, [O daughters of Jerusalem, like the tents of Kedar, like the curtains of Solomon]" (Song 1:5):
         B.   "I am dark" in my deeds.
         C.   "But comely" in the deeds of my forebears.
2.   A.   "I am very dark, but comely:"
         B.   Said the Community of Israel, "'I am dark' in my view, 'but comely' before my Creator."
         C.   For it is written, "Are you not as the children of the Ethiopians to Me, O children of Israel, says the Lord" (Amos 9:7):
         D.   "as the children of the Ethiopians" - in your sight.
         E.   But "to Me, O children of Israel, says the Lord."
3.   A.   Another interpretation of the verse, ""I am very dark:" in Egypt.
         B.   "but comely:" in Egypt.
         C.   "I am very dark" in Egypt: "But they rebelled against me and would not hearken to me" (Ez. 20:8).
         D.   "but comely" in Egypt: with the blood of the Passover offering and circumcision, "And when I passed by you and saw you wallowing in your blood, I said to you, In your blood live" Ez. 16:6) - in the blood of the Passover.
         E.   "I said to you, In your blood live" Ez. 16:6) - in the blood of the circumcision.
4.   A.   Another interpretation of the verse, "I am very dark:" at the sea, "They were rebellious at the sea, even the Red Sea" (Ps. 106:7).
         B.   "but comely:" at the sea, "This is my God and I will be comely for him" (Ex. 15:2) [following Simon's rendering of the verse].
5.   A.   "I am very dark:" at Marah, "And the people murmured against Moses, saying, What shall we drink" Ex. 15:24).
         B.   "but comely:" at Marah, "And he cried to the Lord and the Lord showed him a tree, and he cast it into the waters and the waters were made sweet" (Ex. 15:25).
6.   A.   "I am very dark:" at Rephidim, "And the name of the place was called Massah and Meribah" (Ex. 17:7).

B. "but comely:" at Rephidim, "And Moses built an altar and called it by the name 'the Lord is my banner' (Ex. 17:15).
7. A. "I am very dark:" at Horeb, "And they made a calf at Horeb" (Ps. 106:19).
B. "but comely:" at Horeb, "And they said, All that the Lord has spoken we will do and obey" (Ex. 24:7).
8. A. "I am very dark:" in the wilderness, ""How often did they rebel against him in the wilderness" (Ps. 78:40).
B. "but comely:" in the wilderness at the setting up of the tabernacle, "And on the day that the tabernacle was set up" (Num. 9:15).
9. A. "I am very dark:" in the deed of the spies, "And they spread an evil report of the land" (Num. 13:32).
B. "but comely:" in the deed of Joshua and Caleb, ""Save for Caleb, the son of Jephunneh the Kenizzite" (Num. 32:12).
10. A. "I am very dark:" at Shittim, "And Israel abode at Shittim and the people began to commit harlotry with the daughters of Moab" (Num. 25:1).
B. "but comely:" at Shittim, "Then arose Phinehas and wrought judgment" (Ps. 106:30).
11. A. "I am very dark:" through Achan, "But the children of Israel committed a trespass concerning the devoted thing" (Josh. 7:1).
B. "but comely:" through Joshua, "And Joshua said to Achan, My son, give I pray you glory" (Josh. 7:19).
12. A. "I am very dark:" through the kings of Israel.
B. "but comely:" through the kings of Judah.
C. If with my dark ones that I had, it was such that "I am comely," all the more so with my prophets.
V:ii.5 A. [As to the verse, "I am very dark, but comely," R. Levi b. R. Haita gave three interpretations:
B. " 'I am very dark:' all the days of the week.
C. " 'but comely:' on the Sabbath.
D. " 'I am very dark:' all the days of the year.
E. " 'but comely:' on the Day of Atonement.
F. " 'I am very dark:' among the Ten Tribes.
G. " 'but comely:' in the tribe of Judah and Benjamin.
H. " 'I am very dark:' in this world.
I. " 'but comely:' in the world to come."

The contrast of dark and comely yields a variety of applications; in all of them the same situation that is the one also is the other, and the rest follows in a wonderfully well-crafted composition. What is the repertoire of items? Dark in deeds but comely in ancestry; dark in my view but comely before God; dark when rebellious, comely when obedient, a point made at Nos. 3, for Egypt, 4, for the sea, and 5 for Marah, 6, for Massah and Meribah, 7 for Horeb, 8 for the wilderness, 9 for the spies in the Land, 10 for Shittim, 11 for Achan/Joshua and the conquest of the Land, 12 for Israel and Judah. But look what follows: the week as against the Sabbath, the weekdays as against the Day of Atonement, the Ten Tribes as against Judah and Benjamin, this world as against the world to come. Whatever classification these next items demand for themselves, it surely will not be that of events. Indeed, if by event we mean something that happened once, as in "once upon a time," then Sabbath as against weekday, Day of Atonement as against ordinary day form a different category; the Ten Tribes as against Judah and Benjamin constitute social entities, not divisions of time; and this age and the age to come form utterly anti-historical taxa altogether.

Events not only do not form a taxon, they also do not present a vast corpus of candidates for inclusion into some other taxon. The lists in the document at hand form selections from a most limited repertoire of candidates. If we were to catalogue all of the exegetical repertoire encompassed by davar-aher-constructions in this document, we should not have a very long list of candidates for inclusion in any list. And among the candidates, events are few indeed. They encompass Israel at the Sea and at Sinai, the destruction of the first Temple, the destruction of the second Temple, events as defined by the actions of some holy men such as Abraham, Isaac, and Jacob (treated not for what they did but for who they were), Daniel, Mishael, Hananiah and Azariah, and the like. .It follows that the restricted repertoire of candidates for taxonomic study encompasses remarkably few events, remarkably few for a literary culture that is commonly described as quintessentially historical!

Then what taxic indicator dictates which happenings will be deemed events and which not? What are listed throughout are not data of nature or history but of theology: God's relationship with Israel, expressed in such facts as the three events, the first two in the past, the third in the future, namely, the three redemptions of Israel, the three patriarchs, and holy persons, actions, events, what-have-you. These are facts that are assembled and grouped; in Song of Songs Rabbah the result is not propositional at all, or, if propositional, then essentially the repetition of familiar propositions through unfamiliar data. What we have is a kind of recombinant theology, in which the framer ("the theologian") selects from a restricted repertoire a few items for combination, sometimes to make a point (e.g., the contrast of obedient and disobedient Israel we saw just now), sometimes not. What is set on display justifies the display: putting this familiar fact together with that familiar fact in an unfamiliar combination constitutes what is new and important in the list; the consequent conclusion one is supposed to draw, the proposition or rule that emerges - these are rarely articulated and never important. True, the list in Song of Songs Rabbah may comprise a rule, or it may substantiate a proposition or validate a claim; but more often than not, the effect of making the list is to show

how various items share a single taxic indicator, which is to say, the purpose of the list is to make the list. The making of connections among ordinarily not-connected things is then one outcome of Listenwissenschaft. What I find engaging in *davar-aher*-constructions is the very variety of things that, on one list or another, can be joined together - a list for its own sake. What we have is a kind of subtle restatement, through an infinite range of possibilities, of the combinations and recombinations of a few essentially simple facts (data). It is as though a magician tossed a set of sticks this way and that, interpreting the diverse combinations of a fixed set of objects. The propositions that emerge are not the main point; the combinations are.

That seems to me an important fact, for it tells me that the culture at hand has defined for itself a repertoire of persons and events and conceptions (e.g., Torah-study), holy persons, holy deeds, holy institutions, presented candidates for inclusion in *davar-aher* constructions, and the repertoire, while restricted and not terribly long, made possible a scarcely-limited variety of lists of things with like taxic indicators. That is to say, since the same items occur over and over again, but there is no pattern to how they recur. By a pattern I mean that items of the repertoire may appear in numerous *davar-aher* constructions or not; they may keep company with only a fixed number of other items, or they may not. Most things can appear in a *davar-aher* composition with most other things.[5]

The upshot is simple. List-making is accomplished within a restricted repertoire of items that can serve on lists; the list-making then presents interesting combinations of an essentially small number of candidates for the exercise. But then, when making lists, one can do pretty much anything with the items that are combined; the taxic indicators are unlimited, but the data studied, severely limited. And that fact returns us to our starting point, the observations on history as a cultural artifact that form the premise for the study of history within the archaeology of knowledge. In fact, in Judaism history serves the theological sciences and therefore cannot be said to constitute history in any ordinary sense at all; but that is a trivial and obvious observation. More to the point, history, in the form of events, contributes to a rather odd way of conducting theological science.

For, forming part of the *davar-aher* construction, history constitutes one among a variety of what I call, for lack of more suitable lan-

---

[5] To make this point concrete, here is a survey of sequences of components of such lists:

Joseph, righteous men, Moses, and Solomon;

patriarchs as against princes, offerings as against merit, and Israel as against the nations; those who love the king, proselytes, martyrs, penitents;

first, Israel at Sinai; then Israel's loss of God's presence on account of the golden calf;

guage at this point, theological "things,"[6] - names, places, events,

---

then God's favoring Israel by treating Israel not in accord with the requirements of justice but with mercy;

Dathan and Abiram, the spies, Jeroboam, Solomon's marriage to Pharaoh's daughter, Ahab, Jezebel, Zedekiah;

Israel is feminine, the enemy (Egypt) masculine, but God the father saves Israel the daughter;

Moses and Aaron, the Sanhedrin, the teachers of Scripture and Mishnah, the rabbis;

the disciples; the relationship among disciples, public recitation of teachings of the Torah in the right order; lections of the Torah;

the spoil at the Sea = the Exodus, the Torah, the Tabernacle, the ark;

the patriarchs, Abraham, Isaac, Jacob, then Israel in Egypt, Israel's atonement and God's forgiveness;

the Temple where God and Israel are joined, the Temple is God's resting place, the Temple is the source of Israel's fecundity;

Israel in Egypt, at the Sea, at Sinai, and subjugated by the gentile kingdoms, and how the redemption will come;

Rebecca, those who came forth from Egypt, Israel at Sinai, acts of loving kindness, the kingdoms who now rule Israel, the coming redemption;

fire above, fire below, meaning heavenly and altar fires; Torah in writing, Torah in memory; fire of Abraham, Miriam, bush, Elijah, Hananiah, Mishael, and Azariah;

the Ten Commandments, show-fringes and phylacteries, recitation of the Shema and the Prayer, the tabernacle and the cloud of the Presence of God, and the mezuzah;

the timing of redemption, the moral condition of those to be redeemed, and the past religious misdeeds of those to be redeemed;

Israel at the sea, Sinai, the Ten Commandments; then the synagogues and school houses; then the redeemer;

the Exodus, the conquest of the Land, the redemption and restoration of Israel to Zion after the destruction of the first Temple, and the final and ultimate salvation;

the Egyptians, Esau and his generals, and, finally, the four kingdoms;

Moses's redemption, the first, to the second redemption in the time of the Babylonians and Daniel;

the litter of Solomon: the priestly blessing, the priestly watches, the sanhedrin, and the Israelites coming out of Egypt;

Israel at the sea and forgiveness for sins effected through their passing through the sea; Israel at Sinai; the war with Midian; the crossing of the Jordan and entry into the Land; the house of the sanctuary; the priestly watches; the offerings in the Temple; the sanhedrin; the Day of Atonement;

God redeemed Israel without preparation; the nations of the world will be punished, after Israel is punished; the nations of the world will present Israel as gifts to the royal messiah, and here the base-verse refers to Abraham, Isaac, Jacob, Sihon, Og, Canaanites;

the return to Zion in the time of Ezra, the Exodus from Egypt in the time of Moses;

the patriarchs and with Israel in Egypt, at the Sea, and then before Sinai;

Abraham, Jacob, Moses;

Isaac, Jacob, Esau, Jacob, Joseph, the brothers, Jonathan, David, Saul, man, wife, paramour;

Abraham in the fiery furnace and Shadrach Meshach and Abednego, the Exile in Babylonia, now with reference to the return to Zion

[6] I find myself at a loss for a better word-choice and must at this stage resort to the hopelessly inelegant, " 'theological' things," to avoid having to repeat the formula that seems to me to fit the data, namely, "names, places, events, actions deemed to bear theological weight and to affect attitude and action." Still, better a simple Anglo-saxon

actions deemed to bear theological weight and to affect attitude and action. The play is worked out by a reprise of available materials, composed in some fresh and interesting combination. When three or more such theological "things" - whether person, whether event, whether action, whether attitude - are combined, they form a theological structure, and, viewed all together, all of the theological "things" in a given document constitute the components of the entire theological structure that the document affords. The propositions portrayed visually, through metaphors of sight, or dramatically, through metaphors of action and relationship, or in attitude and emotion, through metaphors that convey or provoke feeling and sentiment, when translated into language prove familiar and commonplace. The work of the theologian in this context is not to say something new or even persuasive, for the former is unthinkable by definition, the latter unnecessary in context. It is rather to display theological "things" in a fresh and interesting way, to accomplish a fresh exegesis of the canon of theological "things."

The combinations and recombinations defined for us by our document form events into facts, sharing the paramount taxic indicators of a variety of other facts, comprising a theological structure within a larger theological structure: a reworking of canonical materials. An event is therefore reduced to a "thing," losing all taxic autonomy, requiring no distinct indicator of an intrinsic order. It is simply something else to utilize in composing facts into knowledge; the event does not explain, it does not define, indeed, it does not even exist within its own framework at all. Judaism by "an event" means, in a very exact sense, nothing in particular. It is a component in a culture that combines and recombines facts into structures of its own design, an aspect of what I should call a culture that comes to full expression in recombinant theology.

We have been prepared for such a result by Jonathan Z. Smith, who has made us aware of critical issue of the recombinancy of a fixed canon of "things" in his discussion of sacred persistence, that is, "the rethinking of each little detail in a text, the obsession with the significance and perfection of each little action." In the canonical literature of Judaism, these minima are worked and reworked, rethought and recast in some other way or order or combination - but always held to be the same thing throughout. In this context I find important Smith's statement:

---

formulation than a fancy German or Greek or Latin one. And Hebrew, whether Mishnaic or modern, simply does not serve for analytical work except when thought conceived in some other language is translated back into that language, should anyone be interested.

> An almost limitless horizon of possibilities that are at hand...is arbitrarily reduced...to a set of basic elements....Then a most intense ingenuity is exercised to overcome the reduction...to introduce interest and variety. This ingenuity is usually accompanied by a complex set of rules.[7]

The possibilities out of which the authorship of our exemplary document has made its selections are limited not by the metaphorical potential of the Song of Songs (!) but by the contents of the Hebrew Scriptures as the textual community formed of the Judaic sages defined those contents within their Torah.

For every Abraham, Isaac, and Jacob that we find, there are Job, Enoch, Jeroboam, or Zephaniah, whom we do not find; for every Sea/Sinai/entry into the Land that we do find, there are other sequences, e.g., the loss of the ark to the Philistines and its recovery, or Barak and Deborah, that we do not find. Ezra figures, Haggai does not; the Assyrians play a minor role, Nebuchadnezzar is on nearly every page. Granted, Sinai must enjoy a privileged position throughout. But why prefer Shadrach Meshach and Abednego, Hananiah, Mishael, and Azariah, over other trilogies of heroic figures? So the selection is an act of choice, a statement of culture in miniature. But once restricted through this statement of choice, the same selected theological "things" then undergo combination and recombination with other theological things, the counterpart to Smith's "interest and variety." If we know the complex set of rules in play here, we also would understand the system that makes this document not merely an expression of piety but a statement of a theological structure: orderly, well-composed and proportioned, internally coherent and cogent throughout.

The canonical, therefore anything but random, standing of events forms a brief chapter in the exegesis of a canon. That observation draws us back to Smith, who observes:

> the radical and arbitary reduction represented by the notion of canon and the ingenuity represented by the rule-governed exegetical enterprise to apply the canon to every dimension of human life is that most characteristic, persistent, and obsessive religious activity....The task of application as well as the judgment of the relative adequacy of particular applications to a community's life situation remains the indigenous theologian's task; but the study of the process, particularly the study of comparative systematics and exegesis, ought to be a major preoccupation of the historian of religions.[8]

---

[7] "Sacred Persistence: Towards a Redescription of Canon," in William Scott Green, ed., *Approaches to Ancient Judaism* 1978, 1:11-28. Quotation: p. 15.
[8] *ibid.* p. 18.

Smith speaks of religion as an "enterprise of exegetical totalization," and he further identifies with the word "canon" precisely what we have identified as the substrate and structure of the list. If I had to define an event in this canonical context, I should have to call it merely another theological thing: something to be manipulated, combined in one way or in another, along with other theological things.

Have we access to other examples of cultures that define for themselves canonical lists of counterparts to what I have called "theological things"? Indeed, defining matters as I have, I may compare the event to a fixed object in a diviner's basket of the Ndembu, as Smith describes that divinatory situation:

> Among the Ndembu there are two features of the divinatory situation that are crucial to our concern: the diviner's basket and his process of interrogating his client. The chief mode of divination consists of shaking a basket in which some twenty-four fixed objects are deposited (a cock's claw, a piece of hoof, a bit of grooved wood, withered fruit, etc.). These are shaken in order to winnow out' truth from falsehood' in such a way that few of the objects end up on top of the heap. These are 'read' by the diviner both with respect to their individual meanings and their combinations with other objects and the configurations that result.[9]

In Song of Songs Rabbah, Abraham, Isaac, Jacob, or the Sea and Sinai, or Hananiah, Mishael, and Azariah, are the counterpart to the cock's claw and the piece of hoof. The event, in Judaism, is the counterpart to a cock's claw in the Ndembu culture. Both will be fixed, but will combine and recombine in a large number of different ways. But then what of "the lessons of history," and how shall we identify the counterpart to historical explanation? I find the answer in the Ndembu counterpart, the mode of reading "the process of interrogating the client"? Again Smith:

> The client's situation is likewise taken into account in arriving at an interpretation. Thus. . .there is a semantic, syntactic, and pragmatic dimension to the 'reading.' Each object is publicly known and has a fixed range of meanings. . .The total collection of twenty-four objects is held to be complete and capable of illuminating every situation. . .What enables the canon to be applied to every situation or question is not the number of objects. . .Rather it is that, prior to performing the divination, the diviner has rigorously question his client in order to determine his situation with precision. . .It is the genius of the interpreter to match a public set of meanings with a commonly known set of facts. . .in order to produce a quite particular plausibility structure which speaks directly to his client's condition, which mediates between that which is public knowledge and

---
[9] Smith, p. 25.

the client's private perception of his unique situation.[10]

That concludes our inquiry, since it draws us to the task of the exegesis of exegesis. Events then form a problem of exegesis, in which, from what a culture defines as a consequential happening, we find our way back to the system and structure that that culture means to form. The work before us will teach us, in the case of Judaism, how from the study of what are defined as events to describe the process of interrogation that has produced the result we see before us, this particular plausibility structure that has persuaded holy Israel, from then to now (as indeed all the Israels that revere the Song of Songs have been persuaded), to read the erotic as the best, the only way to express precisely who is God in relationship to Israel, and who is Israel in relationship to God. The theology of this Judaism - that is to say, our account of the world-view that comes to expression within this literary culture and textual community - will take shape within the exegesis of that exegesis.

The upshot is that in an exact sense, "event" has no meaning at all in Judaism, since Judaism forms culture through other than historical modes of organizing existence. Without the social construction of history, there also is no need for the identification of events, that is, individual and unique happenings that bear consequence, since, within the system and structure of Judaism, history forms no taxon, assuredly not the paramount one, and, it must follow, no happening is unique, and, on its own, no event bears consequence. These statements rest upon modes of the analysis of history as the fabrication of culture, including a religious culture, and require us to review the recent formation of thought on history as culturally ordered, and on the event as "contingent realization of the cultural pattern," for it is only in that context that we may make sense, also, of the representation of both history and its raw materials, events, in Judaism in its definitive canon.

It follows that, when the Judaism of the dual Torah invented history, it not only did so for its own purposes, but it also undertook the work within its own distinctive idiom of thought and expression. And, as we have seen, idiom did not yield the kind of history-writing that, even in that day and age, others nearby undertook. The initial definition of history turns out to have been remarkably congruent to that of what we today classify as social science: the search not for the unique but the exemplary, the inquiry into not the particular but the general, the quest for generalization concerning the social order, rather than the search for the unusual and the different that marked one component of the social order as an event, the other as routine.

---

[10] Smith, p. 25.

The history that Judaism invented therefore differs radically from the history that, in general, people assume ancient Judaism, in the pages of the Hebrew Scriptures for instance, invoked. History served the cause of theological truth, but it was never the source of theological truth. The Torah set forth the truth; history, if truth be told, was not needed to prove any element of the truth that the Torah revealed. History was subordinate, not probative; at best exemplary, but never normative. That conception of history draws us far from the contemporary one. For some time now in the West we have called upon history to serve as arbiter of truth, history as mediator of sensibility and source of explanation. But before its own entry into the Western intellect, in the nineteenth and twentieth centuries, Judaism knew nothing of that other use of history, so different from its own.

Indeed, these honored roles in the court of intellect came to history only in the formative centuries of our own civilization. We should, after all, have to trace the path back to the Protestant Reformation, with its insistence on the priority of historical fact, deriving from a mythic age of perfection, in dictating the legitimacy of social reality in the present moment. Renewed in the romantic reentry into historical discourse, this same preference for history as a medium of organizing the everyday and explaining it characterized the formation of the historical sciences in the nineteenth century: history proves, history teaches, the verdict of history, the lessons of history - these and other accepted formulations bear the single message. Cutting through the detritus and sediment of the long centuries of increment and accumulation, therefore appealing not to *Listenwissenschaft*, but to a different, more autonomous kind of judgment altogether, for the logic of their discourse, the Reformation theologians and the nineteenth century German historians who were their secular continuators identified history, the record of what happened (in this case) in Scripture, as the instrument for the validation of reform. Reform then would accomplish the renewal of times past, times perfect, appealing therefore to the court of appeal formed by history. Describing "Judaism" as a historical religion therefore classifies what was philosophical as historical, a religion that sought the rules of the social order in regularity as one that appealed to the singular and the extraordinary. But history is of more than one kind, in religion as much as in the life of intellect, and the kind of history that Judaism invented in the fourth century and carried on from then to the nineteenth finds more in common with modes of thought familiar to us today, in the social scientific reconsideration of the meaning of historical knowledge, than with the Protestant theological appeal to history as a source of validation of reform, as the source of Reformation.

Turning toward the future, we do well to reflect on the subordination of history by Judaism in light of the current recognition that history forms a discourse of contemporary taste and judgment, events become eventful only because we make them so, and, in all, history is culturally ordered, and events are defined and identified as statements of an intensely contemporary perception. It follows, we now understand, that all histories are the creation of an eternal present, that is, those moments in which histories are defined and distinguished, in which events are identified and assigned consequence, and in which sequences of events, "this particular thing happened here and therefore...," are strung together, pearls on a string, to form ornaments of intellect. And, with that understanding well in hand, fully recognizing that history is one of the grand fabrications of the human intellect, facts not discovered but invented, explanations that themselves form cultural indicators of how things are in the here and now, we find ourselves no longer historians of ideas of history, or analysts of the history of culture, let alone practitioners of the dread narrative history that makes of historical writing a work of elegant imagination. We find ourselves, rather, archaeologists, working from the surface, that is known, through the detritus of the unknown, in quest of a material understanding of a reality that is not known but for its artifacts, not susceptible of explanation and understanding except in categories and terms that are defined by those same artifacts. And that quest is, we all recognize, not a very smooth one.

Today we understand that events in particular, and history in general, form cultural indicators. Accomplishing the analysis of events for what they teach us about the culture that identifies a given happening as eventful, neglecting some other as inconsequential or routine, is important. In the vast canon of the two Talmuds and the Midrash-compilations that took shape in late antiquity, the first seven centuries A.D., under the title, the Oral Torah, history was invented within Judaism for the distinctive purposes of Judaism: it was not a general thing, and was never meant to be. That labor of rewriting and recasting of one thing in light of something else that produced the Judaism of the dual Torah forms a rich set of cases in cultural transformation, in the determination, by a system, of its own past, in the identification, within a system, of its own resources. For, after all, while a system speaks through its canon, and while theologians commonly read the canon to describe the system, in point of fact it is the canon that recapitulates the system, the system that speaks, in detail to be sure, through the canon. History forms part of, not the system but, merely, the canon.

GENERAL INDEX

Abba, 222
Abba Hoshaiah of Taraya, 222
Abba bar Kahana, 215, 224
Abbahu, 216, 228
Abin, 222
Adda bar Ahbab, 222
Africanus, Julius, 107-108
Aha, 202, 206
Akiba, 139-141
Albeck, H., 150-151
Alexander the Great, 106, 115
Ambrosius, 110
Ammi, 230
Ammianius Marcellinus, 41, 105, 112, 117, 119-21
Annales (Febvre-Bloch), 160-162
Annals (Tacitus), 59, 62, 96
Anonymus Valesianus, 111
Apolonius of Tyana, 115
Apologetics, Quintus Tertullian, 51-54, 56, 61, 64, 66-67, 70-71, 73-75
Apuleius, Lucius, 55
Aqiba, 48, 151-53, 167, 222
Archaeology of Knowledge (Foucault), 19
Archimedes, 95
Aristotle, 33-34, 41; *Physics*, 33
Astral piety, daemons and guardian angels, 81-82
Athanasius, 89, 104, 115-116
Athenagoras, 73
Augustine, 101, 117; 120; "City of God," 100; *Civitas dei* (Augustine), 110
Augustus, Gaius, 78, 86-87, 91; speech of Maecenas, 51
Aurelian, Lucius, 88
Aurelius Victor, 120; *Caesares*, 105, 117-118
Azariah, 219

Ba, 195
Ba bar Binah, 206
Barnes, Timothy D., 55-57
Bar Qappara, 219
Basilides, 89
Bede, Saint, 114
Berekhiah, 226

Birai, 224
Bischoff, Heinrich, 40
Bloch, Marc, 161
Brown, Peter, 155
Burrows, Mark S., 15

Caecilius of Calacte, 106
Caesares (Aurelius Victor), 105
Callimachus, 36
Canonical writings and history, 157-179
Carlyle, Thomas, 36
Cassiodorus, Favius, 114
Cassius Severus, 64
Catiline, 43
Cato, Marcus, 36
Celsus, 57
Chestnut, Glenn W., 6
Christianity: foundations for a historical Jesus, 19-27; and political world of Roman Empire, 4-15
Chronica urbis Romae, 110, 119
Chronicle (Eusebius), 77, 86
Chronicon (Eusebius), 110
Chronicon (Hippolytus), 108
Church History (Eusebius), 6-7, 77-78, 84
Cicero, 52, 54, 56-57, 64-66, 73-75
Civitas dei (Augustine), 110
Clemens Alexandrimus, 107, 113
Clement of Alexandria, 63, 79
Codex Laurentianus, 117
Constantine, 103-104, 116; 118; faith and church, 3-4, 6-7, 78-79, 81, 88-89, 101; *Panegyric to Constantine* (Drake), 81-82
Constantius II, 117
Cornford, F.M., 43
Croesus, 31, 40, 42-43, 47
Cyprian, 63
Cyrus II, 31

Daemons, guardian angels and astral piety, 81-82
Darius, 38
De civite dei, (Augustine), 121
De cursu temporum (Hilarian), 108
Demonstratio Evangelica (Eusebius), 77

De mortibus persecutorum (Lactantius), 103-104, 111
Dio Cassius, 30-31, 41, 51
Diocletian, Gaius, 46, 88, 104, 113, 118
Diodorus the Greek, 64
Domitian, Titus, 62, 104
Donatus, 120
Dosa b. Harkinas, 148, 150-152
Drake, H.A., *Panegyric to Constantine*, 81-82

Ecclesiastical History (Eusebius), 8, 12-13, 104
Eleazar, 185, 205; New Year festival, 173
Eleazar bar Abina, 223
Eleazar ben Azarya, 140
Eleazar of Modiim, 140, 197
Eliezer ben Hyrkanos, 138
Ennius, Quintus, 63
Euhemerus, 63-64
Eunapius, 105, 117, 120
Euripedes, *Hippolytus*, 47
Eusebius, 3, 7-8, 10-11, 13, 63; *Chronicle*, 77, 86; *Chronicon*, 77, 86; *Church History*, 6-7; 77-78, 84, 89; *Demonstratio Evangelica*, 77; *Ecclesiastical History*, 8, 104; fate, fortune and omens in formation of Christianity, 29, 32, 44-46; *Life of Constantine*, 8, 78; pagan and Christian history, 103-104, 108-109, 112-116, *Praeparatio Evangelica*, 77, 104
Eutropius, 109-110
Evagrius, 13, 115
Ezra: Apocalyptic s, 128-138; historical teachings, 127-128

Febvre, Lucien, 63-64; and Marc Bloch, *Annales*, 161-162
Felix, Minucius, 63-64; *Octavius*, 74
Festus Avienus (Rufus), 109-110, 120
Fortune and fate, superstitions and paganism, 29-49
Foucault, *Archaeology of Knowledge*, 19
Fredouille, Jean-Claude, 55, 70-71

Gaius Caesar, 36
Galen, 106
Galerius, Gaius, 46
Gamaliel, setting date of Rosh HaShanah, 148, 150-151, 153
Gamaliel II, 139, 141
Genesis Rabbah, as history, 11-13, 209-230
George of Alexandria, Bishop, 117

Germania (Tacitus), 96
Gnaeus Fulvius, 31
Goodblatt, David, 154
Goodman, Martin, 154
Greek and Roman history in formation of Christian history, 29-49
Green, William Scott, 237
Guicciardini, Francesco, 112, 112

Haggai, 227
Hanan, 206
Hananya ben Hiskiya, 138
Hanina of Bet Hauran, 206
Hanina of Sepphoris, 22, 230
Hannibal, 31-32, 36
Hanson, R. P.C., 63
Heinze, Richard, 54, 56; *Tertullians Apologeticum*, 54
Herodotus, 6; 82, 93-95, 112; 121; pagan traditions and Christianity, 29-31, 35-40, 42, 44-47
Hesiod, 92, 97; *Works and Days*, 92
Hilarian, Bishop, *De cursu temporum*, 108
Hilqiah, 228
Hinena bar Pappa, 218
Hippolytus, 107-108; *Chronicon*, 108
Hippolytus (Euripedes), 47, 107-108; *Chronicon*, 108
Historia Augusta, 105, 117-121
Histories, (Tacitus) 96
History of the Jews in Babylonia (Neusner), 165
Hiyya, 195
Hiyya bar Abba, 228
Hiyya the Elder, 204
Hoil, K., 115
Hoshaiah, 206, 222
Huna, 218-219

Iamblichus, 115
Irenaeus, 79
Isaac, 213, 216, 219, 225, 227, 229
Isaac b. R. Eleazar, 185
Isaac b. Eliasheb, 206
Ishmael, 221
Israel, history and Genesis Rabbah, 209-230

Jacob bar Aha, 192
Jerome, Saint, 108, 110
Jewish Antiquities (Josephus), 68
John of Salisbury, 114
Jonathan b. Haggai, 219

Index

Josephus, 9, 86, 113; *Jewish Antiquities*, 68
Joshua, 148, 150-151, 153
Joshua b. Hananiah, 148-149, 224
Joshua b. Qorha, 173
Joshua of Sikhnin, 211
Judah, 174
Judah b. Padaiah, 219
Judah the Patriarch, 222
Judaism: history of events, 234-248; Jewish antiquity and Roman novelty, 68-71
Judaism and Christianity in the Age of Constantine (Neusner), 5
Jugurthine War (Marius), 40
Julian, Flavius, 46
Justin, 61, 73
Justin Martyr, 79

Lactantius, Lucius, 63, 103-104, 106, 108, 111; *De mortibus persecutorum*, 103-104, 111
Law and Rabbinic Judaism, 143-156
Levi, 185, 202, 210-211, 215, 226, 230
Levi b. R. Haita, 239
Libanius, 109
Liber antiquitatum Biblicarum, (Philo), 111
Licinius, 89
Life of Constantine (Eusebius), 8, 78
Livy, 112, 116, 121
Lortz, Joseph, 54, 56-57
Lucian, 52, 57, 65
Lycurgus, 96

Machiavelli, Niccolo, 112
Mack, Burton, *Myth of Innonence*, 15, 19-27
Macrobius, Marcus, 120
Mana, 187-188
Mani, 89
Marcus Aurelius, 59, 99
Marius, Gaius, *Jugurthine War*, 40
Maecenas, Gaius, 51
Martin of Tours, 110
Meir, 141-142
Melito of Sardis, 58-59
Menander, 89
Mishnah, Talmudic Judaism and history, 170-179
Momigliano, Arnaldo, 8
Moore, George Foot, 125-126
Myres, John L, 43
Myth of Innocence, (Mack), 15

Nahman, 188
Nazarius, 117
Nehoray, 139
Nehunya ben Hakana, 141
Nemesius of Emesa, 34
Nepos, Cornelius, 64
Neusner, Jacob, *History of the Jews in Babylonia*, 165; *Judaism and Christianity in the Age of Constantine*, 5
New Year festival, 173-179
Nicias, 39
Nicomachus Flavianus, 120

Octavius (Felix), 74
On the Sublime, 106
Origen, 79-80
Origo Constantini imperatoris, 111
Origo gentis Romanae, 118-119
Orosius, 110-111
Ovid, 97

Paganism, apologetic use of history, 51-75
Palestinian Talmud and uses in history, 181-208
Pamphilus, 104
Panegyric to Constantine (Drake), 81-82
Pericles, 36
Philo, *Liber antiquitatum Biblicarum*, 111
Philostratus, 115
Phineas, 228
Phinehas ben Yair, 138
Physics (Aristotle), 33
Plato, 65, 84, 93, 98
Polybius, 6, 29, 32, 36-38, 40, 43, 93-94
Porphyrios, 108
Praeparatio Evangelica (Eusebius), 77, 104
Publius Sulpicius, 31
Pythagoras, 115

Quintilian, Marcus, 54, 56, 58, 64, 73, 75

Rabbah b. Hahmani, 167
Rabinic law and society, 143-156
Regulus, Marcus Atilius, 43
Reitzenstei, R., 115

Sacred times, historical narrative, 143-156
Sallust, Gaius, 29, 36-37, 40, 43, 95, 116
Samuel bar R. Isaac, 206-207
Samuel bar Nahman, 189
Saturninus, Lucius, 89
Schaeder H. H., 127

Scholasticus, 6-13
Scipio, Africanus, 36
Seneca, 97
Servius, 120
Severus, Alexander, 117
Severus, Septimius, 41
Shwartz, Eduard, 108, 113
Sider, Robert, 54, 56-57, 61
Simeon b. Gamaliel, 174
Simeon b. Halapta, 204
Simeon b. Laqish, 226
Simeon ben Yohai, 141, 221
Simon, 214, 223, 228
Simon Magus, 89
Simon ben Yohai, 140
Smith, Jonathan Z., 243-246
Society and Rabbinic Judaism, 143-156
Socrates, 6, 13, 37
Solon, 47, 96
Song of Song Rabbah and history in Judaism, 234, 248
Sozomen, 16-13, 114
Stock, Brian, 163
Suetonius, 116
Sulla, Lucius, 95
Sulpicius Severus, 109-110
Superstitions, paganism and formation of Christianity, 29-49
Symmachus, Marius, 117, 120

Tacitus, Cornelius, 44, 59, 62-63, 69, 75; 95-96, 104, 106, 111-112, 116, 119; *Annals*, 59, 62, 96; *Germania*, 96; *Histories*, 96
Talmud and history, 158-179
Tanhum, 202
Tanhum b. R. Hiyya, 202
Tannaites: affirmation of history, 138-142; traditional teachings of, 125-127; Zion and Babylon-Rome, 129-131

Tertullian, Quintus, *Apology*, 51-54, 56, 61, 64, 66-67, 70-71, 73-75
Tertullians Apologeticum (Heinze), 54
Themistocles, 36
Theocritis, 97
Theodoret, 6, 13
Theodosius, 105, 118-119
Theophilus, 73
Thucyydides, 6, 32, 35-37, 40, 43, 48, 111, 121
Tilllemont, Louis Sebastian Le Nain de, 115
Tilly, Louise A., 161

Urbach, E. E., 147

Valens, 117
Varro, Marcus Terentius, 75, 121

Wilken, Robert L, 69
Works and Days (Hesiod), 92

Xenophen, 40, 48, 92-93
Yehuda Hanassi, 141 139
Yohanan, 182, 195-196, 206, 222, 224, 226
Yohanan b. Nuri, 148-150
Yohanan b. Zakkai, 168, 173, 193
Yosa bar Halputa, 207
Yose ben Halafta, 139-140, 142
Yose bar Haninah, 216
Yose bar Jacob, 200
Yose ben Kisma, 141
Yudan the Patriarch, 188-189, 199

Zadok, 138
Zeno the Stoic, 113
Zeira, 187, 207
Zenobia, Queen of Palmyra, 88

INDEX OF BIBLICAL AND TALMUDIC REFERENCES

2 Chronicles
  7:14, 205
Daniel
  7:7, 224
  8:13, 218-219
  8:14, 219
  9:11, 217
Deuteronomy
  6:4, 218
  8:13, 219
  12:9, 176
  12:10, 176
  14:8, 228
  28:49, 186
  31:10-11, 200
Ecclesiastes
  1:5, 222
  8:8, 211
Esther
  3:1, 224
  5:1, 210
Exodus
  14:6, 221
  15:2, 238
  15:9, 221
  15:24, 238
  15:25, 238
  16:25, 202
  17:7, 238
  17:15, 239
  19:16, 210
  24:7, 239
  24:9, 151
Ezekiel
  16:6, 238
  20:8, 238
  27:3, 218
  27:6, 230
Ezra
  8:3, 210
Genesis
  2:15, 217
  2:16, 217
  3:8, 215-216
  3:9, 216
  3:11, 217
  3:12, 218
  3:14, 215
  3:18, 218

  3:19, 223
  3:22, 218-219
  3:24, 217
  4:1, 223
  4:9, 218
  6:8, 214
  8:15, 224
  14:1, 223
  15:12, 223
  17:19-20, 224
  17:21, 225
  22:2, 210
  22:3, 221
  22:4, 210
  22:10, 221
  22:20, 222
  23:1, 222
  25:22-23, 226
  25:23, 227
  25:27, 228
  26:34-35, 228
  27:41, 185
  36:27, 229
  36:31-32, 229
  36:36, 229
  36:42, 230
  42:18, 210
  47:29-31, 211
  49:1-4, 212
  49:8, 186
  49:18, 213
  49:28, 225
Hosea
  6:2, 210
  6:7, 216
  7:5, 199
  7:6, 200
  7:7, 200
  9:15, 217
Isaiah
  2:4, 88
  21:9, 224
  21:11, 201
  21:12, 201-202
  24:23, 188
  26:8, 213
  33:2, 213
  41:16, 220
  41:27, 228

44:6, 227
49:14, 141
Jeremiah
  1:5, 227
  2:7, 217
  15:1, 217
  17:12, 227
  31:1, 214
  49:20, 141
  49:21, 224
  49:22, 228
Jonah
  2:1, 210
Joshua
  2:16, 214
  7:1, 239
  7:19, 239
  15:17, 222
I Kings
  6:1, 211
  12:27-28, 200
  12:28, 200-201
  12:29, 200
  21:1, 211
  22:47, 185
II Kings
  20:14, 218
Lamentations
  1:1, 217
Leviticus
  17:8-9, 176
  19:23, 219
  23:4, 151
  23:40, 227
  24:2, 217
Malachi
  1:3, 227
Micah
  4:1-4, 88
  7:8, 204
Nehemiah
  9:8, 214
Numbers
  3:12-13, 195
  8:16-18, 175
  9:15, 239
  13:32, 239
  22:9, 218
  22:21, 221
  25:1, 239
  25:8, 211
  27:18, 222
  32:12, 239

Obadiah
  1:21, 229
Proverbs
  20:21, 230
  25:14, 225
Psalms
  2:12, 220
  17:15, 205
  37:29, 216
  57:3, 212
  58:4, 226-227
  60:10, 196
  78:40, 239
  89:21, 214
  95:7, 202
  97:7, 188
  106:7, 238
  106:19, 239
  115:8, 187
  130:5, 214
  133:4, 214
  140:12, 215
I Samuel
  3:3, 222
Song of Songs
  1:5, 238
  1:6, 195
I Timothy
  3:2, 63
Zechariah
  11:1, 193
  11:17, 197
Mishnah
Abodah Zarah
  4:7 187
Ketuvot
  13:1-2, 150
Megllah
  1:4, 192
Qiddushin
  4:1, 72
Rosh haShana
  1:6, 150
  2:8-9, 148
  4:1-4, 173
Sotah
  9:15, 191, 193-194, 204
Sukkah
  3:12, 173
Taanit
  2:1-4, 199
  4:6, 183
  4:6-7, 174-175

Index

4:7, 176
Zebahim
  13:1, 176
  14:4-9, 175-176
  14:9, 176
Tosefta
Abodah Zarah
  4:7, 187
Palestinian Talmud
Abodah Zarah
  1:1, 199-201
  1:2, 185
  3:1, 206-207
  4:7, 187
Erubin
  3:4, 195
Gittin
  5:7, 186
Haggai
  2:1, 191
  2:9, 191
Megillah
  1:4, 192
  11:12, 191
Sanhedrin
  7:2, 193
  7:8, 191
Sotah
  6:3, 193
Sukkah
  5:1, 185-186
Taanit
  1:1, 201-202
  2:1, 205
  3:9, 198
  4:5, 182, 196
  4:6, 183
Terumot
  8:10, 188
Yoma
  1:1, 206
  3:2, 204
  5:2, 203-204
Apocrypha
Ezra, Fourth Book of
  3:4, 136
  3:4-28, 130, 136
  3:7, 136
  3:22, 130
  3:25, 129
  3:28, 129
  3:30, 129
  3:31, 130

4:11, 132
4:12, 132
4:21, 132
4:26, 133
4:37, 134
4:40, 134
5:29, 129
5:43, 133
5:44, 134
5:46, 133-134
5:55, 130
6:1-5, 134-135, 137
6:8, 136-137
6:26, 136-137
6:38-53, 136
6:38-54, 135
6:55, 129, 136
6:56, 129
7:1-5, 131
7:11, 130, 136-137
7:12, 130, 137
7:14, 130, 137
7:16, 131-133
7:18, 131, 137
7:20, 134
7:21, 130
7:24, 130
7:63, 133
7:64, 133
7:68, 133
7:70, 134-135
7:74, 134
7:96, 131
7:98, 131
7:104, 135
7:106, 136
7:106-110, 132, 136
7:112, 132
7:118, 136
7:129, 136
7:129-131, 130
8:1, 134
8:2, 135
8:6-14, 135
8:41, 135
8:42-45, 135
8:47, 134
8:60, 130
9:18, 134
9:22, 132
9:29, 136
9:29-32, 137
9:34-37, 135

9:37, 130
10:14, 136
10:23, 129
10:45-48, 136
10:54, 131
11:44, 133-134
12:11, 136
12:44, 133
13:26, 133
13:39-47, 137
13:40, 136
14:3, 136
14:3-5, 137
14:5, 134
14:10, 131
14:11, 134
14:13, 133
14:16, 131
14:21, 132, 137
14:22, 137
14:29, 136
14:31, 130
14:32, 130
Rabbah
Genesis Rabbah
  XIX:VII.1, 215-216
  XIX:IX.1, 216-217
  XIX:XI.1, 218
  XX:I.1, 215
  XXI:I.1, 218-219
  XXI:VII.2, 219-20
  XXIX:I.1, 215
  XLII:IV.1, 223
  XLIVLXV.1, 223
  XLVII:V.1, 224-225
  LV:VIII.1, 210
  LVI:I.1, 221
  LVIII:II.1, 222
  LXII:VI.11, 226-227
  LXII:X.1, 228
  LXIII:VII.2, 227
  LXIII:VIII.2, 227
  LXIII:VIII.3, 227-228
  LXV:I.1, 228-229
  LXXXII:I.1, 229
  LXXXIII:IV.3, 230
  LXXXIII:V.1, 220
  XCVIII:I.1, 212-213
  XCVIII:V.4, 213-214
Song of Songs Rabbah
  V:i.1, 238-239
  V:ii.5, 239

www.ingramcontent.com/pod-product-compliance
Ingram Content Group UK Ltd.
Pitfield, Milton Keynes, MK11 3LW, UK
UKHW041431180426
11947UKWH00007B/382